# THE LIFE
## OF
# ERNST CHAIN

Also by Ronald W. Clark

# THE LIFE
# OF
# ERNST CHAIN

## Penicillin and Beyond

## Ronald W. Clark

Weidenfeld and Nicolson
LONDON

ISBN 0 297 78700 4

Printed and bound by
Butler & Tanner Ltd,
Frome and London

# CONTENTS

# ILLUSTRATIONS

All the photographs belong to Lady Chain's collection and are reproduced by her kind permission. Whilst every effort has been made to contact all the copyright owners of the photographs, the publisher apologizes to anyone whom he has been unable to trace. Due acknowledgement will, of course, be made in future reprints.

# ACKNOWLEDGEMENTS

My first thanks are to Lady Chain, who has given me unrestricted access to the extensive correspondence and papers of Sir Ernst. I am grateful to her for reminiscences and for reading the manuscript; and also to her three children for recollections and reminiscences.

Sir Ernst's papers were initially assembled by Lady Chain and then passed to the Contemporary Scientific Archives Centre at Oxford (Honorary Director, Professor Margaret Gowing), where they were catalogued under the supervision of Mrs Jeannine Alton, Deputy Director. A 439-page three-part catalogue of the Chain archive was produced at the Centre, after which the material was lodged at the Contemporary Medical Archives Centre, Wellcome Institute for the History of Medicine, London, under the care of the Centre's archivist, Miss Julia Sheppard. I am most grateful to all of those involved. The greater part of Sir Ernst's correspondence quoted here is held by the Medical Archives Centre in London, its details being given in the catalogue produced in Oxford.

I am also grateful to the Medical Research Council for permission to quote from their archives and to their archivist, Miss Mary Nicholas, for her help in handling them.

I wish to thank Lady Florey for her permission to use her husband's archive at The Royal Society, and Mr N. H. Robinson, the Society's Librarian, for his approval of the wording I have used in quoting from the Florey Papers.

I further wish to thank Mr Robinson for help in consulting other papers held in The Royal Society's Library.

I also wish to thank Dr Norman Heatley for permission to quote from his Notes now deposited at the Wellcome Institute for the History of Medicine; and The Weizmann Archives for permission to quote a letter by Dr Chaim Weizmann.

Those who have helped me in other ways, largely by their recollections of Sir Ernst, include: Sir Edward Abraham; Professor Sir Derek Barton; Lord Beloff; Professor Isaac Berenblum; Mr Donald Callow; Ms Nechama Challom, Curator of the Weizmann Archives; Dr J. Edelman;

Dr Ruth Eisner-Strahl; Professor R. Falini; Dr Henry Fisher; Sir Ian Fraser; Dr Samuel A. Goldblith; Sir Ronald Halstead; Professor H. Harris; Dr Norman Heatley; Professor Dorothy Hodgkin; Professor Ephraim Katzir; Mr D. Kleeman; the late Mr H. G. L. Lazell; Rudolf Lewy; Dr Keith Mansford; Sir Ashley Miles; Mr Nathan Milstein; Professor Albert Neuberger; Mrs Jean Pingree, Archivist, Imperial College of Science and Technology; Professor S. J. Pirt; Mrs Rinna Samuel, Assistant to the President of the Weizmann Institute of Science; Professor Michael Sela, President of the Weizmann Institute of Science; Lord Sieff of Brimpton; Dr Arnold Spicer, formerly adviser to the Lord Rank Research Centre; Dr Trevor Williams; Lord Wolfson; Mrs Haya Wolovsky, Curator of the Weizmann Institute of Science Archives; and Mr D. J. Wright, Librarian, British Medical Association.

Except where made clear by their context, views expressed in this book are my own and should not be attributed to those who have so generously helped me in my research.

# −1−

# A BERLIN YOUTH

The discovery of penicillin and the exploitation of its therapeutic powers which have saved lives literally by the million during the last four decades, reveals history aping art in its coincidences, its ironies and in the strange interlinking records of those involved. The circumstances of the time have lodged in public memory the names of Alexander Fleming, who reported the existence of penicillin in 1929, and of Howard Florey in whose Oxford laboratory its unique therapeutic powers were discovered a decade later. Ernst Chain, who with Fleming and Florey was awarded a Nobel Prize in 1945 for work on penicillin, has remained the relatively unknown scientist in the enterprise, even though he became a leading figure in the development of antibiotics after the Second World War, the man who created in Rome the first international centre for research into antibiotics and whose work led the way to the creation, in the late 1950s, of the 'tailormade' penicillins which were further to transform medicine's fight against bacteria. For the last reason if for no other the life of Ernst Chain would form an intriguing entry in the story of twentieth-century science.

Yet Chain, 'a temperamental Continental' as he half-mockingly described himself, was also to influence – and not in Britain alone – the role which government was to play in medical research, the developing relationship between industry and the universities, and the ethical problems which became more pressing as science gave the medical profession increasing control over life and death. That influence was exercised by a man impatient of bureaucracy, frequently categorical in his views and with a marked inability to mince his words. A tendency to overstatement sometimes led to his proposals being discounted, but his forthright attitude frequently proved effective even though it could make enemies as easily as allies. As a committed Jew he experienced both advantages and the reverse, being supported throughout a long life by the certainties of his faith and by the Jewish communities within whose orbit he

I

moved; but, during the first half of his life, suffering from an undercurrent of anti-Semitic feeling which he believed dogged even his scientific work.

Ernst Boris Chain was born in Berlin on 19 June 1906, of Russian-German parentage. He had an excitable nature of which he later became well aware and this he was not above exploiting to great effect if it would help him in an argument. His father, Michael, the son of a tailor from Mogilev Gubernski, within the Jewish pale of settlement in White Russia, had emigrated to Berlin at the end of the nineteenth century. Here he had taken a degree in chemistry and subsequently, as a chemical engineer, built up the successful Chemische Fabrik Johannisthal in Adlershof, an industrial suburb of Berlin, which produced metal salts such as copper sulphate and nickel sulphate. Thus Ernst, as he later wrote, 'grew up in an atmosphere of chemical industry and chemical research'. His mother, Margarete, a German Jewess, was a close relative of Kurt Eisner, the Social Democratic leader who became Bavaria's Prime Minister in November 1918 and was assassinated less than four months later. Eisner's contacts with the Chain family are unrecorded but it seems likely that they influenced, if only indirectly, the climate in which the young Chain grew up, a climate which encouraged 'regrettably left-wing views', as he later described them.

More important than any political influence was the family's commitment to Jewry, a commitment which was ever present and which at times strikingly asserted itself. At the age of sixty-eight Ernst Chain still remembered being visited as a youth in Berlin by his grandfather from Russia. He was 'a most impressive figure with a large black beard, and [I] was told that he spent every free moment he had in studying Torah and Talmud while my grandmother looked after the more mundane business of daily life,' Chain later wrote. 'I was indoctrinated by both my parents with a maxim that was beyond discussion, that the only worthwhile occupation in life was the pursuit of intellectual activities, and any career which was not a university career was unthinkable.'

Little is known about Chain's early life in Berlin. His father died in 1919, when Ernst was only thirteen, and despite the apparent success of the father's chemical works the family found itself reduced to something approaching poverty, a common enough fate in the first hyperinflationary days of the Weimar Republic. Ernst's mother ran the home as a guesthouse and the son grew up accustomed to a fluctuating household served by an overworked mother and her young daughter, Hedwig.

Simple rather than poor was one relative's later recollection of con-

ditions in the Alt-Moabit home; although in the early 1930s there was
an attempt by the authorities to seize furniture in the house, an attempt
disallowed only because it was needed for the owner's business of letting.
Russian as well as German was habitually spoken, and Ernst's friends
appear to have made up a cosmopolitan collection. 'It was a life full of
music', a distant relative remembers. 'Ernst and his Polish friend Mie-
czyslaw Kolinski often played four-handed duets. Tille Daniler, a Russian
coloratura, sang her *lieder* while Ernst himself took lessons in conduct-
ing.'

Next to music his great love was his cat, Mitzinka. She tore the
furniture to pieces, but when the family moved to a new home in 1931
her owner insisted that the cat be taken with the family in a taxi. Ernst
was studious, had private lessons in mathematics, took a mild interest in
philosophy and is remembered as having visited the Buddhist Centre
which in the early 1920s was opened in Berlin. He was educated at the
Luisengymnasium and the Friedrich-Wilhelm University where, in 1930,
he graduated in chemistry and physiology, a combination of medicine
and science to which much of his life was subsequently to be devoted.
He then worked for a while in the Kaiser Wilhelm Institute for Physical
Chemistry and Electrochemistry run by Fritz Haber at Berlin-Dahlem,
and later was proud to recall the men he had worked under. 'I was
taught by Nernst, Planck, Schlenck ... and during the years I worked
at Dahlem I got to know Hahn, Lisa Meitner, Warburg, Neuberg,
Haber, Freundlich.'

At university it was the biological approach to chemistry which most
attracted him, and having graduated he eventually joined the Chemical
Department of the Pathological Institute of the Charité Hospital, one of
Berlin's most illustrious institutions. Here, in 1927, he obtained his PhD
for research on the optical specificity of esterases. He was to write half
a century later:

Since the beginning of my scientific career I have been interested in the study
of biological phenomena which could be explained in terms of the action of
well-defined chemical substances, and in the study of the structures and mode
of action of these substances. The action of toxins, the phenomenon of bacterial
lysis, growth promotion and inhibition, virulence, regulation of metabolic reactions by hormones come into this category. After more than forty years of
professional activity this is essentially still my personal approach to biochemical
research.

With such interests it was natural that Chain should be particularly
attracted to work on enzymes, the large group of proteins produced by

living cells whose presence affects the speed at which chemical actions take place. Enzymes themselves are not consumed during such actions, only minute quantities are involved, most of them are specific in their actions, operating only on certain substances, and many come into operation most effectively only at certain temperatures. While all this is known today, knowledge of enzymes – frequently named by adding the suffix '-ase' to the name of the substance whose reactivity is increased by the enzyme – was considerably less when Chain started work; indeed, their existence in an unknown territory waiting to be explored appears to have been one of their attractions to him. He recalled years later:

It seems unbelievable now but it is nevertheless a fact that although the bulk of the evidence of the time of these studies (in the early 1920s) pointed clearly to the protein nature of enzymes, this was by no means generally accepted, and I remember very clearly during the time when I studied chemistry and started my first research, in the years 1924–30, that the great organic chemist Willstätter, who devoted the last years of his career to a study of the nature of enzymes and succeeded in developing some new and very effective methods of their purification, came to the conclusion that enzymes could not be proteins, as the enzyme solutions, as they became more active in the course of purification procedure, contained less nitrogen.

However much Chain might in the 1920s have been intrigued by such chemical riddles as the enzymes offered for solution, he had need of more money than the career of chemist seemed likely to offer, particularly as support of his mother and young sister Hedwig became an increasing drain on his almost non-existent resources.

In 1928 he became a naturalized German citizen. The reasons are uncertain, but prospects for the Weimar Republic appeared for a while to be improving, and the move was a natural one for a young man who still saw his future in Germany. What that future was to be remained unclear. For a while he continued to think that his career might be that of a professional pianist, and music was certainly an activity that attracted him for the whole of his life. So much was this so that, visiting Japan for a series of lecture tours at the age of seventy, he insisted that a piano be available, adding:

I need a piano as I have to perform in the middle of June and cannot be a month without any practising. Would it be possible to find a place not very far from the hotel where I could play for about 1–2 hours a day when there is time for this? Otherwise my fingers will get very stiff.

In 1930 he visited the USSR to organize an exchange of musicians and artists on behalf of the German Society of Friends in the USSR, and the following year visited Argentina in the hope of arranging visits by Russian and German musicians. Nothing came of these attempts and a relative remembers that all he gained from the trip to Argentina was the experience of another country and the new suit of clothes in which he came back to Berlin.

Although he returned to resume his chemical studies, music remained a guiding influence. He appeared as a pianist on a number of Berlin platforms and wrote as music critic for the Berlin evening paper *Welt am Abend* 'rather left-wing I'm afraid', as he later described it.

The Chain household had in 1923 been joined by a cousin who was directly to affect the course of Ernst Chain's life and who with only a slight stretch of the imagination can be claimed to have played a part in bringing the benefits of penicillin to the world. This was Mrs Anna Sacharina, some twenty years older than Chain, a widow who had continued to live in St Petersburg after the death of her lawyer husband until she moved to Berlin. The childless Mrs Sacharina, slightly better off than the Chains, spoke Russian, German and French fluently, and took Ernst under her wing, encouraged him in his studies, often referred to a brother-in-law who had failed as a conductor to show that there was no money to be made in music, and influenced his career by constant advice. Remembered years later as a determined, tough little woman, Mrs Sacharina was to be Chain's housekeeper in Oxford throughout the years of the development of penicillin, and accompanied him as with his wife he moved up the ladder of success. 'Aunt' Sacharina, as she was often described, accompanied Chain to Sweden when in 1945 he received the Nobel Prize, travelled with him and his wife when he left Britain after the Second World War to set up a new Institute in Rome, and occupied quarters specially built at Imperial College when Chain left Rome for London in the early 1960s.

In Berlin it was certainly Mrs Sacharina who impressed on him that science offered greater possibilities than music. This eventually echoed his own feelings. More than one colleague has recalled that he began to swing towards science once he realized that although he might become a good pianist he would never become a great one. However, music remained in his blood and the musical wealth of Weimar Germany is rarely absent from his later recollections: 'There were large opera houses conducted by Otto Klemperer, Leo Blech, Erich Kleiber and George Szell, two large orchestras conducted by Wilhelm Furtwängler and Bruno Walter and of course many famous guest conductors.' There was a marvellous choir, the Singakademie under Siegfried Ochs, where Chain heard performances of the St Matthew Passion 'of a standard and quality', as he later wrote, 'such as I have never heard since anywhere else'.

But it was not only music which made Chain later look back to Berlin with an enthusiasm which confirms the view that in drawing him into its field science recruited a potential follower of the arts. 'We had several state repertory and private theatres, again of first quality, with an assembly of great and unforgettable actors and producers such as Max Reinhardt for instance,' he has written. 'There were also great painters, such as Liebermann, Paul Klee and many others.' Describing in his seventies the atmosphere which this artistic wealth generated, he could say to a friend:

This period has gone for ever, suffering the same fate as many similar ones did before it in the past though to us at the time it seemed built for eternity. But I consider myself privileged, as it seems you do, to have been allowed to grow up in it. It has influenced my standards for my whole life in the spheres of music, theatre and science.

The young man who stood on the verge of a career in 1930, as the American depression began to pave the way for economic crisis and the end of the Weimar Republic, had not yet finally decided between the competing claims of science and music. He was to remain undecided for another three or four years until, in England, he was offered opportunities in science too good to refuse.

It was before he left Berlin, however, that he began to praise the virtues of applied as distinct from pure science. Later in life, as experience began to qualify his views, he would usually emphasize the virtues of a proper 'mix' between the two. More than one of his Berlin colleagues, however, remembered how he would say while still in Germany:

In pure science if what you do is a success you write a paper; if it is a failure you write a paper. With applied science it is harder. If what you are doing works it is a success; if it does not it is nothing more than a failure.

This was, perhaps, the natural conclusion to be drawn by the son of a man who had built up a chemical works which had been successful until it fell to hyperinflation.

The shortish Ernst Chain, with his magnificent mane of black hair, was remembered as much for his temperamental idiosyncrasies as for his twin interests of science and music. One colleague recalled:

With guests he was most amiable. He liked jokes and when pleased his face was shining and he reminded one of a purring kitten. At the other end of the scale

I experienced quite a few outbursts with shouting and throwing things about, and he once even hurt himself with splintered glass. He often used the phrase, 'I hate that, I hate that', and liked to seal his verdict with: 'That's me, Ernst Boris Michaelovich Chain – Chaithin!'

The drawbacks of this ebullient and sometimes dogmatic attitude to life were counterbalanced by Chain's abundant energy – a fount of power which even past middle age allowed him to deal with work enough for three men and still come up smiling – and his determination to follow his own beliefs wherever they led and however inconvenient this might be for others or for himself.

He was a natural linguist, an advantage in a life that was to be so largely international. For a year he had studied Russian and he had taken naturally to French. His English was at first somewhat fractured, but within a few months of landing in Britain in 1933 he had acquired a command of the language which quickly moved from tolerable to good. Years later it was noted that a few months after arriving in Rome as head of the Laboratory of Biological Chemistry in the Istituto Superiore di Sanità he was lecturing fluently in Italian to professional audiences. 'With all languages,' he wrote, 'including English, the day comes when you suddenly speak it fluently, however difficult the beginning was, and you will never understand then by what means you acquired the knowledge of the language.' As with the piano, as with the feel for certain chemical reactions, so with languages – Chain was helped by instinct.

His prospects as he worked away in the Charité rested entirely on his own ability. He had no family connections which would be of use to him and as a Jew he suffered from the anti-Semitism which had been simmering away in Germany even before Einstein had won world-wide fame with his General Theory of Relativity during the First World War. Even without the rise of Hitler it would have been natural for him to seek fame and fortune elsewhere. Nevertheless, the circumstances which eventually made Chain leave Germany are not as clear as they superficially appear. The growing strength of the Nazis by 1932 certainly augured ill for a Jew of left-wing tendencies, especially one whose family was related to the assassinated Kurt Eisner. The appointment of Adolf Hitler to the Chancellorship of Germany on 30 January 1933 could well have been the last straw.

Chain himself has on more than one occasion said that he arrived in England on this very day, adding in one version that he landed with only £10 in his pocket. However, his passport records that he landed at Harwich on 2 April. 'I left Germany', he later wrote, 'because I felt disgusted with the Nazi gang, not because I thought my life was in danger. I did not believe that the system would last more than six months at the most.'

A friend wrote to him years later recalling his 'quick decision to go to England' and it would be in character if the decision had been made impetuously, on the spur of the moment. What is not clear is his reason for moving to England rather than to France, a country which, he was to write, he had always 'considered [his] second spiritual country'. The impression of haste, and of minimum discussion with his family, is supported by his later feelings of regret, and of some guilt, at his failure to take his mother and sister with him or at least to make certain that they could follow him. Both were to die in Theresienstadt concentration camp.

# —2—

# THE MOVE TO BRITAIN

The England in which Chain arrived early in 1933 was almost unimaginably more insular in outlook than it is today or than it has been for the last three decades. Louis Blériot had flown the English Channel almost a quarter of a century earlier and had aroused more than one reflection that Britain was no longer an island. Yet to most British men and women the Channel was still a stretch of water which although only twenty-two miles wide effectively divided 'us' from 'them'. Only a small percentage of the population had visited Europe, or ever expected to do so. British superiority was taken as a law of life and considered even more natural when the countries of central and eastern Europe were considered rather than those just across the Channel. Five years after Chain's arrival Somerset Maugham was to comment, not entirely in jest: 'It is good to be on your guard against an Englishman who speaks French perfectly.' And when in 1938 the Prime Minister, Neville Chamberlain, spoke of the Czech crisis as being 'a quarrel in a far-away country between people of whom we know nothing', he was speaking no more than the truth. Central Europeans were sometimes treated with a tolerance of which the British were constitutionally proud, but beneath the tolerance lay an attitude that was transformed into an anachronism only by the events of the Second World War and the revolution in thought, communications and travel that followed it. Thus, however well Chain was treated in Britain, there was a reaction to his extravagant personality, his outspokenness, his natural lack of reserve, to which his sensitive antennae quickly responded.

British reaction to his innate Jewishness was more complex. Anti-Semitism was endemic, even if its worst manifestations were limited to a small minority, and even if the trickle of refugees from Germany had not by 1933 developed into the flood that created genuine problems easily exploited by those who disliked foreigners in general and Jews in particular. Certainly in the academic world, which gave birth to the

9

Academic Assistance Council, every effort was made to aid refugee scientists whatever their race or creed. However, despite this apparently happy situation, Chain sensed an undertow of feeling. In 1939 he believed it to be so strong that he backed away in an Oxford argument 'to avoid any action which could provoke latent anti-Semitism which was very widespread'.

For a young academic from Germany, starting life in England, there were differences between the two countries which called for compromise if friction and disappointment were to be avoided. In Berlin Chain had been brought up in the tradition of strict unquestioning obedience to those above him in the academic hierarchy. This could sometimes be an impediment to the spirit of free enquiry so necessary to progress in science, but it was a framework within which work went on. By contrast, life in an English college or university was suffused by an air of informality which Chain found strange and at times vaguely disturbing. His British colleagues for their part regarded his strict adherence to what he felt was a necessary hierarchical system as an attitude which could be laughed at or ignored but should not be taken too seriously.

Quite as important was the difference between British and German academics in regard to co-operation with industry. In Britain at the time of Chain's arrival, and indeed for many years after, contact between the universities and industry was frowned upon in scientific, and particularly in medical, circles. This was in part a hangover from the days of the industrial revolution when landowners and manufacturing men began to go their separate ways; but it was symptomatic of a difference in attitude to pure and to applied sciences, a difference between 'gentlemen' and 'players', a central division running in a multiplicity of ways down the centre of British life, a division which is sometimes still apparent today.

In Germany, on the other hand, there had been co-operation between industry and the universities at least since the middle of the nineteenth century. The artificial dye industry, founded in Britain, had been exploited by a combination of German industry and academics until it dominated Europe. Most of Europe's tungsten used in specialist steel-making, originally produced in Britain, by this time came from Germany, as did most of the magnetos in petrol engines. The best scientific instruments, as Chain well knew, were preponderantly German. Moreover, while he had been growing up there had been founded in Berlin the Kaiser-Wilhelm-Gesellschaft für Förderung der Wissenschaften (the Kaiser Wilhelm Society for the Advancement of the Sciences), an organization whose series of Institutes specifically encouraged co-operation between industry and academics.

The influence of such a background was seriously to affect Chain's career. In the later part of his life, when the therapeutic value of penicillin had become clear and its commercial prospects undoubted, it enabled him to move more easily than some of his colleagues between university and industry. During his first years in England, however, he often found it difficult to understand the attitudes and values of some colleagues, while his own tended to emphasize, in some eyes, the fact that this bright young man, however agile his brain, was not 'one of us'.

Chain's entry into Britain had been allowed only on condition that, according to the stamp on his passport, he took up 'no paid or unpaid employment', and some three months later the 'condition attached to the grant of leave to land [was] ... varied so as to require departure from the United Kingdom not later than 31st Dec. 1933'. This was the first of numerous variations which continued throughout Chain's early years in England and it is not clear whether he merely ignored the restrictions or received permission from the authorities to take up the work he immediately began to seek.

However suddenly Chain had decided to leave Germany, he appears to have made at least some preparations for arrival in England where, judging by the events of the next few weeks, he metaphorically landed on his feet. His first port of call was the home of his uncle, Boris Haine, who lived in north London and with whom he took lodgings. He was not too enthusiastically received and his uncle recommended that he should get a job, if only that of delivering newspapers, rather than look for scientific work.

To Chain such suggestions verged on the obscene. For him the only two choices were science or music, and it was not until he had become established as an up-and-coming scientist that the possibility of a musical career was finally abandoned. The attractions and the drudgery of science were plain to him from his earliest days and he frequently pointed out how the scientist must never lose sight of his final objective, 'which is a philosophical one, namely to study and to understand the secrets of nature'. If the scientist lost sight of that, he once said, he 'must, in the end, succumb to the fatigue caused by the daily trudge which he is called upon to make through a long stretch of routine operations, forming, as they do, an unavoidable part even of the most fascinating research'.

Since his days in the Charité, Chain had been convinced that his field was biochemistry, the study of the chemical reactions in living animals, plants and micro-organisms. It was a young science, since it became possible to elucidate the complex changes which take place in the thousands of chemical compounds contained in a living organism only after the molecular structure of such compounds had been unravelled. The process developed by slow stages during the nineteenth century as such pioneers as Justus von Liebig and Louis Pasteur began to describe the chemical cycles in nature on which life depended.

Pasteur showed that living organisms caused fermentation, and a knowledge of how intermediate metabolism in the cell takes place was gradually built up. But it was not until 1902 that the first Chair of Biochemistry was founded in Britain – the Johnston Chair in Liverpool University – and in the early 1930s the subject was still, in estate agents' language, 'ripe for development'. It offered great possibilities, and within a week of Chain's arrival in Britain he had written to Frederick Gowland Hopkins, one of Britain's leading biochemists, a Nobel Prizewinner already famous for his work on vitamins, and head of the Sir William Dunn School of Biochemistry at Cambridge. He was interested, Chain said, in working on 'optical activity and enzymes' and on 'the enzymatic degradation of lecithin'. Would it be possible for him to join Hopkins's department? Before receiving a reply he also wrote to University College Hospital Medical School, London, and by 15 April, less than a fortnight after landing at Harwich, had joined the College's Department of Chemical Pathology under Charles Harington. Less than a week later, on 21 April, and apparently uncertain whether he would ever settle down in England, he was writing to the Rockefeller Institute for Medical Research in New York, asking for a job. The succession of letters was an early example of the almost over-zealous enthusiasm which was to typify a whole lifetime of work.

The appointment at University College and the letter to Hopkins, which was to produce results later in the year, followed Chain's approach to J. B. S. Haldane, the physiologist and geneticist. Both Haldane and Hopkins had been sent offprints of Chain's doctoral thesis written in Berlin. In the spring of 1933 Haldane was moving from a Readership in Biochemistry at Cambridge to the Chair of Genetics at University College; as usual, he knew a good man when he saw him and strongly supported Chain – 'what posterity may regard as the best and most important action of my life,' he later wrote. 'Perhaps all my discoveries will be forgotten and I shall only be remembered in the words of the ancient Greek poet Pindar: "He once nourished the contriver of painlessness, the gentle limb-guardian Asklepios (Dhanvantari), the heroic

conqueror of manifold disease." ' As for Chain, he was in no doubt
about the significance of the help from J. B. S. 'In fact the whole of my
career in England is really due to Haldane,' he once said. But if Haldane
was responsible for the start of Chain's career in England, the Jewish
community was at least partly responsible for his keep, and on 23 May
the Liberal Jewish Synagogue confirmed that it would, starting from 1
May, grant him a one-year stipend of £250.

Chain had been lucky in getting his feet on the first rung of the ladder
within a fortnight of arriving in England. Yet it would be difficult to
think of two more incompatible characters than the volatile supremely
self-confident Ernst Chain and the reserved Harington, already putting
knowledge of the chemistry of the thyroid gland on a firm basis and
later to become the respected director of the National Institute for
Medical Research. The difference between the two men, between Harington's quintessential English reserve and Chain's Jewish flamboyance,
was from the first a potential source of trouble.

There was also the difference between the standards of equipment
customary in German laboratories of the time and those usual in Britain.
In Germany, scientists were still benefiting from the attitude which for
half a century had given science a priority position when it came to
sharing out the country's financial cake. In Britain there was resignation
to a less happy state of affairs typified by Rutherford's famous remark:
'We haven't much money so we've got to use our brains.' The contrast
between Berlin and Britain was one about which Chain found it impossible to remain silent, an inability to control his tongue which sometimes aroused resentment. Hans Krebs, who later became a close friend,
has said that in 1934 Chain unburdened himself about the difficulties he
had encountered in Harington's laboratory.

We discussed these difficulties. Sir Ernst held the view, in no uncertain terms,
that one really could not work properly in Harington's laboratory. Considering
that Harington synthesized thyroxine [the hormone found in the thyroid gland]
and established its structure, I thought it was not quite appropriate for a young-
ster of twenty-eight to criticize an accomplished biochemist as to what consti-
tuted proper working facilities. I thought as refugees we ought to be grateful
for any facilities. Neither Harington nor I, at that time, really appreciated what
was in Sir Ernst's mind. It was to Harington's great credit that years later he
told Sir Ernst he had been right in criticizing the facilities. It would certainly
have been impossible to develop penicillin in Harington's laboratory.

The break between the two men came when Chain had been working
in Harington's laboratory for only a few months and differing versions

13

exist as to how it came about. Chain has merely recorded that he 'had a row' with Harington and it seems that there was a regular stream of complaints about lack of equipment. But according to one of Chain's friends the final upheaval occurred when Harington arrived one morning to find him upbraiding laboratory technicians in a way more suitable to a German laboratory, where such workers were expected to know their place and to keep to it, than to the environment of University College.

Once again, and for what was probably a combination of reasons, Chain found himself looking for work. Once again he appears to have invoked the aid of Haldane, never a man to withhold help from anyone who had been fired for sticking to his own point of view. This time he intervened on Chain's behalf with Gowland Hopkins, to whom Chain had first written a few days after arriving in England.

By September 1933 Chain had also been in touch with Norman Pirie, later of the famous Rothamsted Experimental Station in Hertfordshire, but at that time a demonstrator in Hopkins's laboratory. From Pirie there came a warning. There were already three German exiles working in the School of Biochemistry laboratory at Cambridge, he said, and went on to warn Chain that he might find equipment in Cambridge no more satisfactory than it had been in Professor Harington's laboratory.

Eventually, however, Chain arrived in Cambridge to work under Hopkins, whom he described as 'one of the most considerate and kindest of human beings I ever had the good fortune to meet'. Had there been any doubt about the course of Chain's scientific life it would have been resolved by Hopkins who not only excelled in the art of filling others with his own enthusiasm but who was now at the height of his fame as an exponent of the comparatively new specialization of biochemistry. For a quarter of a century he had helped to unravel the details of one of its central problems: that of intermediary metabolism, the complex linked chemical reactions, catalysed by intracellular enzymes, which provide the physical and energetic basis for the processes of life in general and of cellular respiration in particular. While Hopkins was to achieve fame largely for his discovery of the essential part played by vitamins in human health, his lesser-known work on metabolism was in some ways quite as important. There is here a comparison with Chain who during the second half of his life greatly extended the knowledge of how metabolism works although his Nobel Prize was awarded for his work on penicillin. Hopkins was, moreover, a man of far-seeing ideas of what biochemistry and its practitioners might accomplish. He once said:

I have faith that in the end they will reach to a description of living systems which, in so far as they are chemical systems, may be complete. From a know-ledge of individual events they will proceed to an understanding of the organ-ization of those events: that organization which makes the organism. I can see no obstacle to the attainment of such an intellectual synthesis of knowledge. When that synthesis comes it will involve a full understanding of many of life's visible manifestations, which is of course not to say that it will define life itself.

Hopkins's influence on Chain may well have been decisive during the early years in England. None who knew him well, Sir Henry Dale was to write of Hopkins, 'could have failed to experience a quality in his friendship which made the mere description of doubts and difficulties to Hopkins seem to bring a solution within easier reach'.

Hopkins took the young man under his wing, yet despite his almost fatherly help Chain remained a basically worried person who still con-sidered emigration to Canada or Australia, or even switching from the profession of science to that of music, a profession after which he con-tinued to hanker despite Mrs Sacharina's warnings. This tugging in two directions may well have increased the mental uncertainties which wor-ried him for some while during his first months in Britain. He suffered from 'frequent attacks of fear, especially in closed rooms, tube, etc. Melancholic depressions', and these were to grow into something approaching psychosomatic illness. 'During the Cambridge period (Sept. 1933–Aug. 1935)', he later wrote, 'often fear of being poisoned in the lab. different symptoms of fear. Big financial worries, uncertainty of future.'

As conditions in Germany slipped from bad to worse the apprehen-sions of a young Jew whose family lived in Berlin, and who saw no chance of helping them, were natural enough and were only partly alleviated by the fact that he was settling down in Cambridge better than he had expected. Although Chain already had his PhD from Berlin, Hopkins believed that a Cambridge degree would be of value to him and approached the Censor of Fitzwilliam House, then a non-collegiate body, and explained the position to him. Chain subsequently wrote:

I went to see [the Censor], found sympathy and understanding and very soon afterwards I was accepted by him as a PhD student. I received a maintenance grant of £300 per annum, which I considered then royal generosity, through the good offices of yet another distinguished Cambridge figure ... the late Dr Redcliffe N. Salaman FRS, a plant virologist of repute (and the great expert on the potato, who founded the Potato Virus Research Institute which he directed for years) in whose hospitable splendid house at Barley, Royston, I spent many pleasant evenings during my Cambridge stay with his large family over which he presided in a patriarchal manner.

After his one-year stipend from the Liberal Synagogue had ended, Chain had only his £200-a-year salary from the laboratory and his maintenance grant on which to sustain himself. His lodgings were of the poorest kind – 'lino on the floor', as one contemporary friend describes them – and his comment about inadequate food appears to have been amply justified. His musical ability helped and Ashley Miles, then Demonstrator in Pathology at the University of Cambridge, recalls not only that Chain would frequently visit his home to play piano duets, particularly the arrangements of Bruckner and Mahler, but that he obviously enjoyed getting a square meal.

Chain spent 1934 equably enough in Cambridge, worried but surviving. 'I was then in a very difficult phase of my life, uprooted and disorientated', he remembered years later, '... and was right in the middle of the painful process of trying to adjust myself to the new conditions of a refugee existence and to grapple with the various problems and difficulties arising from this situation.' His musical ability continued to open many doors which might otherwise have remained closed, and while his professional self-confidence continued to grow he appeared to many friends as a diffident and almost shy personality never too anxious to stand in the limelight – a strong contrast to the confident young scientist into which he was to develop a decade later. Just as some American presidents have been known to 'grow with the job', so was Chain to grow with success, helped by the attitude of Cambridge colleagues typified by Hopkins's note as he was about to sit for his PhD: 'You need not fear the ordeal: we shall be very merciful.' The doctorate was granted for a thesis on 'Some chemical and biochemical investigations on phospholipins', most of it dealing with original work carried out in Berlin, London and Cambridge.

In the university he met for the first time two scientists whose paths were later to cross his own in the penicillin enterprise. One was Dorothy Hodgkin, whose crystallographic work was finally to solve the riddle of the penicillin molecule's structure. The other was Norman Heatley, working for his PhD on 'The application of micro-chemical methods to biological problems'. The difference between Heatley and Chain was crucial but almost indefinable. Heatley was in no way anti-Semitic but was on the contrary an epitome of the men who later supported Rutherford's Academic Assistance Council. But there was a radical difference between Heatley's and Chain's assessment of how the human problems of life could best be tackled, a difference that transcended politics, race, and the other matters that divide one man from another. Neither Hodgkin nor Heatley had forewarning that chance was to bring on to the centre of the stage a German Jew who was obviously doing his best to fit into the English scene but as yet had hardly succeeded in doing so. By contrast, one of the few who may have sensed Chain's potential status was Hopkins, always a percipient judge of human beings and the man who in 1935 was to guide Chain on to his path.

Georges Dreyer, the first Professor of Pathology in Oxford, had died the previous August after occupying the Chair for more than a quarter of a century. The Sir William Dunn School of Pathology, whose head he had been since its opening, had become his monument, and there was more than normal university interest in who was to succeed him. Here chance was to play an unexpected part. In travelling to the meeting of the Electoral Board which was to decide the succession, Edward Mellanby, secretary of the Medical Research Council, missed his train from Paddington to Oxford and arrived only after the Board had failed to elect Mellanby's candidate, a young Australian, Howard Florey, and had instead elected someone else. But the force of Mellanby's character now persuaded the Board to change its collective mind and offer the Chair to Florey after all.

As the new director of the School, Florey was intent on building up its biochemical work. This was hardly a popular programme in the 1930s even though at the end of 1932 the then head of the Medical Research Council, Sir Walter Morley Fletcher, had thought it worth while writing to Florey with encouragement. 'Let me say that we here see little hope of progress in bacteriology without its biochemical development, and we think also that biochemistry simply cannot afford to dispense with the study of bacteria, who can beat any biochemist at his own game....' Florey's aim was unlikely to have been vigorously pursued by any other candidate, and in the spring of 1935 he began searching for a man to help him. Among his first choices was Norman W. Pirie. Nothing came of this since Hopkins maintained that he would be unable to release Pirie for two years. However, he suggested an alternative: Ernst Chain. 'I find his biochemical knowledge is more than merely adequate,' Hopkins wrote to Florey.

He has really become a well-qualified biochemist. I have just had to read his thesis for the PhD degree here (which he will certainly get) and am struck with the ability it displays. Leathers, who was external examiner, also thought highly of it and of the knowledge he displayed at our oral examination.

I feel that if his race and foreign origin will not be unwelcome in your department, you will import an acceptable and very able colleague in taking him. Incidentally, I have found that his remarkable genius as a musician has made him acceptable in certain social circles here – a point which I think is not without some importance.

Florey took Hopkins's advice and Chain was offered a one-year appointment in Oxford at £200 a year. 'This offer came to me as a very pleasant surprise,' Chain later wrote, 'because really I had no hopes at that time that I would find a university job in England, and I was quite prepared to emigrate to Australia, Canada or some country like that.' Without delay Chain went to Oxford to work under the man with whom his career was to be so closely linked.

We discussed the plans for the future organization of the Department of Biochemistry which Florey wanted me to organize in his Institute. He had been convinced for some years that biochemistry was of very great importance for the development of pathology and that in fact all pathological changes had at their basis biochemical phenomena, and he told me that I would have a completely free hand in developing that section. The only problem that he himself suggested was that I should become interested in elucidating the mode of action of the bacteriolytic substance lysozyme. He himself had been interested in this substance for some years. He had found that it had something to do with the nature of the gut and he believed that it had something to do with the nature of defence mechanisms against bacterial invasion and also possibly something to do with the protection against gastric ulcers.

The chance of building up his own department was an opportunity which Chain was eager to seize with both hands, although his hopes were qualified on the day he arrived in Oxford. In some ways, he discovered, conditions would not be so very different from those in London or Cambridge. Florey was ill and Chain was met at the station by James Kent, Florey's personal assistant. 'He looked like a refugee all right and seemed very depressed in every way,' Kent told Florey's biographer, Gwyn Macfarlane.

We walked to the School of Pathology and as we passed the Dyson Perrins [Laboratory] he caught sight of a Soxhlet apparatus (for extracting the soluble portion of any substance by a continuous circulation of the boiling solvent through it) through a window – they were pretty rare and expensive in those days and I don't suppose there were more than three or four in Oxford. He brightened up at once. 'You have Soxhlets in your Department?' he asked. I said that we had one. 'One?' he shouted. 'I must have six, a dozen!'

Other facilities were also fewer than Chain had expected, and a quarter of a century later he recalled how the cold store was small and not automatically regulated.

Every morning the chief laboratory steward poked his nose into the small existing cold store, and if he found it rather warm, switched on the motor of the ammonia compressor for such time until he thought it had cooled down enough. One of the first things I did in Oxford was to get the cold store enlarged and modernized.

The estimate for the job was exceeded by an amount which he recalled as £15; 'this caused a terrific upheaval,' he remembered, 'and Florey never forgot this incident and reminded me of it until I left the Institute'.

However, his later complaints were often more against the then state of the art than against Oxford, as when he wrote regretfully, 'we had no isotopes, no chromatography, no mass spectrograph, no nuclear magnetic resonance, only the beginnings of infra-red spectroscopy'. Often he must have seemed to his colleagues the inveterate complainer; to others, more perceptive, as the man for whom nothing less than the best would suffice.

Although there was a lack of equipment at the School of Pathology, the building itself had been designed only about a decade previously and in general the facilities impressed Chain more than those he had found at Cambridge; some two years were to pass before he appreciated that when it came to money Oxford was as short of it as Cambridge. He liked Florey and there was no hint yet of the disagreements that were to mar the relationship between the two men and to induce in Chain's mind the bitter belief that he was being unfairly treated. His money was still restricted to a few hundred pounds a year but he appears to have made it go further than in Cambridge and succeeded in renting a flat in North Oxford opposite the Dragon School which he was to occupy for the next thirteen years. It lay, he was to record, 'in one of those quiet and peaceful roads typical of this residential area, lined with cherry, almond and laburnum trees successively blossoming luxuriously in the spring and making North Oxford look like one big garden'.

Here he was joined in 1937 by Mrs Sacharina, who had moved from Berlin to Paris where she had set up a cosmetics business with her widowed sister. Chain was involved in lengthy negotiations with the

Home Office before Mrs Sacharina was allowed to settle in Britain and to some of his colleagues her presence as his housekeeper in Oxford was something of a mystery. This, however, ignored the contemporary problems of getting Jews out of Hitlerite Germany which effectively prevented him from bringing his mother and sister across the Channel – even had they been willing to come, which is uncertain. There was, moreover, the debt which he owed her for giving him the academic opportunities he would otherwise have lacked. During his early years in Britain she, more than any other person, enabled him to keep on an even mental keel for most of the time and thus played a significant if usually unacknowledged part in mothering penicillin into existence.

Chain was not what Dr Johnson would have called a clubbable man. However, music was still a preoccupation which came second only to chemistry in its attractions, and in Oxford, as earlier in Cambridge, it drew him into the company of like-minded men and women whom he would accompany on the piano or with whom he would play four-handed duets. With these exceptions he was self-contained, taking little or no part in communal activities and, a black mark in many eyes, playing no games, a fact not entirely balanced by his enjoyment in hard walking, particularly in the Lake District.

Immediately outside the School of Pathology there lay a group of tennis courts and those working under Florey would occasionally take time off for a few sets. Chain was never among those who played, and more than one colleague later commented on his lack of interest in any sport or game. It was, moreover, a characteristic which he knew set him apart from his colleagues. He recognized, and at times tended to exaggerate, the gulf that was created.

Whether or not lack of exercise affected him is not clear but during his first years in Britain his health continued to cause him worry. 'Periodic fear attacks', ran the notes on his health which he wrote for the period August 1935–February 1936.

Since January increased sudden attacks of palpitations, followed by strange languor. In laboratory from time to time sudden fear of being poisoned (strong palpitations, sudden eruptions of sweat).

During this period a big amount of work was to be done, scientific and musical. The food was inadequate. Death of several intimate friends. Several attacks of weakness, especially in the mornings, the strongest ca 3 weeks before the beginning of the influenza in February.

Apart from the influenza, which put him out of action for a number of weeks, there now occurred a more important event. Chain began to experience severe internal pains which could be diagnosed neither by his doctor nor the hospital to which he was taken. His foreign background, and his excitable nature, began to influence those in charge. The trouble, it was seriously suggested, must be mental rather than physical. The result was that he was taken to what friends and relatives have variously described as a specialist nursing home, a mental hospital and a lunatic asylum. Whatever the correct description, it was only with the help of Colya Seltsovsky, an acquaintance from the Continent, who described the situation to Ashley Miles, Chain's Cambridge friend, that Chain was eventually taken from the home.

The trouble was still a mystery when Mrs Sacharina took control and insisted that Chain visit her doctor in Paris. Here appendicitis was diagnosed, an operation was performed and Chain proudly returned from France with his appendix in a bottle.

The only credit item in the unfortunate incident was that Seltsovsky knew the family of a Jewish businessman, Simon Beloff, and that Chain was brought into contact with Beloff's daughter Anne, later to play an important part in his life as wife and professional colleague.

# —3—

# BIOCHEMISTRY
# AND PENICILLIN

Chain's research under Florey in Oxford's School of Pathology began with investigations into two specific problems. The first was continuation of work he had started in Cambridge: an investigation of the way in which snake venom worked. The second was an analysis of lysozyme, a substance of indeterminate nature discovered a few years earlier by the bacteriologist Alexander Fleming.

Since researches in Berlin's Charité had first united Chain's interests in biochemistry and physiology, he had been intrigued by the biochemical methods in which some substances brought about characteristic biological reactions. This had led him to study the ways in which some snake venoms brought about their neurotoxic effects. The enquiry was a good example of what he once described as his 'principal motivating principle' – essentially 'always to look for an interesting biological phenomenon which could be explained on a chemical or biochemical basis, and attempting to isolate the active substances responsible for the phenomenon and/or studying their mode of action'. In Cambridge he had discovered that some venoms inhibited the conversion of glucose into lactic acid, an essential process in living organisms. In Oxford he carried the investigation further, isolating and purifying the active agent in the venom, identifying it chemically and then discovering how it operated. As a result he established that the substance which did the damage was an enzyme which knocked out one of the enzymes in the victim's body which normally helped control cell respiration. In his own words, he was able to show

that the powerful neurotoxic effect of certain snake venoms was due to their action on the respiratory chain. The link affected in this case was the adenine-nicotinamide dinucleotide coenzyme, which, I showed, was rapidly and completely broken down into two mononucleotides by an enzyme of nucleotidase nature contained in the venom. . . .

Thus, for the first time, he could report that 'the mode of action of a natural toxin of protein nature could be explained in biochemical terms as that of an enzyme acting on a component of vital importance in the respiratory chain'.

He was able to show, he went on,

that the respiration of brain tissue can be completely arrested by minute amounts of snake venoms, and that this is the reason for their neurotoxic action. Thus for the first time the toxic action of a venom has been explained on a bio-chemical basis; the neurotoxin is an enzyme destroying a vital coenzyme required for carbohydrate oxidation. It is now understandable why the venom acts in such high dilution; it is a case of a catalyst acting on a catalyst.

Although Chain's experimental findings were certainly correct, there seems today to be some doubt about the validity of his reported conclusion. The neurotoxicity of purified snake venom, for instance, is at present believed to be associated with the action of a phospholipase on cell membranes.

While the examination of snake venom was continuing, Chain began a number of other, comparatively minor, investigations. One which, Florey wrote to Mellanby on 11 February 1936, 'seems to me well worth a little encouragement', was important for the future since it brought to Oxford the Norman Heatley whom Chain had already met in Cambridge and who had by this time become an expert in micro methods. The work was a comparison of the normal mouse epithelium with that from skin which had been painted with carcinogens for different lengths of time, and correlation of the histological and metabolic changes associated with the onset of malignancy. An expert in micro methods was essential, and in telling Mellanby of the proposal Florey said that he had already been in touch with Heatley 'who Chain proposes as a collaborator'. The research carried out with Isaac Berenblum who had been born in Eastern Europe but had for some years been working in Britain, was eventually abandoned when it was found that there was no difference between the metabolism of normal epithelium and that of tumours. But it was of personal importance in bringing to light the fact that Chain and Heatley were somewhat allergic to each other, a fact not without significance when both were later working on the penicillin project.

Even before the epithelium investigation had been abandoned Florey decided that Chain should turn to the investigation of lysozyme about which few chemical facts were known. Fleming, working at the time under Sir Almroth Wright in St Mary's Hospital, Paddington, had noted the action of lysozyme after a drop of nasal mucus had fallen on to a plate of bacteria. 'In this communication,' he wrote in a paper to the Royal Society, 'I wish to draw attention to a substance present in the tissues and secretions of the body, which is capable of rapidly dissolving certain bacteria. As this substance has properties akin to those of ferments I have called it "Lysozyme".' Sir Almroth, the model for Sir Colenso Ridgeon in Shaw's *The Doctor's Dilemma*, was not enthusiastic about the development of biochemistry in medicine and had some feelings in common with those who in Shaw's play maintained 'that drugs were delusional and could only suppress symptoms without eradicating disease, in contrast to the ability of the phagocytes, when suitably stimulated, to devour the germs and cure the patient'. Fleming nevertheless continued to investigate, found that the material was present in tears, saliva, the white of egg, and various animal and plant tissues as well as bronchial mucus, and described it in a paper 'On a Remarkable Bacteriolytic Element found in Tissues and Secretions' presented to the Royal Society early in 1922.

Although Fleming carried out further experimental work on lysozyme, it attracted little attention and during the next few years the only man to follow up the discovery was Florey, although his findings were as devoid of important results as Fleming's.

However, Florey's interest persisted, partly for a reason that was to become a link in the chain that led to penicillin. The antibacterial power of lysozyme was not particularly great, but the enzyme, for such it turned out to be, occurred in duodenal secretions which personally interested Florey.

Chain's interest was satisfied after a young Rhodes scholar, Leslie Epstein – who later changed his name to Falk – arrived in Florey's laboratory in 1936. 'He assigned me my doctorate thesis subject, "The Actions of Certain Bacteriolytic Principles",' Epstein has written, 'allowed me to choose Dr Ernst Chain, a brilliant biochemist, as my supervisor, and bade me get to work to isolate the substrate of lysozyme' – the specific substance whose reactivity was increased by it.

Chain himself was anxious to investigate the nature and chemical characteristics of lysozyme since his work on snake venom had increased his interest in enzymes which could produce dramatic biological effects, such as lysozyme's antibacterial action. The enzyme also had dramatic characteristics of a non-biological character. Thus a small amount added to a suspension so thick that it was possible to turn a glass of it upside down without the suspension running out, quickly turned the solution into one which would flow as easily as water. Chain wrote:

We were able to show that lysozyme was an enzyme of polysaccharidase nature acting on a polysaccharide which we could isolate from dried bacterial cells of *M. lysodeicticus.* We prepared the latter in batches of several hundred grams by growing the bacteria on agar surface in large Winchester bottles – for the purpose of distributing the agar evenly in these bottles we constructed a Heath Robinson contraption for rolling them. It was for the first time that I was confronted with the problem of producing micro-organisms in large amounts, and this problem has remained with me ever since throughout my professional career, and still confronts me at the present day.

While Chain's work on lysozyme – and, later and more importantly, on penicillin – is among the best-remembered examples of his research at the William Dunn, there was also his investigation, with E. S. Duthie, of the 'spreading factor', a substance present in extracts of testes, bacterial filtrates, venoms and leeches which enhanced the spread of intradermally injected dyes and particulate matter. Chain and Duthie showed this was an enzyme which liquefied a viscous polysaccharide, hyaluronic acid, present in skin, thereby permitting intradermally injected material to spread. Although the investigation had been started without thought of possible applications, it was now realized that the substance had had an important function in the process of mammalian fertilization since it enabled the sperm to penetrate the mucoid layer of the ovum.

Overshadowing both the work on the spreading factor and that on lysozyme was the investigation which was to lead to penicillin. There are different, and in some ways conflicting, accounts of how that work was triggered off. Even without the later discussions as to who was most responsible for transforming penicillin from a laboratory curiosity into a miracle-working drug – a transformation which passed through many separate stages – the process had sufficient inherent complications to make the separate allocation of credit almost impossible to assess with any hope of fairness. The situation was further complicated not by the vulgar hope of personal gain, which was happily absent from the make-up of those most personally involved, but by their conflicting personalities. To understand how the controversy arose it is first necessary to recall how the story of penicillin had developed until the late 1930s when Chain went to Oxford.

Despite the lack of scientific information on the way in which anti-bacterial agents worked, there was a record of 'old wives' cures' going back centuries. It was well known by both medical men and biochemists that in primitive societies moulds had frequently been used in the treatment of wounds and the cure of disease. The Ukraine, Yugoslavia, Greece and Finland were only some of the areas from which there had come reports that substances such as mouldy bread produced results that had no logical explanation but which could not be dismissed out of hand. In 1877 the whole question of antibacterial activity began to be brought on to a scientific basis when Pasteur and Joubert described the inhibiting action of certain organisms on the growth of the anthrax bacillus. Before the end of the century it was found that the growth of other bacteria could be inhibited by naturally occurring substances and the biochemist, able to isolate and analyse such substances, was brought into the field of medicine.

Bacteria-inhibiting properties – or antibiotic properties as they were subsequently called – were observed by William Roberts of Manchester, and in 1876 John Tyndall, the Victorian natural philosopher, spelt out the effects of penicillium noted while investigating the theories of spontaneous combustion the previous year.

The mutton in the study gathered over it a thick blanket of *Penicillium* [Tyndall wrote]. On the 13th [December 1875] it had assumed a light brown colour, 'as if by a faint admixture of clay'; but the infusion became transparent. The 'clay' here was the slime of dead or dormant *Bacteria*, the cause of their quiescence being the blanket of *Penicillium*. I found no active life in this tube, while all the others swarmed with *Bacteria*.

In every case where the mould was thick and coherent the *Bacteria* died, or became dormant, and fell to the bottom of the sediment. The growth of mould and its effect on the *Bacteria* was very capricious.... The *Bacteria* which manufacture a green pigment appear to be uniformly victorious in their fight with the *Penicillium*. ...

Tyndall went on to identify three different strains of penicillium, distinguishing them by their cultural characteristics, but does not appear to have realized that inhibition of the bacteria was due to a chemical substance produced by the mould. Only in the following year, 1877, did Pasteur write:

In the inferior and vegetable species, life hinders life. A liquid invaded by an organized ferment, or by an aerobe, makes it difficult for an inferior organism to multiply.... These facts may, perhaps, justify the greatest hope from the therapeutic point of view.

26

But the full realization that Tyndall and Roberts had demonstrated Pasteur's statement that 'life hinders life' had to wait for the twentieth century.

It came in 1928 when Fleming was studying· the staphylococcus micro-organism for a chapter he was writing in the textbook *System of Bacteriology*. The work involved the use of staphylococcus variants which were allowed to grow in Petri dishes and were inspected from time to time. At one point during the experiments Fleming took a holiday. In an ideal laboratory all the used material would have been cleared away before he left, but Fleming was not that kind of worker and when he returned to St Mary's a number of discarded, but untouched, dishes remained on the laboratory bench. It has usually been assumed that chance alone left one particular Petri dish to the mercy of the chance contamination, but a statement made by Fleming in 1946 throws doubt on this. 'Sometimes, however, it is unavoidable, as in this particular instance,' he wrote, 'when the culture plate had to be opened for examination under a dissecting microscope and then left for future examination.' The result, Fleming noted, was 'that around a large colony of contaminating mould (on one Petri dish) the staphylococcus colonies became transparent and were obviously undergoing lysis [the destruction of cells]'. They had, in other words, been killed off by the micro-organisms that had settled on the dish.

Fleming himself was surprised and, showing the dish to a colleague, exclaimed: 'That's funny.' Other visitors were shown the dish, and one, a Canadian Rhodes scholar, was told: 'You think yourself a clever fellow, explain this one.' During the next few days and weeks Fleming grew the contaminating mould – which had arrived according to legend through an open window but had almost certainly floated up from the room of a colleague on a lower floor – and discovered some facts about it.

While penicillin was thus being studied a decade before the outbreak of the Second World War, it is an interesting fact that the details of its chemical make-up remained uncertain for many years. However, Fleming succeeded in throwing a good deal of light on the life-history of the mould. The material which was to play such an important part in the relief of human suffering starts life as a spore which germinates and produces filaments which contain a number of cylindrical cells. These cells eventually form a thick felted colony. Reproductive cells are also produced and any one colony can in the end produce many millions of spores. These spores can be spread by such means as air currents. Then, if they fall on the right kind of culture medium, they can themselves turn into a mould colony such as can be seen on bread, jam, or similar organic matter which is sufficiently moist.

While the initial colony is a white fluffy mass, its centre later becomes dark green or even black. After a few more days there is a further change to a yellow or reddish colour.

There remained something of a mystery about Fleming's specimen of penicillin, a name which he gave to his active mould broth filtrate to avoid the use of a cumbersome phrase for it. The mystery was hardly removed by the long and elegant life of Fleming written by André Maurois. '[The book] is a brilliant and exciting novel which makes good reading, as all Maurois' biographies do,' Chain once wrote, 'but unfortunately it is as far removed from reality as can be and scientifically without much value.' Explanation had to wait until 1970 when Ronald Hare's *The Birth of Penicillin* showed that growth of the specimen depended on the climatic conditions of the period.

Fleming's mould continued to kill off staphylococci even when diluted 500-fold, and it showed no signs of being toxic when injected into either a rabbit or a mouse. As he was to write in the *Journal of Pathological Bacteriology* in 1932:

In penicillin we have a perfectly innocuous fluid which is capable of inhibiting the growth of the pyogenic cocci in dilutions of up to 1 in 800. It has been used on a number of septic wounds and has certainly appeared to be superior to dressings containing potent chemicals. . . . The practical difficulty in the use of penicillin for dressings of septic wounds is the amount of trouble necessary for its preparation and the difficulty of maintaining its potency for more than a few weeks.

It was in fact extremely unstable, losing most of its effect on staphylococci within ten to fourteen days.

He wrote up the discovery in the *British Journal of Experimental Pathology*, but for the moment did little more. Chain was later to write:

All Fleming had to do to demonstrate the curative effect of penicillin was to repeat the experiment of injecting 0.5 ml of his culture fluid into a 20 g mouse infected with a few streptococci or pneumococci which he had shown to be very sensitive to penicillin. With 1 or 2 units per ml of penicillin he would undoubtedly have obtained a striking curative effect in such an infected mouse.

He did not perform this obvious experiment for the simple reason that he did not think of it.

But, as Chain and others were to point out, there were respectable reasons for Fleming's omission. The instability of penicillin appeared to rule out its use for therapeutic purposes. There was also another reason that may have helped deter Fleming. Ronald Hare has pointed out, after his examination of Fleming's notebooks, now in the British Library, that Fleming believed that penicillin disappeared rapidly from the blood, and also that it took a long time to kill bacteria. If this were the case, its potential value was obviously limited.

The possibility that it might be a new drug of great value was further decreased when Harold Raistrick of the London School of Hygiene and Tropical Medicine carried out a series of experiments in 1932. Raistrick was one of the world's greatest experts on moulds, and the chemicals which they could produce, and his work was planned to discover more about the chemical nature of penicillin rather than to investigate its value as a therapeutic agent. It could apparently be produced only in minute quantities, it was as unstable as Fleming had already discovered, and it appeared to have no practical value. However, there were other results of Raistrick's experiments. One was that the penicillin used by Fleming in 1928 was found to be *Penicillium notatum*. Secondly, it was found that the mould would grow not only on the broth of bullock's heart which Fleming had used but also on a modified form of the artificial Czapek-Dox medium, named after its inventor and consisting merely of glucose and mineral salts in water. But there was a third, more important, result. When Raistrick showed 'that the concentration of penicillin was not quite successful even in the hands of an expert chemist', Fleming later wrote to Florey, 'I am afraid I got discouraged about the problem.'

While Raistrick's findings tended to dissipate any interest in penicillin that might then have existed, there was also the feeling against chemo-therapy which had been nurtured for years at St Mary's by Almroth Wright. As Sir Henry Dale was to put it in a kindly way: 'Neither the time when the discovery was made nor, perhaps, the scientific atmo-sphere of the laboratory in which [Fleming] worked, was propitious to such further enterprise as its development would have needed.'

Chain was to describe the situation more forcibly: 'I believe it to be a particularly striking example of how prejudice in scientific thinking can interfere with progress.' And to Lady Fleming he wrote after Sir Alexander's death:

I still believe that in the Wright atmosphere of St Mary's the mere thought of replacing immunotherapy by chemotherapy was considered absolute blasphemy. I think if this atmosphere could have been a little less despotic and people less prejudiced against the new concepts, Fleming could not have resisted the temptation to repeat his toxicity tests on infected animals with the crude culture liquid, without any chemical purification whatsoever, and there is no doubt in my mind that in this case, on injecting the crude culture fluid into infected animals twice or three times, he would have observed a sufficiently dramatic curative effect – though perhaps not such a clear case as we obtained with the purified material – to encourage him to engage a good chemist and proceed with the purification at all costs.

The strength of Sir Almroth Wright's opposition was revealed years later when in 1979 V. D. Allison wrote: 'Wright had been the reverse of enthusiastic about the curative value of penicillin when the manuscript of the first paper was submitted for publication. So much so, that he had demanded the omission of the short paragraph suggesting its employment for surface infections – meaning local infections.' But Fleming stood his ground and the offending sentence ('It is suggested that [penicillin] may be an efficient antiseptic for application to, or injection into, areas infected with penicillin-sensitive microbes') was published without alteration.

However, while Fleming did not foresee the use of penicillin as a chemotherapeutic agent he did appreciate its more limited antibacterial use. He wrote as early as 1929:

Penicillin, in regard to infections with sensitive microbes, appears to have some advantage over the well-known antiseptics. A good example will inhibit staphylococci, *Streptococcus pyogenes* and pneumococcus in a dilution of 1 in 800. It is there a more powerful inhibitory agent than is carbolic acid and it can be applied to an infected surface undiluted as it is non-irritant and non-toxic. If applied, therefore, on a dressing, it will still be effective even when diluted 800 times which is more than can be said of the chemical antiseptics in use. Experiments in connection with its value in the treatment of pyogenic infections are in progress. In addition to its possible use in the treatment of bacterial infections penicillin is certainly useful to the bacteriologist for its power of inhibiting unwanted microbes in bacterial cultures so that penicillin insensitive to bacteria can readily be isolated.

Whatever the strength of the various factors inhibiting a determined follow-up of the discovery, there was a further very practical consideration: the effect of penicillin on bacteria appeared to be extremely variable, the reason for this only becoming clear in the 1940s as the factors present in Fleming's initial discovery began to be understood. The penicillin involved is quite common and as Chain was to say, 'it can be isolated from most of the back and front gardens of London houses; it must have landed on innumerable Petri dishes of bacteriologists in this country'. However, special, even exceptional, conditions are needed to produce the results that Fleming observed. The penicillin contaminant must have had time to grow, at the right temperature, to considerable strength; the staphylococci, by contrast, should be hit before they become fully grown. Fleming had left his Petri dish for several weeks at a temperature of 18-20°C which was warm enough for the penicillin to grow reasonably fast but was not warm enough to bring the staphylococci up to full strength. This was the factor of chance and good luck which was to lead to the saving of so many lives in the years which lay ahead.

To these exceptional conditions, needed before the anti-bacterial characteristics of penicillin can be visible, there is added the requirement that its spores should settle and reproduce before the eyes of a trained observer such as Fleming. The odds against such a happening are enormous. Ronald Hare, who was later to work on the purification of penicillin, has expressed it in this way.

And if, as Ehrlich used to say, scientific discovery depends partly on *Geld* or money, partly on *Geduld* or patience, partly on *Geschick* or brains, and partly on *Glück* or luck, it was the last of them that was almost entirely responsible for the discovery of penicillin. It was, surely, the supreme example in all history of the part that luck may play in the advancement of knowledge.

Chain himself had one rider on this verdict. After citing as other examples of luck in science the discovery of radioactivity by Madame Curie and of X-rays by Roentgen, he noted:

We ourselves at Oxford, in the discovery of the curative properties of penicillin had plenty of luck. Therefore it is petty and irrelevant to try to detract from the importance of Fleming's discovery by describing it entirely to good luck, and there is no doubt that his discovery, which has changed the history of medicine, has justly earned him a position of immortality.

Generous as the judgement is, it does not represent the entire story. A hint of the rest is given by a later reported comment of Fleming. 'I would have produced penicillin in 1929 if I had had the luck to have had a tame refugee chemist at my right hand. I had to stop where I did.' However, he did have the help of two medical students, Ridley and Craddock.

In these early days one man did, however, consider the therapeutic possibilities of penicillin although nothing came of his idea. John F. Fulton has revealed in the *Journal of the History of Medicine* that

Among the records of the Yale School of Medicine an application [was] made in 1930 by a man who has since become a prominent member of our faculty for a grant to study the possibility of extracting the *Penicillium* mold for therapeutic purposes. The grant was turned down.

Thus the situation in the late 1930s was that Fleming's discovery of penicillin's possibilities had been stillborn. That it failed to remain so was due to events in the William Dunn. These led to a survey of the relevant literature by Chain and the start under Florey's direction of what was to be intensive research into penicillin. There is, however, some vagueness about the events themselves although it does seem that search of the literature was probably carried out after Chain and Florey, walking across the Parks after work one evening, finally decided that it should be carried out. However, Isaac Berenblum, who had earlier carried out work with Chain and Heatley on cancer research with the help of Heatley's micro-apparatus, distinctly remembers a significant teatime meeting in the William Dunn at which both Florey and Chain were present. The talk, he says, turned to antiseptics, and then to those that could not be used internally. At this point Florey first recalled Fleming's discovery of penicillin and then mentioned Raistrick's experiments in which penicillin had appeared to be unusably unstable.

Chain, says Berenblum, overheard the conversation and, in character, chipped in with the opinion that in that case Raistrick could not be such a very good chemist. It *must*, he is remembered as adding, be possible to produce it in stable form. This assertion, it can be claimed with considerable plausibility, played its part, if not indeed the vital part, in leading to the work from which penicillin finally emerged as the live-saver it was.

One certain outcome of Chain's interest was his search of the literature dealing with bacterial substances, a search which turned up some two hundred items, 'many more references than I had expected to find', as he described it. Although the number sounds large, two hundred or more references to antibiotics were included in *Les Associations microbiennes* by Papagostas and Gate, itself listed in a 1930 paper by Goldsworthy and Florey on lysozyme. Chain also wrote that

In some cases it was shown that the antagonistic action of one microbe against the other was due to the production, by the antagonistic species, of metabolites and anti-bacterial action, but almost nothing was known about the chemical nature or pharmacological properties of these substances. In numerous discussions which Florey and I had on the subject, it became clear to us that here was a neglected field of research worth a systematic study. It seemed to us that such a study could bring to light antibacterial structures of a novel type which, either in their original or in a chemically modified form, could become of therapeutic interest.

Among the papers which Chain had studied during his search of the literature was of course Fleming's 1929 report on penicillin.

When I saw [it] for the first time [Chain wrote] I thought Fleming had discovered a sort of mould lysozyme, which in contrast to egg-white lysozyme acted on a wide range of gram-positive pathogenic bacteria. I further thought that in all probability the cell wall of all these pathogenic bacteria whose growth was inhibited by penicillin contained a common substrate on which the supposed enzyme acted, and that it would be worth trying to isolate and characterize the hypothetical common substrate. For this purpose it would, of course, be necessary to purify the supposed enzyme, but I did not foresee any undue difficulties with this task for which I was well prepared from my previous research experience.

Soon after Chain had read the Fleming paper, he and Epstein made some tentative investigations into penicillin. These experiments, which were to consolidate Chain's interest in Fleming's material, were made possible by a coincidence almost as startling as the events which had originally brought penicillin to Fleming's attention.

After reading Fleming's paper, Chain later said: 'Something seemed to click in my mind.' He remembered a Miss Campbell-Renton who worked in the laboratory.

I went at once to find her and ask her whether I had seen her carrying a Petri dish with a mould culture along the corridor that separated our laboratories, and she said she had. I asked her if she knew the strain of the mould and if, by any chance, it was *Penicillium notatum*. She looked surprised and then said 'yes', it was, and that she had been using some of it for some time in the bacteriology lab to separate unwanted bacteria from cultures of *B. influenza* which was not sensitive to penicillin. I was astounded at my luck in finding the very mould about which I had been reading, here, in the same building, right under our very noses. I could hardly believe it was true. Miss Campbell-Renton agreed to give me a sample and told me that it had been obtained from Fleming by Professor Dreyer, Florey's predecessor, who had thought for a time that it might have some relationship to his interest in bacteriophage – but that he had lost interest when it was seen that it had nothing to do with that subject.

Chain later stressed that it was important to make one statement about the incentives behind the investigations on which he embarked with Epstein.

As far as I am concerned the problem of reinvestigating penicillin was a biochemical one.... I was interested to find out the reasons for [the] extraordinary instability of the active principle. I believed that the substance in question was a very unstable enzyme and probably denatured by the methods this group of scientists used, and I thought I would start tackling this problem using the much milder methods of enzyme chemistry with which I was familiar from my earlier work. It never struck me for a fraction of a second that this substance could be used from the chemotherapeutic point of view because, evidently, a substance which is so unstable that it goes off while you look at it, does not give very great promise with regard to practical applicability. Later on it turned out that it was not at all as unstable as it looked at the beginning and this was then a different matter, but we could not know this when we began the work. The substance was described in the literature as non-toxic, or I should rather say the crude culture fluid containing an unknown and probably a very small concentration of the active principle was described as non-toxic.

I believed at this time that the active principle was an enzyme, that is to say was of protein nature. Under these circumstances, it would be expected to be non-toxic. If it were just an ordinary protein, it would have no acute toxicity; nevertheless, it would have been quite impossible to use it as a chemotherapeutic agent for the reason that it would obviously produce anaphylactic phenomena. Altogether, at that time, my particular interest was to try to find an enzyme similar to lysozyme, which would act on something in the cell of the pathogenic bacteria. For me it would have been a very interesting problem in any case, even if it should have turned out to be a protein and of no practical value, because it would have shown us something about the structure of the cell of pathogenic bacteria and we should have isolated a constituent of obviously vital importance from the bacterial cell which was common to a large number of important pathogens. So, irrespective of the eventual practical outcome of the work, it was bound to produce some results of really considerable interest to the biochemist.

At this point the murk surrounding the early days of penicillin becomes even thicker. Neither Epstein nor Chain has described their first work with penicillin in any detail, and Chain's notebooks for the period have not been found. Epstein has merely reported that the results were unimpressive. However, Chain is known to have obtained crude preparations of penicillin by extractions with methanol.

Early in 1939 Florey produced the first recorded link between Chain and penicillin. It came in an application to the Medical Research

Council, made by Florey on 27 January, and in a request for £200 per year for expenses, itemized £75 a year

For a continuation of work on Lytic substances. Mr Epstein and Dr Chain [it read] have devised a simple means for growing bacteria in bulk – some 150 gms per week of dried M. Lysodeikticus. From the organism they have prepared 10 gms of a 'polysaccharide' which gives about 10 per cent of reducing substance on treatment with lysozyme. They wish to carry out further purification and to characterize the substrate of lysozyme more exactly. With the knowledge obtained from the investigation of this lytic enzyme investigations are planned on the specific lysins in sera as well as the nature of the antibacterial substance in 'penicillin' and 'actinomycetin'.

But lysozyme continued to demand attention and despite the early stroke of luck, the first enquiries into penicillin were not vigorously followed up. It was only in September 1939 that Florey could write to tell Mellanby that 'we have . . . actually started work on Penicillin'.

In his letter dated 6 September, Florey went on:

There is little doubt that Chain has a flair for dealing with enzyme protein and the proposals now made have a very practical bearing at the moment. I can get clinical co-operation from Cairns for any products we produce and I have tested on animals.

Like Florey, Cairns was an Australian, professor of General Surgery in Oxford, already recognized as one of Britain's leading surgeons. In the clinical work soon to be necessary as a result of the penicillin investigations about to be started in the William Dunn, he was to be invaluable.

In October the Medical Research Council received the application which was eventually to produce such dramatic results. Both Florey and Chain had a hand in its instigation, but Florey was later to go on record as saying: 'Eventually Chain proposed, and I agreed to go along with it, that we should make a thorough investigation of antibacterial substances. That is why we looked at penicillin.'

The application, made by Florey on Chain's behalf, was for an annual grant of £300, plus an expenses grant of up to £100 a year. Chain would be able to work full time on the project since his duties as a University Demonstrator would be in abeyance during the war. The aim of the work would be:

Preparation from certain bacteria and fungi of powerful bactericidal enzymes, effective against staphylococci, pneumococci and streptococci.

Work carried out in this Department over a number of years [the application continued] has shown that the bacteriolytic principle of egg-white lysozyme is an enzyme which exerts its action by hydrolysing a complex polysaccharide present in the bacterial membrane.

Although chemically most suitable for use as an antiseptic *in vivo*, its practical application is limited by the fact that its action is almost entirely confined to non-pathogenic organisms. There are, however, accounts in the literature of substances with chemical properties very similar to those of lysozyme, which act powerfully on pathogenic bacteria, especially on staphylococci, pneumococci and streptococci. These substances have been obtained from filtrates of certain strains of penicillium, actinomycetes and of certain soil bacteria. Of these substances only the bactericidal principle from soil bacteria, which is especially effective against pneumococci, has been studied in some detail. Recently prominence has been given to this substance in the American medical literature, since it has not only a strong bactericidal effect on most types of pneumococci *in vitro*, but also can cure and protect animals from infections with virulent pneumococci. The chemical properties of the bactericidal substance are very similar to those of lysozyme; there can be no doubt that it is an enzyme belonging probably to the same group of enzymes as lysozyme.

Filtrates of certain strains of penicillium contain a bactericidal substance, called penicillin by its discoverer Fleming, which is especially effective against staphylococci, and acts also on pneumococci and streptococci. There exists no really effective substance acting against staphylococci *in vivo*, and the properties of penicillin, which are similar to those of lysozyme, hold out promise of its finding a practical application in the treatment of staphylococcal infections. Penicillin can easily be prepared in large amounts and is non-toxic to animals, even in large doses. Hitherto the work on penicillin has been carried out with very crude preparations and no attempt has been made to purify it. In our opinion the purification of penicillin can be carried out easily and rapidly.

A further bactericidal principle, similar to penicillin, but effective against the enteric group of bacteria, has been found in filtrates of certain strains of actinomycetes. As in the case of penicillin, very little chemical work has been done on this substance.

In view of the possible great practical importance of the above mentioned bactericidal agents, it is proposed to prepare these substances in a purified form suitable for intravenous injections and to study their antiseptic action *in vivo*. In addition to their action on staphylococci and the enteric group of bacteria, these substances may, by their action against streptococci and pneumococci, make it possible to reduce the large doses of the sulphanilamide drugs at present necessary, and thus obviate some of their toxic manifestations.

Thus penicillin was only one of three candidates for investigation. In addition there was pyocyanase, a substance produced by *Pseudomonas* and discovered by Emmerich and Löw in 1899; and actinomycetin, a metabolic product of an actinomycete discovered in 1924 by Gratia and Dath.

Penicillin was the first of the three to be considered. This was presumably due to the little earlier work on the substance, although he later maintained that when Florey learned of this earlier work his reaction was 'what reason have you to think that you would be successful where other competent chemists failed'.

Chain once explained:

As far as I am concerned the problem of reinvestigating penicillin was a biochemical one. There was described in the literature an obviously very active antibacterial substance – I mean from Fleming's description it was obvious that the mould secreted a very active antibacterial principle; and other people, another group of very competent chemists who had started to investigate the nature of this substance after Fleming, had reported that it was extremely unstable and went off, as you would say, while you looked at it. . . .

Any doubt about the spur which drove him towards penicillin was dissipated when he later wrote

I became interested immediately in penicillin after seeing Fleming's paper not because I hoped to discover a miraculous drug for the treatment of bacterial infection which, for some reason, had been overlooked, but because I thought it had great scientific interest. In fact, if I had been working, at that time, in aim-directed scientific surroundings, say in the laboratory of a pharmaceutical firm, it is my firm belief that I would never have obtained the agreement of my bosses to proceed with my project to work on penicillin.

Florey took much the same view and has been quoted as saying of the early penicillin research, 'I don't think that the idea of helping suffering humanity ever entered our minds.'

What did attract him – comparable to the chemical riddle of penicillin with its fugitive characteristics that attracted Chain – was what he has called 'a stimulus of a more materialistic nature'. In 1937 the department had an overdraft of £500, he told Chain, and no further equipment was to be ordered, stressing the situation by adding 'even a piece of glass rod', words that lodged in Chain's mind and affected his attitude to scientific funding for the rest of his life.

After an unsuccessful approach to the MRC for a very modest support of my research project, [I] decided that it was essential for us, if we were to make any progress at all, to become as independent as possible of both university and government financial support and to look for private funds. I thought that a long-term project that would keep us going for a number of years would suit us best, so that we would not have to go through the agonizing experience of fund-raising every year, and I started to think intensely about possible subjects for a project. The systematic study of antibacterial substances produced by micro-organisms seemed ideal for the purpose.

Thus the scene was set for the enquiry into penicillin which, quite coincidentally with the outbreak of war in September 1939, began to take the centre of the stage.

In 1939 information about the chemical composition of penicillin was slight, but it was known to be produced from moulds whose tangle of fine threads threw off fruiting bodies which in turn produced spores. When the spores came into contact with the right kind of medium they began to germinate. Thus *P. roqueforti* made the blue veins in Roquefort cheese and *P. camemberti* gave Camembert its distinctive taste. *P. expansum* destroyed half the American apples that were lost in winter storage and *P. digitatum* did the same for oranges.

The structure of penicillin only became apparent during the 1940s. The nucleus of the penicillin molecule, it was gradually understood, consists of two rings of atoms. One is a five-sided thiazolidine ring containing atoms of sulphur, carbon, hydrogen, oxygen and nitrogen arranged in a specific way; the other is a beta-lactam ring containing atoms of carbon, hydrogen, oxygen and nitrogen; and the five-sided and four-sided rings have a common side, so that the nucleus of the penicillin molecule can be diagramatically drawn as:

$$(CH_3)_2C \text{------} CH\text{-}COOH$$

$$S \qquad N \qquad \qquad \text{Penicillinase}$$
$$\qquad \qquad \qquad \qquad \qquad H_2O$$
$$HC \qquad CO$$
$$CH$$

I. Penicillin

$$NH\text{-}COR$$

The penicillin nucleus is called 6-aminopenicillanic acid, or 6-APA. When originally used therapeutically, however, penicillin consisted of the nucleus to which there is attached a side chain of atoms whose composition and structure governs both the absolute activity of the penicillin and the spectrum of bacteria against which it is effective. The side chains can be of considerable complexity, that of benzylpenicillin, the penicillin most used therapeutically consisting, for instance, of five carbon atoms each linked to a hydrogen atom and a sixth carbon atom linked to two hydrogen atoms – the whole side chain making up phenylacetic acid. By 1971, little more than three decades after research had started on penicillin as an antibiotic, some 1,800 different penicillins had been prepared and studied at the Beecham laboratories, while the number known throughout the world included many thousands more.

It is natural, in view of the legends that were to spread, that both Florey and Chain should stress that their investigation was not started with the specific hope of dealing more efficiently with the wounded of the Second World War. Nevertheless, the autumn of 1939, which saw the German invasion of Poland and the first casualties of the Royal Air Force, did witness three events which, though fortuitous in their timing, paved the way for the preparation of therapeutically usable penicillin. One was the recruitment into the penicillin project of Norman Heatley, who was to play a key role in the enterprise. Another was the preparation by Chain of an application for support by the Rockefeller Foundation without which penicillin would almost certainly have been stillborn. The third was the start of penicillin manufacture on an experimental basis in Oxford and the accumulation of the first data on which the antibiotics industry was eventually to be based.

These events took place as Chain, who had had annually to renew his permission to remain in Britain until he had become naturalized earlier in 1939, found himself working in a nation at war. He had taken his summer holiday in Belgium and had hurried back to Britain at the end of August to arrive only a few days before the German invasion of Poland. On 25 August Florey had proposed to Mellanby that Chain, A. G. Sanders, a part-time worker in the laboratory, and he himself should form a small research unit, adding: 'I have agreed to give 1/3 of my time to the War Office for gas research, whatever that means.' He and Chain were soon heading a small group specializing in blood transfusions, but although Chain had taken a Red Cross First Aid course he was later forbidden to practise in the organization on the grounds that he was alien born. His military call-up was deferred – presumably on the grounds of the work he was doing – but three years later the deferment was cancelled, and at the height of the penicillin research Florey had to write in desperation to the Medical Research Council. In the laboratory work went on much as before, hampered only by the blackout regulations and similar restrictions.

Earlier in 1939 Heatley had been awarded a Rockefeller Foundation grant to work from September onwards with Linderstrøm-Lang and Holter in Copenhagen. The declaration of war on 3 September changed all that, and Florey proposed that Heatley should work on at the William Dunn in developing the micro-apparatus which would be needed for the penicillin project. While Heatley was glad to work on at the laboratory he felt that if collaboration with Chain was involved it would be wiser to decline. The decision reflects adversely on neither man; but in both background and temperament they were as dissimilar as the proverbial chalk and cheese, and it is clear from the surviving records that within the confines of a smallish laboratory the scope for disagreement would be considerable.

Heatley explained his position to Florey in the presence of Chain and of Isaac Berenblum, and Florey assured Heatley that he would be accountable to him and not to Chain. This solved the immediate problem although minor disagreements were to continue.

In October, on Florey's suggestion, Chain made his own application to the Medical Research Council for financial support. The outcome was a grant of £300 per year, which continued until 1943, and an expenses grant of £250 a year from 1939 to 1940. These, in Chain's opinion, were merely 'little bits and pieces of £50 and £100 ... which really did not lead us anywhere', and he now proposed that Florey should make an attempt to get money from the Rockefeller Foundation. 'It was to be a joint study', Chain wrote, 'in which I would be concerned with the isolation of the antimicrobial substances, whereas [Florey's] part would be the biological assay of the products and the study of their pharmacological properties.'

The suggestion was made at a lucky moment, since Dr H. N. Miller of the Foundation's headquarters in New York was about to visit Oxford. In November 1939 Florey met Miller and discussed the possibilities of a block grant to the Institute. Chain reported:

After Miller left Florey came down to my laboratory and said that Miller told him that provided that we could submit a *biochemical* programme, there was a good chance that we could get a grant. But the programme had to be of a biochemical nature and not of a medical nature, and Florey asked me whether I would be prepared to work out a programme which would be suitable for the Rockefeller Foundation. I said this would be very easy and set out at once to work.

Chain's programme contained three sections. One dealt with the continuation of his work on toxins and snake venoms. A second concerned the spreading factor and the third dealt with bacterial antagonism. Chain later wrote,

I suggested that it would be a fruitful occupation to investigate *systematically* this field which so far had been completely neglected from the chemical point of view. It seemed to me that here was material which could occupy us for at least a ten-year period without having to produce any fresh ideas at all. Florey agreed to this; he took this memorandum, wrote a covering letter and sent it to the Rockefeller Foundation.

The covering letter from Florey, dated 20 November 1939, read:

I have been fortunate in having in the department Dr E. Chain who has, I have no hesitation in saying, a very great flair for the elucidation of enzymes as well as other biochemical problems. He has been the guiding chemist in all the work so far done here and, under the new proposals, he would continue in that capacity. I might also point out that, where necessary, this chemical work is correlated with biological investigations such as those needing animal experiments.

In view of the fact, rightly stressed by both Florey and Chain, that penicillin was not developed specifically to deal with war wounds, it is worth putting into the other side of the balance the words with which Florey ended his letter to the Foundation: 'It may also be pointed out that the work proposed, in addition to its theoretical importance, may have practical value for therapeutic purposes.' Practical use was not, as is sometimes suggested, entirely ruled out; from the start the intellectual and the utilitarian acted as double spurs to progress.

The application to the Rockefeller Foundation asked for wages for three technical workers and £600 for 'one fully qualified biochemist for one year'. The bill for one year's chemicals and apparatus was put at £500 and the equipment required was listed in detail. The total came to £2,452, £1,670 for wages and an equipment grant of £782, and it is a tribute to Chain's advocacy that not only was the initial grant approved but that between 1940 and 1945 the money from the Foundation totalled £6,140.

To Chain, and to Florey, this was support on a scale they had never before known, yet it was to be no less than was required for the research that lay ahead. For as work continued in the William Dunn it became increasingly clear that all the three stages of penicillin production posed problems far larger than had been expected.

The first of the three stages was fermentation, during which a penicillin mould was grown on a liquid, the culture medium. The second stage was extraction, in which the penicillin which had accumulated in or on the liquid was extracted and purified. In the third stage the penicillin was dried and put into ampoules.

Initially the penicillin was grown in shallow trays of Czapek-Dox medium, a refinement on the rough digest of bullocks' hearts which Fleming had used in 1928. Attempts were made to improve the yield by adding glutamine, a colourless amino-acid, various other chemicals, and even such household products as Marmite. They had little effect and the only major improvement came when boiled brewers' yeast was added to the medium. This not only increased yield by about 10 per cent but reduced the time needed to bring the mould to maturity from three weeks to ten days.

A further improvement in 'output' came after Heatley had discovered that it was possible to harvest penicillin from beneath a mature mould without disturbing the mould itself, and then to grow a second 'crop' from the broth once this had been brought up to its previous volume. The second 'crop' matured in only two-thirds of the time needed for the first. The process could, moreover, be repeated up to twelve times.

The extractors which gathered the 'crop' in the second stage of the operation were of various kinds; even the best, according to Chain's description, would be judged primitive by today's standards.

The basic unit, of which there were six working in parallel, was a glass tube containing amyl acetate down which fell a shower of droplets of cooled brew which had been acidified with phosphoric acid immediately before entering the jets. The droplets, which yield their penicillin to the solvent, coalesced at the bottom of the tube and passed to waste through an automatic syphon, while a gummy material (which with more vigorous shaking caused stable emulsions) collected at the solvent-water interface in a bottle at the bottom of each column and was periodically removed. Fresh solvent was fed in continuously at the bottom of each column and a corresponding amount of penicillin-rich solvent passed out at the top through a trap to a collecting bottle, after which it was dealt with by hand. There were special devices for controlling rates of flow, liquid levels, and the position of interfaces, and there was a system of coloured lights and a bell which gave warning shortly before any of the containers needed replacing ...

Other similar and slightly Heath Robinson methods included percolating the medium through columns of wood shavings on which the penicillin developed, and growing it on strings which had been saturated with the culture medium.

Another method, proposed by Heatley, was that penicillin should be extracted from ether into a neutral buffer. An account made with the aid of Heatley's laboratory notebooks says that Chain maintained the method would not work, that Florey was encouraging, and that Chain agreed only reluctantly, saying: 'Then if you think it will work, why don't you do it yourself? That will surely be the best and quickest way to show that you are wrong.'

The method overcame one difficulty: that penicillin appeared to be stable only when it was in, or at least near to, a neutral state between acidity and alkalinity. But low temperatures decreased the inactivation rate, and if the solvent extraction process was carried on at or near 0°C, it was possible to end up with a liquid in which most of the antibacterial activity had been retained.

Yet a further difficulty still remained: it appeared impossible to dry or crystallize the solution without its antibacterial characteristics disappearing during the process.

Eventually freeze-drying which involves the freezing of the liquid and then the removal of the water from it by volatilization at low pressure and temperature, was used. In Nature the process takes place on mountains where ice or snow disappear without passing through a liquid state. Although it had already been applied in the laboratory it had only gone into general use after the start of the war in September 1939, for the drying of blood serum. Its use to produce certain enzymes without reducing their activity was found to be successful, and Chain thought that the antibacterial agent in penicillin might be retained in the same way. The idea worked. 'I obtained,' he wrote, 'as was to be expected, a very nice brown powder which kept the entire activity of the medium undiminished, without any loss whatsoever.'

This brown powder contained everything that had been in solution, but first attempts to purify it produced the earlier problem: loss of biological activity. This difficulty was overcome by using dry methanol as a solvent, diluting the solution with water and then freeze-drying the result. It was during this set of experiments that the extraordinary antibacterial activity of penicillin was appreciated in full for the first time, for it was found that it would stop bacteria from growing even at a dilution of one part in a million.

This remarkable power, which showed that it was twenty times as strong as the strongest sulphonamide, led Chain to believe that the penicillin they were using must be comparatively pure. In fact the brown powder, as then produced, contained only 1 per cent of pure penicillin, and it was a remarkable piece of luck for the work that none of its impurities were toxic.

While these early attempts to find the best way of making penicillin were continuing it was thought necessary to improve on the comparatively primitive methods of measuring the antibacterial strengths of the various batches. The result was Heatley's cylinder plate method which was to be used as standard in the antibiotics industry for a number of years. A hole was bored in a glass plate on which bacteria were being grown, and a small hollow glass cylinder was fitted into the hole. A sample of the penicillin under trial would then be dropped down the cylinder and at its bottom there would develop a 'zone of inhibition' within which the bacteria were prevented from growing. The diameter of this zone indicated the antibacterial strength of the penicillin.

The cylinder plate method was the first of various successful attempts to bring some form of standard measurement into the field of antibiotics – a word not coined until 1943, when it was used by Selman A. Waksman, the discoverer of streptomycin, a drug effective against various micro-organisms, including the one which causes tuberculosis.

Among the next developments was definition of the 'Oxford unit', at first known as the Florey unit and designed primarily for the convenience of workers at the William Dunn School. There were two definitions of the unit. One was 'That amount of penicillin which when dissolved in 1 c.cm of water gives the same inhibition as ... (a certain partly purified) standard (solution)'; the second, 'The amount of penicillin contained in 1 ml of a certain phosphate buffer solution containing ether.' This was approximately the same as the international standard set up three years later by the permanent commission of the Health Organization of the League of Nations and, while purely arbitrary, roughly corresponded to the amount of penicillin which, when dissolved in 50 millilitres of broth, would just inhibit the growth of the test staphylococcus.

By 1943 there were known to be at least three different penicillins, and the standard was determined by pooling samples from British and US firms and the Northern Regional Research Laboratory at Peoria, Illinois, and then recrystallizing them. The ten grams of the result was deposited at the National Institute for Medical Research at Hampstead, London, and then dispensed in 30 mg amounts in hermetically sealed phials. The international unit was then defined as 'the specific activity contained in 0.6 micrograms of the International Penicillin Standard' – activity roughly the same as that of the original 'Oxford unit'.

While research continued at Oxford into the most effective ways of producing penicillin and of investigating its antibacterial properties, Chain was trying to solve the complex riddle of exactly what the material was and of how the atoms in its molecule were put together. Early in his investigations he received a shock. Penicillin, he found, passed easily through cellophane filters; this meant that it could not possibly be a large molecule and this in turn meant that it was not an enzyme as he had previously believed.

I was at first disappointed with the finding [he later said] for my beautiful working hypothesis dissolved into thin air, yet the fact of the instability of penicillin remained and became even more puzzling as it could not be explained on the basis of being a protein. There was at that time no other antibacterial with that degree of instability known, and it became very interesting to find out which structural features were responsible for the instability. It was clear that we were dealing with a chemically very unusual substance and thus it was of obvious interest to continue with the work. Only the nature of our problem had changed; instead of studying the isolation and mode of action of an enzyme with strong antibacterial properties, our task was now the elucidation of the structure of a low molecular substance which combined high antibacterial power with great chemical instability.

It was a challenging task, very suitable for Chain's particular talents, as his interest in biochemical problems had developed since his Berlin days into what was almost a vocation. At the very least it was an ability raised to extreme levels; just as some men have what seems to be an instinctive 'feel' for handling horses, and others have an uncanny appreciation of the way in which a mountain can best be tackled, Chain had a flair for understanding how the more complex problems of biochemistry could be solved.

This great ability could be balanced at times by his acute sensitivity to what he sometimes regarded as personal slights when none was intended. For years after Fleming and Florey had been elected to the Athenaeum Chain felt himself as 'not then considered worthy of this honour' and the situation as a 'snub'.

His touchiness no doubt contributed to the argument which had arisen after Heatley had proposed carrying out extraction work. It had initially been proposed that Heatley should concentrate on production while Chain applied himself to the chemical problems. Solvent extraction could fall under either head and both men maintained that it came into their own orbit. But Florey backed Heatley, a fact which Chain remembered nearly forty years later, claiming that

This was once again a clear breach of an agreement between Florey and myself and I expressed with a gesture my disappointment and annoyance that one could not trust any undertaking given by Florey. I gave in in the end, because I could not afford a serious row at that stage because of my special position in the country which was very weak. I had become a naturalized British citizen just a few months before this conversation took place and had to avoid any action which could provoke latent anti-Semitism which was very widespread. I had to bear in mind the fact that the Jewish community would not be very pleased if controversies of any kind with anti-Semitic undertones came into the open. Florey knew of my weak position and exploited it repeatedly; he also knew that he would find support in any action he took by the then secretary of the MRC, Mellanby.

Years after the event he was to write:

I have always considered, and still do, that Florey's behaviour to me in the years 1941 until October 1948, when I left Oxford for Rome, was unpardonably bad. I could give many examples of this, but I prefer to cover the relevant episodes with silence, as I have done in the past. They were undoubtedly due to human weakness.

Chain's feelings in the early 1940s about anti-Semitism and his belief that Florey treated him badly, can be almost endlessly debated. There was some substance in both feelings but both were exaggerated in Chain's mind by the fact that he saw himself to be a constitutional odd man out. Their real importance was that Chain believed them to be factors affecting his career, a belief which remained even when his professional success had decisively removed any influence that they could possibly have had.

# —4—

# FIRST RESULTS

The main experiments which demonstrated that a new therapeutic tool might be emerging, and which transformed penicillin from a laboratory curiosity to a potential 'wonder drug', took place on 19 March and 25–26 May 1940.

The first was carried out by Dr John M. Barnes who worked in the William Dunn laboratory but was not a member of the penicillin group, and was watched by his collaborator, the Spanish Dr Joseph Trueta who had become famous for his system of wound immobilization during the Spanish Civil War. Years later Chain explained how it was that Barnes came to carry out the crucial tests on which the future of penicillin was to depend.

Before I went to Barnes I had come to Florey at least four times over a period of several weeks, with fractions I had isolated, with the request to assay them and carry out toxicity tests. The last time I appeared in his laboratory with this request, Florey turned to Mrs M. Jennings (who was standing next to Sanders engaged with Florey in attempts to extirpate lymph nodes from rats in order to understand the function of the lymphocytes) saying, pointing to me, 'In one of my weak moments I promised this man to test his fractions and here he comes pestering me again.' After these humiliating remarks in front of others not involved in the project it became clear to me that Florey was not really interested in penicillin and I decided to ask my friend Barnes to do the first preliminary experiments.

These remarks, put on record by Chain late in life, provide a clue to the inability of Florey and Chain to see eye to eye on many matters. The trouble arose, as Chain was to admit, from human weakness. To be fair, it was a weakness, different in kind but equally strong, on the part of both men. Florey sometimes threw off casual remarks without appreciating the seriousness with which others might take them. Chain for his part was at times unable to consider such a remark as anything less than

47

a seriously planned attempt to score off him. Thus there were occasions when neither made sufficient allowance for the misunderstandings that can, and often do, confuse human relationships.

The experiments about which Chain felt so strongly consisted of injecting about 30 milligrams of the brown penicillin powder into the abdominal linings of two mice. It had already been shown that even when a milligram of the powder was diluted in a litre of distilled water it still inhibited the growth of staphylococci and it would not have been surprising if the powder had produced toxic effects. Instead the two mice remained entirely unaffected. So it did now appear that a bacteria-in-hibiting substance could be used without danger – at least on some species of animals in certain circumstances. 'The barriers were removed to our hopes and our dreams, and the fears that our purified extract would be harmful were all banished,' Chain later said, '... [it was] the crucial day in the whole development of penicillin and the day on which every-thing became possible to us.' However, though Chain was delighted at the success of the experiment, it should be remembered that in Florey's initial request to the Medical Research Council for penicillin support he had stated that penicillin was 'non-toxic to animals, even in large doses'.

There had, however, been two almost extraordinary strokes of good luck in these experiments. In the first place the 'purified extract', it was later discovered, formed only about 1 per cent of the injected material; about 99 per cent consisted of impurities, any one of which could have been toxic and could have suggested that penicillin was unusable as a therapeutic agent. Secondly, it was lucky that mice were used for the experiment rather than guinea-pigs; for it was subsequently found that for some complex reason guinea-pigs were vulnerable to penicillin.

The same afternoon Florey appeared in the laboratory, having heard that the experiment had taken place. 'I thought', he said, according to Chain, 'that we were going to do the penicillin work together.' To which Chain replied: 'We were indeed, but as you remember on several occasions I could not get you to carry out the necessary tests as you were too busy with other work.' 'This will be different in the future,' Chain was then told by Florey. From this exchange it seems likely that the most important outcome of the experiment was that Chain's approach to Barnes so irked Florey that he decided to carry out further tests him-self and so became more deeply drawn into the penicillin investigation.

The experiment on the two mice in March had appeared to confirm the non-toxicity of penicillin, but Florey then repeated it with a fresh batch of the mould. Chain has written:

48

It is one of the scenes in the penicillin development which stands out most vividly in my memory. He injected about 20 milligrams of this material and found again that it had no toxic effect. He was so sceptical about this that he thought he had missed the vein in this injection and said: 'Let me have some more material', which was a difficult request to comply with at that time, because we had extremely little material and every milligram counted. However, we produced some more material, another 20-milligram lot, and this was again non-toxic.

It was at this point that a fresh and potentially valuable discovery about penicillin was made. Chain continued:

We noted that the urine of the injected mouse, when we turned it over, had a deeply brown colour, so we knew that at least the pigment which was produced by the mould and had accompanied penicillin in the extraction process had passed unchanged through the body and was excreted in the urine. Naturally we were extremely interested to see whether the same applied to the active antibacterial principle we had injected. We took a drop of the brown coloured urine and tested it by the agar plate method and we found that there was an enormous antibacterial power in a drop of the urine. We knew then that here we had a substance that was non-toxic, and not destroyed in the body and therefore was certain to act against bacteria *in vivo*.

The experiment which finally showed that this was so began on the morning of Saturday, 25 May 1940. Eight Swiss albino mice were ready in Florey's laboratory, together with eight doses each of 110 million haemolytic streptococci – those which were causing 0.2 per cent of mothers to die in childbirth from puerperal fever. Florey began by injecting each mouse intraperitonally with one of the doses. Four of the mice were then replaced in their cages. One hour later two of the remaining mice were given 10 milligrams of penicillin by subcutaneous injection; the two others received 5 milligrams and, some hours later, another four further doses of 5 milligrams each, spread over a period of ten hours. Heatley spent most of the following hours in the laboratory. 'The controls were looking very sick,' he wrote in his personal diary after visiting the laboratory in the small hours, 'but the treated animals seemed very well. I stayed at the lab. until 3.45 by which time all four control animals were dead. It really looks as if P. may be of practical importance.'

The belief that they might be on the verge of a major discovery strengthened during the next few hours. Heatley's diary continues:

Left the lab. at 3.45 when it was already beginning to grow light.... Went to the lab. at 11.45 and found all four treated mice alive and well. Had a discussion till 1.15 with Professor and Chain, who wanted me immediately to produce 100 litres of Penicillium broth per week. Chain ordered £200-£300 worth of stuff straight off including 500 litre flasks.

Chain, according to an Australian, Dr Hugh Bary, who was in the laboratory that morning, 'was beside himself with excitement'.

This typically enthusiastic optimism after these first results turned out to be more than justified. The effect was quite as great on Florey, who now decided that more of the William Dunn resources should be concentrated on penicillin and that an attempt should be made to produce enough to carry out a small clinical trial on man. This would be necessary before any pharmaceutical company could, in circumstances where other wartime demands were swallowing up resources, be persuaded to tackle the problems of making the drug on a sufficient scale. Florey now brought in Edward Penley Abraham specifically to help in the purification and chemistry of penicillin.

From May 1940 penicillin was no longer a laboratory curiosity but a potential life-saver. In the process of developing that potential the elucidation of its chemical composition had to be tackled with great urgency, the methods of purifying it had to be improved and, quite as important, different ways of making penicillin in more than minute laboratory amounts had to be investigated. After telling Heatley that 200 litres of broth would be required weekly just for further mouse tests, Florey added: 'We are going to have to move on to man. Until we get to that stage this is all just as much a laboratory curiosity as was Fleming's mould. Remember, a man is three thousand times as big as a mouse.'

Production of penicillin was only one of the hurdles to be surmounted. Very little was as yet known about the substance and it became increasingly necessary that its structure should be elucidated. This was stressed by Chain himself who, in Parks Road the morning following the mouse experiment, met Dorothy Hodgkin, whom he had known in Cambridge and who was by now working in Oxford. He was greatly excited, she remembers, told her briefly of the experiment that had just been completed, and added: 'Some day we will have some crystals for you to work on.' They were to come in fact only after the lapse of more than three years and were to be produced in the United States, by then brought in to the mainstream of the penicillin enterprise.

Once it had been shown that penicillin in greatly increased amounts would be required, production of many more sterilizable containers in which the fungus could be cultivated on a shallow layer of medium became a major priority. Bottles, flasks and trays were all tested; all had disadvantages but in the summer of 1940 various kinds of tins and trays began to be used. Tall rectangular tins such as those used for motor oil or sheep dip were charged with medium, sterilized in the upright position under pressure to above the normal boiling-point of their contents, then incubated on their broad sides with the screw cap replaced by a cotton plug. Biscuit tins, each fitted with a spout, were found useful but were difficult to obtain. Old-fashioned bedpans were pressed into service.

While these makeshifts continued Chain and Abraham increased their attempts to elucidate the structure of penicillin itself and to purify the still minute amounts of the material that could be produced.

The work went on throughout the summer of 1940, and in August was reported in the columns of *The Lancet*. This lengthy account, signed by Florey, Chain, Abraham, Heatley, and other Oxford workers, explained how the penicillin investigation had started and continued:

During the last year methods have been devised here for obtaining a considerable yield of penicillin and for rapid assay of its inhibiting power. From the culture medium a brown powder has been obtained which is freely soluble in water. It and its solution are stable for a considerable time and though it is not a pure substance its antibacterial activity is very great.

The paper then described in detail five experiments, each involving between forty-eight and seventy-five mice, in which the effects of penicillin had been tested on a staphylococcus, a streptococcus and a clostridium, a genus of bacteria which includes those of tetanus and gas gangrene. The results were clear-cut and the paper noted that

penicillin is active *in vivo* against at least three of the organisms inhibited *in vitro*. It would seem a reasonable hope that all organisms inhibited in high dilution *in vitro* will be found to be dealt with *in vivo*. Penicillin does not appear to be related to any chemotherapeutic substance at present in use, and is particularly remarkable for its activity against the anaerobic organisms associated with gas gangrene.

At the end the writers reported that they had had 'financial assistance from the Rockefeller Foundation, the Medical Research Council and the Nuffield Trust', a wording which brought a protest from Mellanby. 'I read your penicillin paper with great interest and it seems clear that you are on to a very good subject. I hope it develops as well clinically as it promises', he wrote, before adding:

I noted at the end of the paper that you gave a great boost to the Rockefeller Foundation for having supported this work and that the Medical Research

Council had to play a very minor role. I doubt whether this is in accordance with the facts and, if you go out of your way to say that one member has got a Rockefeller fellowship, I think it is only reasonable that you should also mention the fact that several other members of the team were being supported by the Medical Research Council. The list would prove a striking one. I understand that the grants that are being held by individuals mentioned in the publication as part authors of this particular work are as follows:

*Financial Support given by Medical Research Council for Penicillin Research*

|  | Personal | Expenses |
| --- | --- | --- |
| Professor H. W. Florey | — | £50 |
| Mrs M. A. Jennings (part-time) | £200 | — |
| Miss J. Orr-Ewing | 200 | 350 |
| E. Chain | 300 | 100 |

I shall be surprised if the Rockefeller Foundation are supporting the work to anything like this extent...

Having said this, I salute you.

Florey replied that some of the money listed by Mellanby had been for non-penicillin work, and added:

You will therefore see that the correct figures for assistance from the Medical Research Council for penicillin work during the past year are £300, for Chain, £200 for Mrs Jennings (who was on another job till quite recently - I applied to you to allow me to use her for the penicillin work instead of the work on mucus secretion). Miss Orr-Ewing's grant (£200) was given for the plaster work and she has given a certain amount of time only to the penicillin work (for this I had your approval). The expenses grant was £100. At a maximum, therefore, it amounts to £800 against about £1,300 from the Rockefeller people. You will thus see that there are good reasons for thanking the Rockefeller Foundation for their generous assistance to penicillin work.

Mellanby was partly mollified and concluded in his reply:

When ... you proceed to point out that only £800 of the total grant of £2,000 a year now being given you by the Medical Research Council is being devoted to the penicillin work, I feel you are engaged in special pleading. However, the Lord be with you and, if you can get the penicillin to cure cases of human bacterial infection, I will forgive you a good deal more than your misdeeds in the present instance.

The support of the Medical Research Council was, in fact, slightly more than its detractors were later to claim, but it was nevertheless comparatively slight. As far as Chain was concerned, the issue was seen, sincerely if largely mistakenly, in far more personal terms. 'It is because

I don't play cricket,' this obviously Jewish immigrant would complain to friends. 'If I only played cricket it would all be different.' That was, of course, an exaggeration even greater than Chain must have suspected it to be; but to discount the implications completely would be to ignore an attitude that still flowed strongly through much of English life.

Whatever support might have been given to penicillin research in 1939 and 1940, it is clear that the medical world, let alone the general public, only slowly came to realize that a new and revolutionary drug was appearing above the horizon. The paper of August 1940 did, however, alert Fleming, who a few days later telephoned Florey to say that he would be visiting the William Dunn School within the next few days. His arrival was a surprise to some of the staff and Chain, on hearing the news that he was coming, remarked: 'Good God! I thought he was dead.' Fleming was given a tour of the penicillin work by Florey and Chain but after his first enquiry: 'What have you been doing with my old penicillin?' made little comment.

He remained cautious, and speaking to the Medical Research Club later in the year said: 'Penicillin has not yet been tried in war surgery and it will not be tried until some chemist comes along and finds out what it is and, if possible, manufactures it.'

Fleming's early caution about penicillin contrasted strongly with Chain's natural exuberance, but the contrast of their approaches was only skin-deep, and the differences between them were not as great, or as personal, as is sometimes made out. To quote Chain:

He was a man of few words who found it difficult to express himself, but he gave the impression of a warmhearted person though he did everything to appear unemotional and aloof. I felt that we were brought nearer to each other through the intermediation of his charming second wife .... Being both of Continental origin, she of Greek descent, I myself with a Russian-German-Jewish background, we understood each other very well and she was ideally suited to act as an interpreter between the temperamental Continental and the restrained Scot. Though Fleming and I were as different as could be with regard to background, interests and character, I had the impression that he had feelings of sympathy towards me, and this was certainly mutual as far as I was concerned.

Despite Fleming's caution in 1940, the tempo of the penicillin investigation was speeded up following the publication of *The Lancet* paper. This was natural enough since a few months earlier the 'phoney war' which had lasted from September 1939 was turned by the German attacks in Europe into one which was quickly causing heavy casualties.

Thus in the summer of 1940 investigation and production of penicillin entered a new phase.

It was a phase during which progress was made at what seems from today's standpoint to have been an extremely slow pace. The appearance of slowness lies in forgetfulness of the huge technological improvements which have been made during the last four decades and the lack of analytical tools available to the biochemists of the 1940s compared with those available today. Chain himself has stressed this in a short history of antibiotics, written just before his death in 1979, in which he says:

I believe that the main reasons why the antibiotics, particularly the ones mainly soluble in water and insoluble in the commonly used organic solvents, were not isolated and used many years earlier are (1) the absence, at the time, of sufficiently sensitive separation techniques, such as became available through the discovery of partition chromatography on paper and its numerous modifications, and (2) the absence of the sensitive spectrometric analytical methods, such as infra-red and ultra-violet spectroscopy, mass spectroscopy, nuclear magnetic resonance and electron spin resonance. It took twenty-five years to isolate and to elucidate the structure of what would now be considered a relatively simple substance, the first coenzyme discovered, nicotinamide adenine dinucleotide, a task which would now be accomplished in a few months.

In 1940 one problem that had to be solved, once it had been decided to expand the production of penicillin, was that of the culture vessels. The ideal material for them was glass, but delivery time was six months and cost of the mould, £500, was prohibitive. Norman Heatley describes how

It happened that Florey knew a consultant physician in Stoke-on-Trent, Dr J. P. Stock, to whom he wrote sending sketches of the kind of vessel required and asking what firms, if any, might be persuaded to produce them. Stock passed the sketches to James MacIntyre & Co. Ltd of Burslem and informed Florey by telegram. The following day Heatley went to Stoke, but his train was delayed and he was only able to visit the firm on the next day, 31 October. He found that they had already made three (unfired) prototypes which the modeller was able to trim with the knife to a finally selected design. Three finished vessels arrived in Oxford on 18 November, and the first main batch of 174 were ready, as promised, on 23 December. They were fetched by van that day, washed, charged and sterilized the next, and half of them were inoculated on Christmas Day 1940. These rectangular containers stacked well in autoclave and incubator. Each held one litre of medium in a layer 1.7 cm deep, and hundreds of them were eventually obtained. They effectively solved the culture vessel problem.

What they did not solve was the different problem of transforming the entire production of penicillin from a laboratory operation to an industrial process. Chain had been among the first to see that this transformation would be necessary if penicillin was ever to be made in the amounts needed. At first he had little success, and records that

We approached at that stage practically all the large drug manufacturers in the country, but found very little interest. That is to say, everybody said 'yes, you have made an extremely interesting observation, but the production of the substance on a commercial scale is quite impractical because your yields are so impossibly low'. In fact our yield of penicillin was only about 5 units per millilitre of culture fluid; which, of course, was quite impractical for large-scale production; it would have meant thousands of litres of culture fluid to treat a few cases. However, nobody made the obvious suggestion that the thing to do was to try to increase the yield, in other words, to put at least a part of the activities of the research organizations of these firms to the task of improving the yields of penicillin and make it into a practical proposition.

There were two respectable reasons for industry's caution. Most firms were already working all out on government orders, the prospect ahead was one of increasingly violent military operations, and the threat of ever-heavier enemy bombing was still important enough to deter the diversion of men and materials into anything that was not vitally necessary to the war. Second, it seemed obvious that efforts would be made to synthesize this drug of apparently remarkable power instead of making it by fermentation. Synthesis could well have advantages which would make obsolete the difficult fermentation, harvesting, and purification processes and there seemed little point in investing large sums of money and manpower in these while synthesis was still a feasible prospect.

This was part of the story, but only a part as Chain was to point out years later when advocating the creation of a state-owned penicillin factory in Britain:

The risk for the firms was however non-existent, as the Government had agreed at this time to guarantee any losses. Even this guarantee was not sufficient to stimulate the commercial firms into activity and the author got the impression that lack of enterprise, imagination and technical knowledge were the real reasons which prevented the commercial firms from successfully entering the field of penicillin production.

However, a few companies did do their best to help in the early stages. Imperial Chemical Industries was working on penicillin in 1941

and producing small amounts the following year. In fact the first penicillin which Florey obtained from commercial sources was 5 grams
which ICI sent him in February 1942, one month before the first ship-
ment arrived from Merck in the United States. Burroughs Wellcome
began large-scale production in September 1942 and the following
month Kemball Bishop, who had been sending supplies since August,
began regular deliveries of penicillin broth in milk churns in October.
Boots and Distillers also began sending supplies.

As commercial companies began to assume greater importance, and
as it became clear that production of penicillin could not indefinitely be
confined to a university laboratory, so did the question of patents begin
to raise its non-academic head. Before the Second World War there
were two facts which in Britain made it difficult to patent a drug such
as penicillin. The first and legally the more important was that no means
existed for patenting a natural product; it might, indeed, be possible to
patent a technological process involved, but it seemed unlikely that
anything done at Oxford would be covered although expert opinion
seemed to differ on this, and the more expert the opinion the greater
the difference. The position in America could well be different, both
because American patent laws were different from British and because
the method of submerged culture to be used there did involve the use
of various 'tricks of the trade' that could no doubt be patented.

This difference between British and American law was in some ways
less important than the attitudes with which patenting of medical
materials and methods were regarded in the two countries. Both Mellanby, the head of the Medical Research Council, and Sir Henry Dale,
the President of the Royal Society, believed that it was unethical to
restrict by patenting the use of life-saving drugs such as penicillin. When
Chain called for this he failed to convince either Mellanby or Dale, and
for the rest of his life maintained that it was their attitude that was
responsible for the payment by Britain to the United States of many
millions of dollars when for some years Britain found it necessary to use,
under licence, the submerged-culture methods developed in the United
States from 1941 onwards.

This attitude to the patenting of penicillin production became an
obsession with Chain, so much so that it played a significant part in his
subsequent career and thus in the development of the antibiotics industry
during the three decades that followed the end of the Second World
War. He was influenced first by his dislike of watching Britain pay large

sums to America for developments that had been initiated in Britain – a further indication of his loyalty to the country which had seen him over the hump in 1933. Another factor was his background within the German chemical engineering industry. During the first half of the twentieth century the links between German academics and their industrial counterparts were of a strength virtually unknown in Britain. To Dale, Mellanby and many others there was a gap between academic research and industry as wide as that between gentlemen and players. To Chain, no such gap existed. He said later:

I could not believe that we would not find other substances of equal, perhaps even greater, versatility than penicillin. It was just too much to accept that Fleming had stumbled on the only antibiotic of use to man – the odds of this happening were astronomical. I saw a whole tremendous virgin field and we were the leaders and would remain so if we got enough money. I argued our position again and again with Florey and we had bitter fights.

He considered it quite unethical, he was later to say, '*not* to take out patents protecting the people in this country against exploitation by foreign commercial organizations'. In these arguments Chain was apt to overstate his case, a weakness of which he was well aware, as when he admitted to his colleague Robert Robinson, 'Actually I do have the habit of letting myself be carried away by some trends of thoughts, and I can well imagine that in these circumstances my way of talking could sound very much like a lecture – sorry for that.'

The dispute over patents was to have a long-term influence. For the rest of his life Chain tended to distrust not only the views of the Medical Research Council but the workings of many government-funded scientific and medical organizations. Certainly it was an important factor in leading him, after the war, to emigrate to Italy and remain there for fifteen years.

He was not the man to give in easily when he felt confident he was in the right and, in his own words, the patent issue became a bitter controversy between the MRC and himself. He has written:

I had several violent discussions on this point with the then secretary of the Medical Research Council, the late Sir Edward Mellanby, but was told that patenting of drugs was unethical and contrary to the traditions of medical research in Britain. I replied that, quite apart from economic considerations, in my view it was unethical in respect to the people of Britain, and those of other countries, *not* to protect a discovery of this magnitude for it would then be free for exploitation for any unscrupulous group; but my arguments did not carry weight and I was told, in no uncertain terms, that I would be very ill advised to pursue the matter any further.

# —5—

# PROGRESS
# AND PROBLEMS

The end of 1940 found the penicillin enterprise in a state which warranted both optimism and pessimism. The efficacy of the new drug as a therapeutic agent appeared to be beyond doubt, although its value to humans still had to be put to the test. By contrast, great difficulties still barred the way to production in quantity, while there remained glaring gaps in knowledge of the drug's structure and some apparently insoluble problems in explaining how it actually worked.

It was found that penicillin was an organic acid, readily soluble in some organic solvents but insoluble in others. It was stable in water only in the form of salts in a pH ranging between 5 and 8, and quickly lost its biological activity in aqueous solutions of higher acidity or alkalinity. In addition, and important from the therapeutic point of view, penicillin, with the exception of ampicillin which was still to be discovered, acted against a number of Gram-positive bacteria – those which were capable of being stained by the method devised by the Danish physician Hans Christian Joachim Gram – and against the Gram-negative gonococcus and meningococcus. It was inactive against Gram-negative bacilli. The Gram-positive bacteria included most of the pathogenic cocci, the Gram-negative most of the bacilli responsible for gut infections, the various salmonellas causing food poisoning and *S. typhosa* causing typhoid fever.

Problems were arising all the time in the pencillin work but many were at leastly partly resolved between the beginning of 1941 and the end of the war in 1945, a period during which the word 'antibiotic' was popularized as a noun by Selman Abraham Waksman, discoverer of streptomycin, the first drug to be effective against Gram-negative bacteria and particularly interesting at the time because of its activity against the human tubercle bacillus. Dr T. B. Flynn, the editor of *Biological Abstracts*, had written to him saying that for indexing purposes he was looking for a word which would describe such compounds as penicillin, actinomycin and pyocyanase. Waksman replied that after going over the matter carefully he had decided to take an old word and put a new meaning into it. The word he took was 'antibiotic' which, as far back as 1891, had been used as an adjective meaning 'against life'. In some ways this was comparable to the word 'symbiotic' which stood for collaboration with living systems. The word 'antibiotic', he proposed, should be turned into a noun to include microbes that had an injurious effect on other microbes. He sought other opinions – from Florey, who proposed 'bacteriostatic', and Dr J.H. Cohn of Geneva, who favoured 'antibiotin'. However, he stuck to 'antibiotic' and it first appeared in *Biological Abstracts*, possibly in 1943.

During the same central years of the war, the chemists began to elucidate the structure of penicillin and then to discover how it achieved its therapeutic effect. At the same time industrial expertise, largely in the United States, made it possible to produce the drug in what, only a year or so earlier, would have seemed unimaginable quantities. Almost as important, during the early 1940s penicillin went through a political sea change, becoming not only 'a weapon of war' but the subject of renewed discussion about whether its production could, or should, be protected by patents. These developments, in all of which Ernst Chain was to be deeply involved, and during which the manufacture of antibiotics grew into a multi-million-dollar branch of the pharmaceutical industry, did not take place in separate self-contained compartments. Academic and industrial research were increasingly linked as the potential of antibiotics became more apparent. Medical ethics and industrial finance became ever more closely allied, and in the evolving situation pre-war practices and attitudes gradually changed.

It was the work in the William Dunn which had triggered off these developments, but before long penicillin was being developed extensively in the United States. In particular American work on deep fermentation, on solving the chemical engineering problems involved, and the widespread and systematic search for better-yielding strains of mould all helped to provide a new dimension to the 'wonder drug' that had come from Oxford as the Second World War was starting.

Despite these later developments a key initial role had been played by the 'Oxford team'. This was a phrase to which Chain strongly objected, on the grounds that its members had not been brought together as a single body specifically to solve the penicillin problem but had been brought in to deal with separate aspects of the problem as they arose.

There was also, it seems likely, Chain's belief that the phrase suggested an overall direction and control by Florey which he felt should be qualified. Nevertheless, the men and women in the William Dunn School did work on different parts of a co-ordinated plan as from 1941 onwards the prospect of a new therapeutic agent of extraordinary value changed from phantom to reality. Chain and Abraham, later joined by Robert Robinson, the leading organic chemist of the day, worked together on the biochemical aspects of the problem while Heatley developed both his assay methods and the equipment with which penicillin could be produced on a laboratory scale. Arthur D. Gardner and J. Orr-Ewing carried out bacteriological studies and M. A. Jennings helped Florey with pharmacological and biological investigations. C. M. Fletcher, who acted as liaison officer between the Radcliffe Infirmary and the Dunn School, and Dr Florey's wife Ethel were active in clinical testing. To Chain 'the gradual unveiling of the astonishing properties of penicillin' during this period was 'a most exciting and quite unforgettable experience', and he later wrote that he and his colleagues were 'profoundly grateful to Providence for having privileged us to perform this task'.

The slightly over-dramatic way of describing his view of the penicillin enterprise provides a clue to one of the three very different ways in which Chain played such an important part in the project the contagious enthusiasm with which he infected those with whom he worked. To a few his apparently inexhaustible flow of ideas and suggestions for overcoming difficulties, his reluctance to admit that any problem was unsolvable, acted at times as an irritant and one of his colleagues once complained of Chain 'buzzing around and making a nuisance of himself'. Yet others remembered him as a perfectionist of the type for whom best was the enemy of better. But this was more than anything a difference of temperament and the overall impression of those who worked with him is that his constant exhortations, his perpetual refusal to accept that failure was possible, opened the way to success which might otherwise have remained closed.

Secondly, there was Chain's manual dexterity as an experimenter. Here he was not in the first rank, but neither was he the chemical equivalent of Rutherford whose theoretical genius was equalled by his inability to perform practical experiments with any certainty of success.

Thirdly, there was Chain's virtually unique knowledge of the relevant literature and his almost photographic memory. Donald Callow, a later recruit who came to be regarded as 'Chain's pair of hands', has recalled how Chain, requiring a reference, would be able to cite not only the volume and page of the journal concerned, but even the position on the page where the reference could be found. His knowledge was kept up to date by a practice which illustrates his ability to charm birds off trees – or books out of libraries. While the William Dunn naturally had an adequate library it was a physiological rather than a chemical institution, and it lacked current runs of some foreign chemical journals. These, however, were available in the Radcliffe, and with the Radcliffe Chain organized his own private arrangement for borrowing four volumes at a time for up to twenty-four hours. Callow was the designated messenger who would regularly call at the Radcliffe, return the volumes from which Chain had abstracted the required information, and at the same time borrow another four.

Ability to consult the literature was important during the long haul from the autumn of 1940 onwards as the task of uncovering the structure of penicillin went on simultaneously with the search for more efficient ways of making this new weapon in the medical armoury.

Chain's importance in the work was acknowledged when Florey wrote to Dr Margoliouth, Secretary of Faculties in the University Registry, recommending that he should be appointed University Demonstrator in Chemical Pathology:

His biochemical work is of a very high standard. He has collaborated with many members of the department as can be seen from his list of published works. He is a man full of fruitful ideas and has been a great stimulus in the department. In particular his work on penicillin is likely to have important therapeutic applications. He has delivered eight lectures every term to pathology students on the biochemical aspects of pathology.

The following year Florey successfully applied for an extension of Chain's grant beyond the normal three years and commented: '[He] is the chief chemist involved in penicillin and other anti-bacterial work which is going on here. He is doing splendid work....' The view was reinforced the following year when Florey told Mellanby that Chain had 'been largely responsible in the first instance for elucidating the chemical properties of penicillin. He has a very considerable flair for isolating natural products and has been behind most of the chemical work done in this department.'

It is possible to highlight a number of events which during these years marked progress towards the transformation of penicillin from a laboratory curiousity to the first of a series of revolutionary drugs. Among the first was an understanding of the reasons behind the failure of penicillin to inhibit the growth of certain bacteria which were expected to respond to it. The bacteria included a staphylococcus which could spread at an alarming rate in hospitals and in the autumn of 1940 Chain decided to attack the problem. With Abraham he confirmed his suspicions that the staphylococci were mutants of the normal forms and produced a penicillin-destroying enzyme. The enzyme was isolated, named penicillinase, and its action described in *Nature* on 28 December 1940. Later, when the structure of penicillin was known, it was found to work by opening the B-lactam ring of the penicillin molecule, a discovery which suggested that if a specific inhibitor of penicillinase were discovered then the problem of the penicillin-resistant staphylococcus might be solved. This was to be so, although after nearly twenty years and the expenditure of many million dollars, that barrier to the wider use of penicillin was not to be entirely removed.

There was, however, one immediate and unfortunate reaction to the discovery of what it was that was counteracting the effect of penicillin. Mellanby wrote to the Wellcome Foundation in February 1941:

I think it is now clear that Florey and his colleagues had not got far enough in working out the conditions of production [of penicillin] on a small scale to be able to apply these results to large-scale preparation. The mere fact that they have discovered penicillinase, an enzyme which breaks down penicillin, seems to indicate that much more preliminary work will have to be done on this biological product.

The purely scientific investigation in Oxford formed only one part of the work which had to be done before the potential of penicillin could be transformed from dream to reality. Supplies also had to be increased. One way of getting them, devised by Heatley, was his method of feeding fresh medium into the penicillin-producing containers as the old medium was drawn off; eventually, up to a dozen 'refills' were being used in succession, considerable production time being saved with each. Another process which had been used by Raistrick, and also by a worker in Fleming's laboratory, although Fleming never mentioned it, was to start the extraction process by acidifying the medium and then mixing it with ether, which took up the penicillin while leaving the initial impurities in the medium. But the process had to be carried on at about 0°C, with the result that the gallon-size bottles being used had to be dealt with in the department's refrigerated room. The 'penicillin girls' who did the job

- and volunteers for such disagreeable and ill-rewarded duties were hard to get - had to work in woollen balaclavas, gloves and overcoats.

While Chain and Abraham concentrated on the dual tasks of discovering more about the nature of penicillin and the ways in which it could be produced in quantities which were not too discouragingly small, preparations went ahead for the next crucial tests: tests of penicillin on human patients. Here the records exist in some detail, certainly in enough to provide a graphic illustration of the difficulties to be met when the efficacy of a totally new drug is to be tested. One problem was that penicillin was available in only strictly limited amounts. Furthermore, it was in an impure form; just how impure was not proven and there would have been considerable misgivings had it been realized that the penicillin available at the end of 1940 was only 1 per cent pure.

The first human being to be treated in Britain with penicillin was a woman who was dying from cancer, and she was for long believed to have been the first patient in any country to have received the drug. This was not so since Dr Martin Henry Dawson of New York, who had read *The Lancet* paper of August 1940, had already treated an endocarditis victim with penicillin obtained from Johns Hopkins. The patient had died but Dawson's belief in penicillin continued and early in 1941 he obtained a small amount from Chain. He had been unable to culture this initial supply and his early attemps to use the new drug were brought on to the record only years later.

In the case of the Oxford woman it was known that she had virtually no chance of recovery but it was decided to see what effect penicillin would have on a human being, and on 17 January 1941, after being told all the circumstances, she agreed to be injected with 100 milligrams, an amount that in relation to the quantity given to mice should be safe for a human. Unexpectedly the patient immediately experienced a fit of shivering and high temperature medically known as a rigor. One possibility, investigated after her death, was that the cause was one of the impurities in the penicillin, later found to number thirty. It might, however, be due to the penicillin itself and it was essential to decide quickly which was the case.

To solve the problem Abraham used chromatography, a valuable method of chemical analysis which was only just being developed. A solution of the penicillin which had been injected was allowed to run down a length of absorbent material. Its different components ran at different speeds and each could thus be dealt with separately. Each was tested on rabbits and it was found to the relief of all that the fever-inducing component in the powder was contained in one of the impurities and not in the bacteria-inhibiting penicillin.

The next test was frustrated by a circumstance more easily understandable but just as tragic. It was made on Albert Alexander, an Oxford policeman who had been infected from a simple scratch from a rose-bush. He was treated in the Radcliffe Infirmary with the latest of the sulphonamides but without success. He lost the sight of one eye and the infection spread to his lungs. Then the first dose of penicillin was given. The results were described with that one word which doctors are chary of using – 'miraculous'. The following day, as the penicillin treatment continued, so did the improvement in Albert Alexander's condition. But one gram of penicillin was being used every twenty-four hours and supplies were running out. It was found possible to continue the treatment with penicillin recovered from the urine. Then this supply ran out. Albert Alexander continued to fight on against the infection but finally succumbed. Tragic as the case was, it reinforced the fact that penicillin could deal with the most intractable infections – if only it were available in the quantities required. There was another point made by Florey: 'If this forlorn case had value it was that it showed that penicillin could be given over five days without toxic effect in man.'

During this period it was found that the excreted penicillin was different in one important respect from that which had been originally administered: when given to a patient it produced no pain. This led to patients asking for doses of it from the collections of what became known as the 'Milk Run' which an assistant from the William Dunn – for some while Mrs Florey – made each morning to the Oxford hospitals from which excreted urine could be collected.

Penicillin's lack of toxicity to man or other animals for long remained a mystery, although an early clue was provided in 1940 when Arthur D. Gardner, working under Florey, found that small doses of the drug caused the cell walls of bacteria to grow into large and fantastic shapes and thereby prevented their normal multiplication. This, it was discovered six years later, was because penicillin prevented the formation of an essential component of the cell wall, thereby weakening it, whereas mammalian cells and penicillin-sensitive bacteria did not contain this component. Thus penicillin prevented the growth of the bacteria but had no effect on their host.

The case of Albert Alexander in 1941 was to have three interlinked results. One was the use of existing penicillin supplies on children, whose bodies would require smaller amounts of the scarce drug than those needed for adults. Another was an all-out drive to increase production in the William Dunn. The third, which was to have the most important effect on the future, was the co-option of the Americans in the penicillin project and the start of a new and revolutionary method of production which was to transform the manufacture of antibiotics.

During the summer of 1941 five more patients, four of them children, were treated with penicillin in Oxford. Although one of the children died from extraneous causes, all the other patients were cured, their troubles having ranged from an infected blood clot in the brain to a carbuncle. These results were written up in a *Lancet* paper of 16 August 1941, which ended with the unqualified statement:

From experiments *in vivo* and *in vitro* much evidence has now been assembled that penicillin combines to a striking degree two most desirable qualities of a chemotherapeutic agent – low toxicity to tissue cells and powerful bacteriostatic action. Its capacity to prevent multiplication covers a wide range of bacterial species, including some of the most common and destructive organisms with which man may be infected, and this bacteriostatic action is in no way interfered with by body fluids or pus, and only to a limited extent by very large numbers of organisms.... Enough evidence, we consider, has now been assembled to show that penicillin is a new and effective type of chemotherapeutic agent, and possesses some properties unknown in any anti-bacterial substance hitherto described.

By the time that the second *Lancet* article appeared, penicillin had begun to gain an official position that was to put its manufacture and use on to a new level. There were a number of reasons for this change which was also to affect Chain's future and they can only with difficulty be disentangled. It was almost certainly triggered off by a report which Florey received from Switzerland early in 1941. The Germans, he was told, wished to examine any available samples of penicillin. They were, he had little doubt, considering its use in the Services and he warned Mallanby that it seemed

very undesirable that the Swiss and hence the Germans should get penicillin and I think it would be well worth while to issue instructions to the National Type Collections not to issue cultures of *Penicillium notatum* to anyone with possible enemy connection and to send a letter to Fleming to the same effect. There may be others in this country with the culture but if so I don't know who they are.

Mellanby's reply was revealing. Florey's letter, he wrote [23 April 1941], raised a matter of some difficulty. He went on:

I sympathize with your position but I do not see how the Medical Research Council can ask their National Type Collections to restrict their despatch of special cultures to different countries and especially to a neutral country like Switzerland. On the other hand, I realize that you must have a free hand in this matter yourself and only send cultures of *Penicillium notatum* to those to whom you feel inclined. It does not seem to me that this is a serious matter, because I expect you are miles ahead of any possible competition. I do feel, however, that you must get some more clinical tests through as soon as possible and then publish the lot.

If the sulphonamide compounds had not proved to be so efficacious, I think you might have had a strong case for withholding publication from the point of view of national interest and, although I do not doubt that penicillin may prove to be superior to the sulphonamide compounds, I have difficulty in believing that this superiority is so great that national interests dictate the withholding of publication. I hope you have been able to arrange for the increased production of penicillin by bringing in industrial interests or otherwise.

Two points should be noted. One is the tardiness with which the military potential of penicillin was appreciated, the early accounts being freely published in *The Lancet* some months after the outbreak of war. But this was paralleled in a far more significant way by the publication of early speculation on nuclear fission which appeared in Britain, France, Germany and the United States in the autumn of 1939 and the spring of 1940 when nuclear weapons were already being discussed as midway between science fiction and nightmare. Second is the legality of trying to restrict the spread of therapeutic information despite various Red Cross agreements signed in Geneva. There was also the ethical aspect and at least one of those working on penicillin was to comment: 'I don't see why the Germans should not have had the use of penicillin to save their wounded.'

This appears to have been legally the case. Major-General James G. Magee, Army Surgeon General of the US Army is reliably said to have told Harvey H. Bundy, Office of the Secretary of War, on 20 June 1942, that neither international treaties nor the accepted rules of war allowed for any distinction between friendly and enemy wounded. In practice this did not appear to raise any insuperable difficulty. 'It would be short-sighted, however,' Magee added, 'to fail to recognize that knowledge in certain fields of medical science may bear more directly on the military situation than on the welfare of the individual.' He was therefore not in favour of spreading information about penicillin too widely. 'The free dissemination of such information', he continued, 'can be of very material aid to the enemy. It, therefore, becomes an instrument of warfare and its publication on the grounds of humanitarianism cannot be justified.'

Its military value was in fact to be appreciated not only by the Germans but also by the Dutch resistance movement and the French Maquis, two groups which have claimed to have tried, unsuccessfully, to make penicillin in secret.

But with penicillin, as with many 'secrets', it was the technological expertise involved in manufacture, rather than the existence of the material itself, which mattered most. Once the British workers had revealed in *The Lancet* that a new and powerful drug had been discovered, it was inevitable that those elsewhere in Europe would follow up the discovery. As early as the summer of 1941 Ernest Gäumann of the Swiss Federal Institute of Technology was asked, by the firm of CIBA among others, to help develop penicillin in Switzerland. The Germans, moreover, thought so much of penicillin's possibilities that they sent to Japan by submarine copies of German medical journals describing its importance. The Japanese *Asahi* in 1944 gave its readers details of penicillin production in the United States and in the same year it was even claimed, incorrectly, that it was penicillin which had saved Churchill from a bout of pneumonia at the Cairo Conference. By early 1944 Japan had set up its own Penicillin Committee and it was later claimed that more than 16,000 strains had been tested before the end of the war.

Certainly by the spring of 1941 the potential importance of penicillin to the Allied war effort was becoming clear.

Dear Florey [wrote Mellanby], After discussing this with you, I have come to the conclusion that the only way that this most important matter may be pursued is for you and Heatley to go to the United States of America for three months.

This is a subject of the highest medical importance and it is quite clear that you cannot get this substance made by firms in this country. I regard it as most important that you go to America and get the facilities there under way.

The first that Chain was to know of this development was when he arrived at the laboratory one morning to find Florey standing beside a packed suitcase. Asked where he was going, Florey said: 'The United States', and added that he would be leaving with Heatley within half an hour. 'No other word of explanation came from him,' Chain later wrote. 'I left the room silently but shattered by the experience of this underhand trick and act of bad faith, the worst so far in my experience of Florey. It spoiled my initially good relations with this man for ever.'

The account, given by Chain many years later, has a touch of the over-dramatic. Yet there is no doubt that he felt strongly and that the incident further darkened relations between the two men. For Florey, it has been pointed out that in wartime all travel in and out of Britain was shrouded in the maximum secrecy and that he was being no more than wise in saying nothing about the coming transatlantic venture. It seems a poor explanation until one considers the character of Mellanby and the strict warnings and injunctions which almost certainly surrounded the official arrangements for the journey. Florey was meticulously correct in such matters and having been warned to give no hint of the journey would doubtless have carried out his instructions to the letter. This would have been good enough but for the way in which the news was broken to Chain, and but for Chain's unconscious habit of seeing incidents as personal slights when none were intended. He himself would have eagerly seized the chance of explaining penicillin production to the Americans and the fact that this task would be going to Heatley while Florey concentrated on the high-level contacts with corporations and government departments no doubt irked him. Nevertheless, 'underhand trick and act of bad faith' looks in the light of sober reflection like an example of the overstatement of a good case to which Chain was prone. But like the casual disagreement on the tennis court before the First World War which set Sir Henry Tizard and Professor Lindemann, later Lord Cherwell, at each other's throats, the incident between Florey and Chain was to have long-range effects that neither man can have foreseen. Certainly it marked a deterioration in the relationships between Florey and Chain which were to be restored, with good grace on both sides, only when Chain left Oxford after the war. It is possible to regret what Chain was to call such 'human weaknesses' – by implication his own as well as others' – but they were endemic in the penicillin story. The relations between Florey and Fleming, between Robert Robinson and others, as well as between Chain and many others could be cited. They should perhaps be remembered not so much as weaknesses but as evidence that these were men of flesh and blood, motivated as much by human feelings as other mortals. When scientists can so easily be isolated in the public imagination from the everyday world, it is salutary that they should sometimes be seen as made from clay, if not-so-common clay.

Florey and Heatley left England late in June 1941 and flew via Portugal in a blacked-out Clipper to New York where they arrived on 2 July. With them they took samples of the precious brown powder prepared in Oxford, and they worried ceaselessly throughout the journey that changes in temperature might be affecting its potency. Also with them went copies of the paper, giving details of the latest Oxford experiments, which was to appear in an August issue of *The Lancet*. This was necessary since both men appreciated that the evidence of penicillin's efficacy as a therapeutic agent was even now remarkably slim; it was certainly slim enough to warrant all the reassurance that they knew would be necessary if the Americans were to be persuaded to pour money, men and materials into production of a mysterious drug of unsubstantiated worth.

Yet the appearance of penicillin with Florey and Heatley was not quite as great a surprise to the Americans as is sometimes supposed. The abortive request for penicillin experiments to be made had been lodged by the unidentified Yale scientist following publication of Fleming's paper in 1928, and in 1930 Roger Reid of Pennsylvania State College compared cultures of twenty-three moulds in an unsuccessful attempt to find a bacteria-inhibiting substance comparable to the one which Fleming had described. However, both E. R. Squibb & Sons and Merck obtained samples from Britain and as one historian of the subsequent American penicillin effort has written: 'Merck was ... actually working, struggling might be a better word, with penicillin when the British arrived.'

The drug had even been taken up clinically and on 15 October 1940 'the first dose of penicillin ever administered systematically to a human being was given intracutaneously' to a patient suffering from subacute endocarditis. Although the patient eventually died, it was verified that penicillin itself was not toxic, a factor of importance in the complex series of negotiations that followed Florey and Heatley's arrival. In addition, by 1941 workers at Beth Israel Hospital and Columbia Medical College in New York, as well as at the Mayo Clinic in Rochester, Minnesota, had begun to study the chemistry and action of penicillin although these investigations were not followed up.

In the summer of 1941 Warren Weaver of the Rockefeller Foundation was among those whose co-operation Florey quickly gained. Another was Dr A. N. Richards, a former Rhodes scholar whom Florey had known years earlier and who had just been appointed chairman of the Committee of Medical Research of America's Office of Scientific Research and Development (OSRD). With the support of these two men, and of Dr Charles Thom, a mycologist in the US Department of Agriculture and a recognized authority on penicillin, Florey succeeded, in a remarkably short time, in gaining the Americans' confidence and in persuading them to embark on an ambitious programme of penicillin production. Eventually a resolution was passed by the Committee of Medical Research that 'the Chairman be authorized to suggest to interested persons the desirability of a concerted program of research on penicillin involving the pooling of information and results; and if the responses are favorable, to proceed to arrange for a conference on the subject'.

While Florey was busy coping with the problems of co-operation – notably those of patents and the fears of commercial companies that they might be infringing America's Anti-Trust laws – Heatley dealt with the on-the-ground problems of production as they arose. Both private companies and government organizations were approached. Among the former there were not only Squibb, Merck and Lederle but also Pfizer, which like many other participants in the penicillin story had been brought in by a personal example of what the drug could do. The president of Pfizer, a company which made citric acid and vitamin $B_2$ by a process of submerged fermentation, was John L. Smith. Smith had a friend whose young daughter was suffering from a severe erysipelas infection which appeared to be incurable. Penicillin succeeded where all else had failed and with no further encouragement Smith enabled his chief engineer John Mackeen to build within five months a pilot penicillin plant consisting of fourteen 10,000-litre fermenters. At first only small quantities were produced and the penicillin was impure, but despite this most of the penicillin which was soon to be saving lives in the Tunisian and Sicilian campaigns came from Pfizer.

Of the government agencies to which the British were directed the most important was the Northern Regional Research Laboratory of the US Department of Agriculture at Peoria, Illinois. It had been opened a few years before the outbreak of war, largely to find a practicable way of disposing of the large quantities of agricultural wastes which were polluting the rivers of the Middle West. Prominent among the substances was corn steep liquor, the liquid left behind after the corn has been soaked and the kernel removed. It was found that if glucose was added to this, addition of penicillin mould resulted in the production of gluconic acid. The laboratory had been using *Penicillium chrysogenum* as the mould and on Heatley's arrival began experimenting with a number of other penicillium strains. Some, they soon discovered, produced up to twenty times the amount of penicillin that had been produced in Britain. Then it was found that even better results were obtained if lactose instead of glucose was used with the corn steep liquor. As Chain was to write:

Thus this laboratory fulfilled the practical purpose for which it was originally intended mainly through the problem which we brought to them. They could not have solved their corn steep problem with gluconic acid production alone but they did solve it completely and most elegantly with the problem of penicillin production, because the value of corn steep went up a hundredfold from the moment they had shown that a good penicillin yield could be obtained on it.

The discovery of corn steep liquor's effect can hardly be overrated. It 'was possibly the greatest single factor in making the commercial production of penicillin feasible', according to Dr Robert D. Coghill, head of the Peoria fermentation division. Although *parti pris*, the statement he made in 1944 was to be fully substantiated by events:

An extension of this work has resulted, in our laboratories, in a [huge] increase in the yields of penicillin surface cultures, i.e., from 2 to 2,000 Oxford units per cc in small Erlenmeyer flasks ... when one considers that a yield of 100 units per cc represents only 0.06 mg of pure penicillin per cc, half of which is lost during recovery operations, it is obvious why the two-unit yield with which we started looked rather discouraging.

The initial discovery was followed by a stroke of good luck when a strain of penicillin detected on a rotten cantaloupe in a local market was found to give better results than any in their collection. This strain was given to a number of other US laboratories and improved by genetical methods; in fact, most of the strains being used for commercial production more than ten years later originated from the Peoria cantaloupe.

Quite as important as the finding of more productive moulds was the technique of deep fermentation which was pioneered at Peoria. From the days of Fleming's initial work on penicillin it had been the practice to grow the mould on the surface of the trays or bottles holding the culture-medium. While this allowed the production units to be individually protected against contamination, it involved much labour and limited the production area to two dimensions. If it were possible to grow the mould not merely on the surface of the medium but when submerged within it, then a third dimension would be added and the area available for growth would be magnified in volume. A single step would thus greatly increase the amount which could be harvested.

In the United States the problems, which later in Europe were to stretch all Chain's abilities, were soon seen to be threefold. First, there had to be found a strain of mould which was capable of a new order of growth. Second, it was necessary to supply sterile and uncontaminated air to the medium if continuous growth were to be maintained. Finally, the culture-medium and the air had to be kept not only at a specific temperature but sterile and in such a constant state of motion that mixing was continuous.

It was the smallness of penicillin yields that seemed likely to discourage pharmaceutical firms. It was thought that something like a kilogram would be necessary even for a proper clinical evaluation, and if the prospect was only of micrograms the operation seemed unlikely to be viable. When the possibility of larger yields from deep fermentation opened up, another problem arose: fear of prosecution under the Sherman Anti-Trust Laws which inhibited companies from pooling information among themselves.

By good fortune a blueprint for Anglo-US collaboration had already been produced on the completely disconnected subject of radar following the visit to Washington in September 1940 of a British mission led by Sir Henry Tizard. By the time Florey and Heatley arrived in America the mission had produced results well outside the radar sphere, a US technical headquarters had been set up in London, the British Central Scientific Office had been established in Washington and Richards' Committee on Medical Research was preparing to open a liaison office in London.

While it was the workers at the Peoria plant who achieved the first successes in the deep-fermentation process, a number of private pharmaceutical companies, notably Merck, Squibb and Pfizer, made their own important contributions and when Florey returned to London in the autumn of 1941 it seemed likely that Britain's supply of penicillin was assured.

However, while the early problems of collaboration were being overcome or circumvented, the situation was dramatically changed. In December 1941 the Japanese attack on Pearl Harbor brought the United States into the war and thus diverted into American channels penicillin which would otherwise have come to Britain.

This was an unexpected setback as far as immediate supplies to Britain were concerned but the Americans continued with their penicillin investigation as enthusiastically as ever. Its extent can be judged from the details in *The Chemistry of Penicillin*, the 1,094-page record published in 1949 by Princeton University Press. In this are given details of the 1,750 communications on penicillin work written by 299 American scientists

in twenty-two research groups and 130 British scientists in eleven research groups, most of them unavailable elsewhere. Increasingly,
throughout the war, the results of this work were incorporated into
drugs which provided a new dimension to the hope of recovery among
battle casualties.

Merck, Squibb and Pfizer turned over the whole of their production
to the Committee on Medical Research for its clinical research programme – at first without charge, later at less than cost and eventually
at commercial prices. As had been the case in Britain, one of the most
difficult early problems was allocation of limited quantities, a task carried
out by Dr Chester Keefer of the Evans Memorial Hospital, Boston, who
had to ensure that the maximum of information was obtained by the
use of as little material as possible.

If American experience paralleled the British in this respect, there was
one great difference when it came to production since the Americans
were the first to grapple with the problems of chemical engineering,
seen after the war to lie at the heart of efficient penicillin production.
Typical was the question of size when submerged culture was considered. Should they use 10,000-gallon tanks, for which there was no
operating experience; or would it be better to use 1,000-gallon tanks
which had already been operated but which would need ten times as
many motors, agitators, tanks and valves? This was typical of the questions which Chain himself had to answer after the war when production
of penicillin was started at an industrial level throughout Europe.

In the wartime United States, following the advocacy of Florey and
Heatley, the Americans put all they knew into the drive for penicillin.
By the spring of 1944 they were, with the Canadians, building twenty-
two plants at a cost of nearly $20 million and production had risen from
425 million units in June 1943 to 18,700 million in February 1944.

Every available method was used for the work, and this very soon led
to the situation which Robert Robinson described a few years later.
'The early struggles of investigators in Britain', he said, 'have been lost
to view, submerged in a flood of organized research by teams of
workers. It is as if Horatio's holding of the bridge had been followed up
by an attack by mechanized troops in force.'

As American work increased, and as it became clear that production
on the far side of the Atlantic was rapidly outstripping Britain's, the
private nature of the enterprise began in both countries to be changed
by what was at first state intervention and then changed to state control.
Official intervention came under circumstances which were very differ-

ent in the two countries. This was natural enough since Britain's industry had been under strain since the outbreak of the war in September 1939, and under air attack since the summer of 1940, while America had been free of all such problems until the Japanese attack on Pearl Harbor in December 1941.

In America, pharmaceutical and chemical firms were guided towards penicillin research from the meetings of A. N. Richards' Committee on Medical Research first held in the autumn of 1941. The Department of Agriculture, the Division of Chemistry of the National Research Council and the War Production Board all collaborated with the private firms, and from the start government agencies had what was to be an increasing control over penicillin production and the allocation of supplies.

This presented formidable legal and industrial problems. As one study of the situation put it:

Richards and Rush recognized the simple truth that the commercial interests would not develop penicillin unless they were guaranteed some enjoyment of the fruits of their labors and investment. Somehow the companies that participated in the development of penicillin had to be permitted exclusive rights to their discoveries. Once the research and development of penicillin were completed, no one could be allowed to jump on the penicillin bandwagon for a free ride. The CMR thus found itself in the awkward position of needing to devise a system by which private companies would gain patent rights to processes and products developed, at least in part, with public money.

The system was eventually devised, but had to be rebuilt in a more complex form once it was realized that Anglo–US exchange of information was essential if the penicillin programme was not to be delayed.

In Britain, where progress had depended at first almost entirely on the work of the Oxford group, the story developed along different lines. Here five private companies – Boots Pure Drug Company, British Drug Company, Glaxo Laboratories, May & Baker, and Wellcome Laboratories, formed the Therapeutic Research Corporation for the pooling of information on penicillin, and a Penicillin Sub-Committee which was later renamed the Penicillin Producers' Conference. Although these groups had the blessing of the Medical Research Council, it was only in the summer and autumn of 1942 that penicillin began to be drawn under the British official wing. It was to be a complex process which eventually led to the Anglo–US co-operation on which Chain was to hold such strong views; a process, moreover, which had been fortuitously started by an acrimonious argument about the respective credits for discovering the drug and later its therapeutic value.

This argument had begun in the summer of 1942 after Fleming had persuaded Florey to send him supplies of penicillin, still in extremely short supply, to treat a seriously ill friend in St Mary's. The patient recovered and on 30 August *The Times* published a leading article explaining the merits of the new wonder drug. This was followed next day by a letter from Sir Almroth Wright pointing out the part which St Mary's had played in its discovery. However, no mention was made of Florey, or of the work in the William Dunn School which had transformed penicillin into a practical therapeutic agent. It was left to Robert Robinson to point out from Oxford in *The Times* of 1 September:

Now that Sir Almroth Wright has rightly drawn attention to the fact that penicillin was discovered by Professor Fleming and has crowned him with a laurel wreath, a bouquet at least and a handsome one, should be presented to Professor H. W. Florey of the School of Pathology at this university. Toxic substances are produced by the mould alongside penicillin and Florey was the first to separate 'therapeutic penicillin' and to demonstrate its value clinically. He and his team of collaborators, assisted by the Medical Research Council, have shown that penicillin is a practical proposition.

Despite the dog-in-the-manger attitude of which Fleming is sometimes accused, he wrote to Florey the following day saying: 'I was very glad to see Robinson's letter to *The Times* this morning. Although my work started you off on the penicillin hunt, it is you who have made it a practical proposition and it is good that you should get the credit.'

To laymen the situation was complicated enough to create mild confusion. It should not, however, have produced the spate of stories which now began to transfer the early clinical trials from Oxford to St Mary's and had Oxford using churns of crude penicillin sent to them from St Mary's. Some of the stories had an extraordinarily long life and more than thirty years later the BBC televised a film in which Fleming was shown arguing the case for 'antibiotics' in 1928 – although the word had not been coined until 1941 – and could be seen preparing penicillin for Albert Alexander, the patient in the Radcliffe at Oxford with whom he had no personal connection. The publicity given to penicillin in the summer of 1942 deepened the differences between Fleming and Florey which had already revealed themselves and have been commented upon in the *Dictionary of National Biography*'s obituary notice of Lord Florey, which runs as follows:

When the tremendous fact of penicillin therapy became news Florey was unwilling to talk to reporters. Fleming had less reserve, and articles appeared in which he was portrayed as the hero of a long struggle to harness the discovery, producing large amounts of penicillin at St Mary's Hospital, London, for use there or at Oxford under his direction. Such distortions, continuing uncorrected for many years, created a general impression that only Fleming's name should be associated with penicillin.

Florey, who in 1942 believed that Lord Moran, a governor of St Mary's, might be backing the Fleming claims, and who felt with some reason that his professional reputation was under attack, wrote on 11 December 1942 to Sir Henry Dale, then president of the Royal Society: 'I have now quite good evidence, from the director-general of the BBC in fact, and also indirectly from some people at St Mary's, that Fleming is doing his best to see the whole subject is presented as having been foreseen and worked out by Fleming and that we in this department just did a few final flourishes.'

Florey had as little luck with Sir Henry on this subject as he had had on the patent issue. There was really nothing that could be done without washing dirty linen in public, he was told. He had much the same reply when, two years later, he wrote to Mellanby:

It has long been a source of irritation to us all here to witness the unscrupulous campaign carried on from St Mary's calmly to credit Fleming with all the work done here.... My policy here has been never to interview the press or allow them to get any information from us even by telephone.... In contrast, Fleming has been interviewed apparently without cease, photographed, etc.... with the upshot that he is being put over as 'the discoverer of penicillin' (which is true) with the implication that he did all the work leading to the discovery of its chemotherapeutic properties (which is not true).... You of course know how dishonest this is and might reply 'why worry'.

Once again, he was advised that silence was the only course to be followed, and was told by Mellanby:

In time the public will realize that in the story of this development of penicillin, the thing that has mattered most has been the persistent and highly meritorious work in your laboratory. The dish you have turned out is so good that you must swallow the rather nauseating but temporary publicity ingredient with a smile.

Of those involved in the argument, Chain took what can be considered as the most understanding view. 'The British hospitals', he said, 'were struggling for their pennies, remember. Then here, suddenly, was a pot of gold for St Mary's. It was an opportunity to be grasped – and if I had been the manager of the hospital, I might have done the same.'

However unjustifiably Fleming was given the Oxford limelight in 1942 he was nevertheless responsible for giving increasingly strong muscle to official support for production of penicillin in Britain. This support was to grow somewhat haphazardly, at the mercy of numerous authorities, just as had happened over the development of radar slightly less than a decade earlier. It was hastened by the cure of Fleming's friend in St Mary's, since it induced him to throw all his available influence behind the production. His colleague, Harold Raistrick, who had experimented with penicillin ten years before, suggested that the best thing to boost production would be to interest the Prime Minister, Winston Churchill. Fleming did not know the Prime Minister but he did know Sir Andrew Duncan, the Minister of Supply. Duncan conferred with Sir Cecil Weir, director-general of stores and equipment in the ministry and therefore in charge of medical supplies. As a first move, the mass production of penicillin was urged by Duncan and the Minister of Health at a meeting of the War Cabinet. Then, on 25 September 1942, six ministry officials, two senior officers from the Army Medical Directorate, Alexander Fleming, Howard Florey and Harold Raistrick, as well as representatives from Kemball, Bishop and Company, one of the firms already producing penicillin, met in London.

The outcome was the formation of the General Penicillin Committee which met for the first time on 13 October 1942, 'to increase and accelerate the production of penicillin, to effect the pooling of information, and to ensure that material produced was put to the best possible use'. This was the first of four committees concerned with the drug to be set up in Britain during the second half of the war. It was followed by the Increased Production Committee, a technical Ministry of Health committee on which the manufacturers were represented; the Clinical Trials Committee of the Medical Research Council, and by the Penicillin (Civilian Supplies) Committee, a departmental committee of the Ministry of Health set up to consider the allocation of penicillin when supplies were available for civilians.

From the end of 1942 onwards these organizations steadily brought research into the nature of penicillin, its production and its distribution – first to members of the armed forces and then to civilians – under varying degrees of official control. Their operation was at times confused by the number of ministries involved – Supply, Production and Health among others – and by the fact that private enterprise and public policy appeared at times to be inextricably entwined. In addition, with the Americans quickly becoming the main producers, Anglo–US relations were deeply involved.

Anglo–US commercial rivalry further confounded the issue. 'Perhaps', as Abraham has sagely remarked, 'this was an almost inevitable consequence of the interaction of human frailty with a highly complex situation in which there were great prizes, both academic and financial.'

There was also the veil of secrecy now hanging over what would in normal times have been open medical research. The first reports of a new 'miracle drug' which would obviously have wartime uses were openly published in Britain and America and there was some feeling among scientists in both countries against hiding this medical advance. In Britain the Official Secrets Act was invoked to prevent publication of chemical information on penicillin and in the United States semi-secrecy was maintained until the disastrous Cocoanut Grove fire in Boston in November 1942 when it was openly reported that supplies of the new drug were rushed to the scene in the hope of saving the hundreds of civilians who had been badly burned.

Although the restriction to a limited circulation of the reports giving fresh information on penicillin chemistry probably hampered progress, restriction was given added force as the new drug began to be used by the services. The first British servicemen to benefit from it were a small number of RAF fighter pilots treated in the Oxford area in 1941. By 1943, however, supplies were available for troops in the Middle East.

It was decided that supplies of penicillin should be given to the Army and that a small research team, manned by the Royal Army Medical Corps and the Medical Research Council, would be set up to investigate its use on battle casualties. Ian Fraser, who as a Lieutenant-Colonel had been Officer in Charge of a 1,200-bed army hospital in West Africa, was put in charge of the unit. Together with the other members who were to make up the penicillin team, he first spent a fortnight at Oxford, and later reported:

We had to learn all about [penicillin's] background, its origin, its method of growth, and as well we had to prepare to give lectures on this subject to the various units to which we were later to be attached.... I spent each day at either the laboratory or at St Hugh's [which Cairns was using as a hospital] learning the various techniques and arranging how in the forward areas we with no sophisticated equipment could carry on.

When Fraser's unit was ready for operations, the conquest of North Africa had been completed and Anglo-American forces were preparing for the invasion of Sicily, to be followed by the advance into Italy. His first disappointment was to discover how little penicillin was available. In addition, most of the drug was in the form of the calcium salt; this was for surface use alone and there were only limited supplies of the sodium salt which could be injected.

The first use of penicillin in the field was subject to a number of restrictions. To quote Ian Fraser:

We were not to use it in osteomyelitis as a full-scale prolonged trial of this had been carried out for several months in Oxford. To this I readily agreed. (ii) We were not to use it in Gonorrhoea as again its full value had been well established by prolonged tests. I did not see that this was a likely problem for an army when fighting on the beaches. (iii) It was suggested that as the drug was in such short supply we should not give it to any of the enemy. I refused to accept this and I said that I must be allowed to use my own judgement in the matter.

The unit was first set up in a 2,500-bed hospital in Algiers but Fraser decided that it should operate as near the battlefield as possible, and it was eventually working as a tented unit at Salerno, only 1,000 yards from the actual fighting. Although the number of men who could be treated was too small to be statistically significant, the benefits of penicillin quickly became obvious. In the early days, when so little was to be had, it was diluted with a neutral powder, such as sulphonamide, which was then sprayed on to open wounds. While this had some value, the results were not comparable to those later obtained when supplies improved and casualties could be injected. The speed with which penicillin could be given was important and Fraser later wrote that

it was really on the invasion of Italy and Sicily, when the drug went in almost with the bullets on the beaches, that the most dramatic results were seen. Florey had the great excitement of waiting in North Africa and seeing the wounded men arrive with their wounds in a state never seen in history before. This meant not only the saving of life, but saving pain and saving of function. I remember seeing him on the quay at Sousse as I brought back the first casualties from the invasion of Sicily. He looked as happy and as anxious as an expectant father waiting to see and hear the news.

By this time American supplies were outstripping British. Despite the urging first of Sir Cecil Weir and then of Oliver Lyttelton, the Minister of Production, who took over responsibility for penicillin, deliveries rarely came up to expectations – a situation virtually endemic in a nation as hard pressed as was Britain.

Not only labour but also money was short and doubts began to be raised even about the future of the Oxford team. Everything appeared to rest on Florey. If he were to be killed, would money be found for continuing his work? Despite the Rockefeller grant, research had expanded so quickly under wartime demand that it was now being run almost on the proverbial shoestring.

This situation, and the fear that the Oxford 'team' could even be split up through lack of finance, came to the ears of Lord Nuffield. His Foundation and his Provincial Hospitals Trust had for some years been supporting numerous charities, many of them in Oxford and many of them concerned with medicine. Now, in March 1943, Nuffield offered to make £35,000 available to Florey over seven years in order to secure the positions of his staff over that period. Details were soon settled and on 25 June Dr Landsborough Thomson of the MRC was told that the Nuffield Provincial Hospitals Trust would take over responsibility for the salaries of Chain, Abraham, and a number of other penicillin workers – a total of £2,300 a year.

Any danger of failing support decreased the following year when Churchill threw his influence behind penicillin production. His action was triggered off by a long statement by David Robertson in the House of Commons on 13 February 1944 which severely criticized lack of British official action, and maintained that the armed forces would be short of penicillin on D-Day, when Europe was to be invaded, which was to come later in the year. 'What Department is responsible for penicillin?' the Prime Minister asked the following day. 'Let me have a report on the statement by Mr David Robertson, MP.'

Oliver Lyttelton, the Minister of Production, was to field the enquiry, but before he could do so Churchill had given his own private boost to penicillin production in a speech made at the Royal College of Physicians on 2 March.

Then there is penicillin which has broken upon the world just at a moment when human beings are being gashed and torn and poisoned by wounds on the field of war in enormous numbers, and when many other diseases hitherto insoluble cry for treatment. It is a great satisfaction to be able to congratulate St Mary's Hospital on their association with penicillin.

A signed copy of the Prime Minister's words was sought, and secured, by Lord McGowan, head of ICI, for use in an appeal he was making for St Mary's.

Meanwhile Lyttelton was preparing the first of a number of progress reports on penicillin for the Prime Minister. On one, which described production in America and Britain, Churchill wrote: 'Let me have proposals for a more abundant supply from Great Britain.' And on another, which gave a somewhat optimistic estimate of future prospects, he wrote: 'Good, good. Press on. Report soon.'

Churchill's interest continued. Lyttelton was regularly asked how production was progressing, and he was told on 18 December:

Your report on penicillin, showing that we are only to get about one-tenth of the expected output this year, is very disappointing. It is discouraging to find that, although this a British discovery, the Americans are so far ahead of us, not only in output but in technique. I hope you are satisfied that we have the right people in charge and that labour and material difficulties are being tackled early enough and energetically enough. Pray let me have a realistic estimate of 1945 production.

Lord Cherwell, the former Professor Lindemann who had become Churchill's scientific adviser, had been asked for his comments on the situation and had been critical of the quality of British penicillin, a point referred to by Churchill when he replied to Lyttelton.

I am glad that we are at last producing really substantial quantities [of penicillin] here. I am disturbed, however, to hear that the quality of penicillin produced in this country is said to be inferior to that from the United States. If so, I trust that this will soon be remedied. We must not sacrifice quality to quantity. No doubt you will let me have a further report when supplies become clearly surplus to Service needs, outlining proposals for increased distribution to the civilian population.

By 1944 it was not only Britain that was concerned with the possible medication of civilians with penicillin. The chemical structure of the drug, and the most efficient ways of making it, were still covered by the Official Secrets Acts in Britain and by their equivalent in the United States. But its existence was known throughout the world and following the three-power Conference at Teheran in 1943 an Anglo–US medical mission that almost included Chain visited Moscow to confer with Russian doctors on the production and use of penicillin.

Chain was to have gone in the role of interpreter but a problem arose when applications for visas were made to the Foreign Office. 'This raises the difficulty about Dr Chain who is a naturalized British subject of Russian and German origin,' said a Foreign Office minute. 'I understand that Florey is very anxious to take him and that his presence would be very useful, though not absolutely essential.'

'Very useful but not absolutely essential' was the role suggested by Florey when he wrote to Mellanby on the subject, adding:

I have had a certain amount of trouble with Chain who is working himself into a frame of mind that he is not getting sufficient credit for his work on penicillin. There are some signs that he overestimates his position and I have done what I can to correct this, but I regard it as essential that you should tell him what his functions are and that if he should not wish to go under these conditions, then say at once that he need not go.

Whether the Russians were unwilling to accept a German-born representative as the Foreign Office feared might be the case, or whether Chain refused to travel merely as an interpreter, is not clear. However, Florey flew to Russia with only his American colleague on what was to be a three-month visit.

Elsewhere throughout the world the news of penicillin spread quickly and even before the end of 1943 the authorities in Britain began to receive requests for the drug from other European countries, as well as from places as distant as Afghanistan. By the start of 1944 requests were arriving in larger and occasionally embarrassing numbers. Some were dealt with without delay or dispute. Thus when Sir Samuel Hoare, the British Ambassador in Madrid, reported of badly frost-bitten British and US escaped prisoners reaching Barcelona from across the Pyrenees that: 'Though medical treatment of these cases at Barcelona is adequate, the risk of amputation would I understand be diminished by early use of penicillin', supplies were sent at once. A further consignment was later sent to help civilian refugees arriving in Switzerland, but supplies to neutral countries were subject to a judgement that was governed by more than purely humanitarian motives.

The Ministry of Health, for instance, was advised by the Foreign Office to satisfy a request for penicillin by the President of the Portuguese Industrial Association, who pointed out that

In this exceptional case it would in our opinion be a gesture that would be very much appreciated and from which we would probably derive political and economic advantage out of all proportion to the sacrifice we might be making in supplying the penicillin.

But the request was turned down, and the British authorities in Lisbon were told that similar requests had 'not the slightest chance of being authorized unless we can back it up strongly from the political angle'.

Switzerland, which on one occasion received supplies by parachute, was more favoured, and a later Foreign Office minute on one Swiss request ran: 'It was decided to meet [it] because the Swiss Government have done so much for British prisoners-of-war, and also because the position regards the supply of penicillin has improved during the last few months.'

Sweden, Spain and Turkey were other countries which applied to Britain for the drug. More than one factor governed the British response as is shown by a Foreign Office comment on a request from Switzerland: 'Personally I think we ought to [send penicillin] because I feel sure that if we refuse they will go to the Americans and get it.'

This was a reflection of the growing unease in Britain throughout 1944 at the vigour with which the Americans were supplying penicillin even to such pro-Axis countries as Spain and Argentina, while Britain was in practice debarred even from providing details of manufacture, as is shown by one memo from the Ministry of Health:

Our position in the matter of penicillin is not a happy one. HMG gets the odium of refusing to tell the Spaniards how to manufacture penicillin ... and the US Government gets the 'kudos' for gifts made possible by the larger manufacturing capacity of the US. It is unlikely that any of the cheering Spaniards present at the 'major celebration' mentioned in the last paragraph of [an enclosed] cutting from the *New York Herald Tribune* paused to reflect that but for the action of British scientists in making this British discovery available to the Americans, no penicillin could have been produced in the USA.

Despite the continuing problems of supply, Britain did her best to help her allies. Members of the Red Army were among those who benefited after supplies had been sent to the British Military Mission in Bucharest. Here thirty-five cases of officers and other ranks, men and women, were treated, and the report to the War Office stated:

The outstanding point is the unbelievable success of penicillin which was very clearly demonstrated and the enthusiasm and gratitude which the Russian patients, sisters and Medical Officers, showed. For the first time also the Russian staff at Colonel Bentley's request treated eight cases of typhus. As far as we know this is the first time penicillin has been used for the treatment of typhus and Colonel Bentley reports results most encouraging. Staff believe all eight cases of typhus were cured by penicillin.

# −6−

# PENICILLIN
# IN PRODUCTION

By the end of 1944 many of the problems of producing penicillin in quantity were being overcome. The theoretical groundwork carried out in Oxford had been transformed by the American mass-production approach. The problems that now loomed ahead were not so much industrial as purely scientific. For despite the successes at Oxford and in the United States, the structure of the penicillin molecule itself, the way in which its component atoms were linked together, still remained uncertain. Until this riddle was solved there were barriers to the synthesis of penicillin, the manufacture of the drug from available chemicals which would eliminate the difficulties of making it by fermentation processes. It was to these problems that Chain and many others in the developing world of antibiotics devoted much of their intellectual energies during the last years of the war.

From the early days of penicillin research there had been doubt about whether its molecule contained an atom of sulphur. In 1941 sulphur was reported to be present but the penicillin concerned was probably less than 10 per cent pure and when, a year later, a purer sample was apparently found to lack sulphur it was assumed that the sulphur in the earlier specimen had been due to an impurity. Abraham has stated that

Chain and I missed the presence of sulfur in 1942 because the microanalysis in the Dyson Perrins Laboratory reported that our best preparation of penicillin was sulfur free. At our first meeting with Sir Robert [Robinson] he asked us if sulfur was present and we told him of the report of the analysts. In retrospect, of course, we should not have accepted the analytical report so readily.

The breakthrough which some chemists believed might open the way to synthesis – the 'artificial' creation of penicillin as it might be termed – came in the latter half of 1943 as workers on both sides of the Atlantic began to discover independently what the individual atoms in the penicillin molecule really were and how they were put together. Three workers in the Squibb group succeeded in crystallizing the sodium salt of benzylpenicillin, a success which led to the recognition of sulphur as a constituent of the molecule. At virtually the same time the presence of sulphur was discovered in Oxford in a number of penicillin derivatives. But it soon became clear that the British and the American penicillins were different in certain ways, notably the greater reluctance of the British variety to crystallize. When the Oxford team heard in August 1943 that the American penicillin had crystallized as a sodium salt, Abraham converted their best preparation to a sodium salt and took some to Dorothy Hodgkin. They found that the material took up water and then set to a mass of crystals when placed on a microscope slide.

Some time afterwards Dr Robert Coghill, visiting Oxford from the United States, watched Chain repeat the experiment:

Chain placed his amorphous preparation on a microscope slide and we each had a good look at it. No crystals; we discussed the whole perplexing situation for the better part of an afternoon with Chain pacing his laboratory. Every once in a while he would stop and look through the microscope. At one of these stops he took a mere glance and shouted: 'It's crystalline!' We each took another look, and sure enough, long beautiful needle crystals had taken the place of the powder of an hour or so ago. Chain was excited and elated – and justifiably so.

But even though one doubt about the components of the penicillin molecule had now been removed it was still unclear as to how they were strung together, since the results of both British and American workers would fit either of two configurations, the 'thiazolidine–oxazolone' and the 'b-lactam'. 'Different pieces of evidence seemed to favour one formula or the other', the authors of Sir Robert Robinson's Royal Society obituary memoir have written. 'For example, penicillenic acid, an oxazolene, is formed from penicillin in very mild conditions, but desthiopenicillin, a b-lactam, is also easily obtainable from penicillin by the action of Raney nickel.' In 1943 Abraham wrote down the beta-lactam formula and went to Chain saying:

'I think that this must be the structure.' We had to admit by this time that there were only two reasonable structures: the beta-lactam and the oxazolone. So I said to Chain at the time, on the basis of the evidence coming from the titrations, it must be the beta-lactam. Then we went to Wilson Baker in the Dyson Perrins Laboratories and talked about writing our report. Both structures were mentioned in the report because although we were sure that the correct structure was the beta-lactam, we were also certain that Robinson wanted the other structure to be the right one. As a result, we wrote a rather neutral report. It would not have been fair to Robinson to have written the report with his name on it and not to include the oxazolone because, after all, it was his structure. In fact, he wrote an appendix to the report disclaiming the beta-lactam structure.

Feelings ran high and the Royal Society's memoir of Sir Robert says that he 'found it hard to believe that a b-lactam structure could show the chemical reactivity of penicillin but was finally convinced'. According to other reports Sir Robert needed a great deal of convincing, and is claimed to have ended one discussion by throwing a bottle of ink at Chain and shouting to his retreating figure: 'I do not want to see that wretched little man again.'

The riddle was only finally solved in the summer of 1945 with the help of X-ray crystallographers led by Dorothy Hodgkin, with whom Chain and Abraham had remained on close terms throughout the penicillin work. The use of X-ray diffraction data to help solve problems of structural chemistry is based upon the fact that the intensities of the X-ray reflections from a crystal are related to the positions in space of the atoms within the crystal. The resolution of any particular crystal structure depends therefore upon finding a set of atomic positions which will, according to calculations, give intensities of X-ray reflections similar to those observed. The calculations are of great complexity and Dorothy Hodgkin and her helpers had been working on them for a considerable time, a period which with the help of electronic computers later available could have been reduced to a matter of weeks.

The approach to success is recorded in a series of letters and notes from Dorothy Hodgkin to the Medical Research Council to whom she wrote on 5 February 1945:

We have determined a large part of the crystalline structure of potassium and rubidium penicillin and consequently a large part of the molecular structure also. But to be certain of the most interesting details of the structure we need to carry out very much more extensive calculations.

Even at this crucial stage lack of hard cash came into the penicillin story, and there were doubts of whether the estimated £1,000 for further computing work would be forthcoming. Chain was confident that the MRC could not refuse. Work and further negotiations went ahead together and on 27 April Dorothy Hodgkin was able to tell the MRC:

At present our work appears to be going very well. We have now placed the atoms in penicillin fairly closely in three dimensions in a way which gives very good general agreement with all our X-ray data. But we still need to carry out some further calculations in order to be quite certain of the chemical structure.

Within a few weeks the work was completed on a government Hollerith machine. Dorothy Hodgkin reported:

In May this year our analysis reached a stage at which we felt reasonably confident that we had found the atomic positions within the crystal structure of potassium penicillin with an accuracy of the order of ±0.3 A[ngströms]. This accuracy is sufficient to determine the essential chemical character of penicillin – which atoms are bonded together by primary chemical bonds in the structure and their stereochemical relation one to another.

Penicillin was thus found to exist in the form of a beta-lactam ring to which was attached a side chain. While the beta-lactam ring was common to all penicillins the side chain varied, and on its composition there depended the various characteristics of the different penicillins. But all appeared to have one thing in common: their antibiotic properties disappeared when the chain was broken, as it easily could be, a fact which accounted for many of the difficulties in early penicillin research.

Once the location of each atom in the penicillin molecule was known, these locations were shown on a model made by sticking a number of pins vertically into a ground plan, one pin for each atom, then sliding a bead up each pin until it occupied the position which had been calculated for it.

Chain was among the first to be invited to look at the model. It naturally pleased him considerably and he exclaimed with great satisfaction: 'But it is the beta–lactam model after all.' This was, he was later to add,

the first demonstration that the chemical structure of a compound can be determined entirely by physical methods. Very soon afterwards when very large computers became available, crystallographic methods were successfully applied to the determination of much more complex substances and of much larger molecular weights, such as proteins and nucleic acids, and it may well be that our work on the determination of the penicillin molecule was the last case when the structure of a natural product was elucidated by classical methods of organic chemistry.

As is so often the case with scientific and technical advance, the solution was discovered elsewhere almost simultaneously, workers at Merck under Karl Folkers also deciding on the fused thiazolidine—B-lactam model.

The structure of penicillin, as revealed, did now begin to explain some of its characteristics, notably its instability under certain conditions. This characteristic, which had intrigued Chain from the first, was quickly seen to be due to the four-member lactam ring, not previously found in natural substances, which could easily be broken.

With the elucidation of penicillin's structure in the summer of 1945 the project on which Chain had embarked in 1938 reached a new and significant stage. Penicillin was by now being made in the United States in ever-increasing quantities, and also in Britain where pharmaceutical firms began not only to use the methods developed in Oxford but the deep-fermentation methods licensed from America. The chemistry of penicillin was now understood to a degree very different from that of only a few years previously.

This increase in knowledge about the structure of penicillin gave fresh impetus to those who were trying to find a way of producing it synthetically rather than by fermentation. It was appreciated that even when deep fermentation had replaced surface culture the process would still be comparatively slow and expensive, and the resulting drug could easily be contaminated. The difficulties of synthesis were known to be enormous, and as early as 1942 Florey had written to Sir Charles Sherrington: 'I am afraid the synthesis of the substance is rather distant, but if, say, the price of three bombers and the same energy was sunk into the project, we could really get enough to do a considerable amount.'

The synthesis of some of the B-vitamins had begun to make the problem look less impossible of solution, yet there were problems other than those of chemistry. Firms which had invested large sums in fermentation plant were hardly likely to rejoice at the prospect of such plant being made obsolete by successful synthesis. There was also in the United States, when it came to collaboration, the threat of anti-trust suits. Despite these problems the OSRD began to take matters in hand and reached agreement between the end of December 1943 and the start of January 1944 for nine companies, two universities and the Northern Regional Research Laboratory to study the chemical problems of penicillin synthesis. The firms involved passed information to the OSRD in a restricted way. 'In other words,' it has been stated, 'they did not believe in a *wholesale* exchange of material; knowing the status of a particular company's research, the OSRD would forward only those data necessary to help in the firm's synthesis of penicillin.'

In Britain a similar move was proposed in the summer of 1943. Here, also, it was realized that there could be complicated implications, as Mellanby pointed out to Sir Robert Robinson after the latter had proposed the formation of a Committee for Penicillin Synthesis. 'We must protect ourselves', he said, 'against allowing public money to be used to help those who, without any hesitation, would take out a patent in their own or their firm's interest on fundamental points in the synthesis of penicillin. . . .' But the state of the art had reached a point where such a committee was obviously needed, and Mellanby concluded by saying that 'if we do not set up such a committee the outcome will probably be chaos'.

There were other implications of a greater attack on the problems of synthetic manufacture, and Sir Andrew Duncan, the Minister of Supply, was told early in 1944 that 'the pharmaceutical industry were inclined to hold back from the manufacture of penicillin until such time as it could be made synthetically'.

This was to be a constantly reiterated point of view, but the Synthesis Committee was set up at the end of 1943 and held its first meeting on 13 January 1944. Sir Robert Robinson was chairman and members included Chain, Heilbron, Professor Todd, Arthur Mortimer from the Ministry of Supply and representatives of Glaxo, ICI, Wellcome, British Drug Houses, May & Baker, and Boots, with Harold King of the National Institute for Medical Research as secretary.

Work continued until the committee was wound up during the first months of peace, but no answer to the problem of producing synthetic penicillin had been found by that time.

Whether success was held back by insufficient collaboration between British and American scientists is an infinitely debatable point, but Chain was constantly reiterating his belief that better interchange of information was needed. He wrote to Sir Edward Mellanby in April 1944:

As you know on several occasions in the past the American workers obtained detailed information about the progress of the work by our group on the chemical structure of penicillin much earlier than we were informed about their work. For example, they were told the structure of penicillamine, the part of the penicillin molecule which is common to all types of penicillin, several months before we obtained proper evidence that phenylacetic acid was a constituent of penicillin II, the type on which most of the American work was done. Had we known earlier about this we should have been able to formulate an adequate expression for the penicillin molecule several months before we were in fact able to do so, because all the C-atoms in the penicillin molecule, except one, would have been accounted for by the two constituents, penicillamine and glyoxal, discovered by us, and phenylacetic acid found in penicillin II by the Americans.

A further example of delays of this sort which have proved very harmful to the development of our work is the finding of Coghill and Stodola that a crystalline product was formed after inactivation of penicillin II by benzylamine. This reaction was discovered during the summer of 1943 by one of Coghill's collaborators, but we heard details about it only in February 1944. The reaction of benzylamine on penicillin II has provided a most essential piece of evidence for the confirmation of our original formula for penicillin, which was proposed in October 1943. We could not have got this evidence ourselves because the Coghill-Stodola reaction does not work smoothly with the penicillin I type, with which all our work was done.

Chain ended his letter with the suggestion that a personal visit to America should be made by one of the British scientists working on penicillin, and added that he himself would be glad to go.

This suggestion was not accepted. One reason was no doubt that however great Chain's technical qualifications might be – and they were never doubted – there were qualms about the way in which he might handle the delicate questions of allied co-operation. It seemed quite certain, in fact, that the work of the Synthesis Committee would almost inevitably produce a heightening of the problems which concerned the release of information on industrial processes, problems arising as much from commercial motives as from the need to keep information from the enemy. This was illustrated as late as May 1945 after Sir Robert Robinson had proposed that a statement prepared by him should be made available to a conference of penicillin producers to be held in Britain. 'The suggestion', Dr C. R. Harington of the National Institute of Medical Research was told by A. N. Richards, chairman of the Committee on Medical Research of the OSRD, '. . . is not acceptable to us. It contains in outline form all our essential information as to penicillin structure and therefore its distribution to individuals or groups who are not bound by contract arrangements would seem to us to violate our obligations.'

During the period which had elapsed between the first meeting of the Synthesis Committee at the beginning of 1944 and the mid months of 1945 which saw the end first of the war in Europe and then of the war with Japan, there had been two results of the new allied attempts to make penicillin synthetically. One was a renewal in Britain of the discussion about who, if anyone, was to benefit financially from the manufacture of penicillin by fermentation. The other was a demand from many quarters in Britain for closer genuine Anglo–US collaboration in penicillin manufacture, a demand which did eventually take Chain to the United States.

The first of these questions, basically dealing with patent rights, was one about which the Government gave an impression of guilty conscience far stronger than was warranted. 'Patent rights and any other developments which may occur during the war', the House of Commons was told by Mr Peat, Joint Parliamentary Secretary, Ministry of Supply, as early as 2 February 1944, 'have been pooled and will be made available to any manufacturer who is in a position to make penicillin.' It might well have been an answer from the Minister of Circumlocution, and further attempts later in the month to clarify the situation met with no greater success. '[If Mr Robertson's questions] had been answered in detail,' the House was informed, 'the answer would have given full information as to the position and the scope of the production and development of penicillin in this country.' And Mr Peat further stated: 'I believe that penicillin, at this moment, is as vital to us as the most secret weapon we are producing, and if I gave this information, it would lay our production of penicillin open to air attack, because if this Question had been answered, it would have given the location –.' That was perhaps pitching the story rather high in view of the numerous top priority targets already known to the Germans and their decreasing ability to hit even the massive forces assembling in Britain for the invasion of Europe.

The question of patents, ostensibly settled when Dale and Mellanby had decided that patenting was unethical whatever the legal position might be, had continued as an unhappy argument as the Americans had gone ahead with their development of deep fermentation. Anglo–US co-operation, which had grown stronger as British and American medical sources began to pool their results, failed to resolve the problem, and as penicillin production began to soar during the later years of the war so did the potential for disagreement.

However, it was only in 1944 and 1945 that the fortuitous occurrence of two events propelled the patent position into public argument. First, there came the Rockefeller Foundation's Annual Report for 1944 which mentioned, if only in passing, the grant of $5,000 which had supported Florey and Chain's initial work in 1939. The report was commented on by the leading London paper, the *Evening News*, which pointed out that this alone appeared to justify the Americans in exploiting penicillin, a statement which led to a question in the House of Commons and to

Mellanby stating that the MRC had supported Florey with some £7,000 between 1927 and 1939.

It was, of course, only since 1939 that the MRC had financed the penicillin investigation and the 1927 date was a ripe red herring. Nevertheless, the MRC had a better case than Chain was to admit, a fact which Mellanby made clear in a letter to Sir Robert Robinson of 21 March.

If there is a competition as to who started to finance Florey for his research the earlier, I think the Medical Research Council will win handsomely. Certainly in 1927 Florey was receiving money from the Council for his work, and I think that he has never asked the Council for financial help without receiving it. This is certainly the case since I became secretary in 1933. In 1939 he made a specific request for more money in order to allow him to start investigations on penicillin, and this was granted at once, so that since 1939 he has in fact received about £7,000 from the Medical Research Council for his work on penicillin. This figure would have been much higher, had we not last year allowed the Nuffield people, who were very anxious to join in the work, to finance part of the research, to the order of several thousand pounds.

It might have been thought that by the spring of 1944 any Anglo-US problems of collaboration on penicillin would have disappeared following Fleming's approach to the authorities roughly a year earlier. This was not the case. Problems had tended to proliferate rather than disappear, a situation probably inevitable in view of the complexities of the situation. This is made clear in a four-page memorandum by Vannevar Bush, head of the Office of Scientific Research and Development, dated 31 July 1944. This reviewed the steps which had been taken since the autumn of 1943 to co-ordinate attempts to solve the problem of penicillin synthesis. Then, in three sentences, it came to the nub of the problem that was never to be entirely solved to everyone's satisfaction.

Although the OSRD and the Medical Research Council [of Britain] now possess virtually the same powers with regard to the disposition of patent rights relating to the scientific information being interchanged, neither the OSRD nor the MRC is in a position to implement its undertakings with its own contractors or fully protect their interests without agreeing with each other upon a co-ordinated program as to the disposition of patents and patent rights. Some further agreement with the United Kingdom is therefore essential in order to insure fair recognition to each participant in the joint research for those contributions which he may have made.

The problem of assessing the relative contributions of the participants in this joint research program for the purposes of recognition in the disposition of patents and patent rights is one of vast complexity.

Various steps to improve the situation were proposed. Some of them were taken, but the imbroglio almost inevitably created when it had been decided to merge British and US penicillin efforts had not finally been settled when it disappeared under the pressure of post-war developments.

This only slowly became clear, the difficulties of the situation being outlined by Mellanby to Chain in March 1944 when he turned down Chain's suggestion that he should visit the United States to help resolve outstanding difficulties.

In April 1944 he told Chain that the previous October he had suggested to Vannevar Bush that there should be complete collaboration between American and British chemical workers on the subject of penicillin chemistry.

They consented to such an arrangement on condition that we made a formal agreement, which was complicated by many problems as regards patenting. At the same time they also stated that, until such an agreement was signed, sealed and delivered, all collaboration should cease.

During the past few months I have been making the greatest effort to get an agreement among our people here which would satisfy the American authorities and conform to their rules [he went on]. This has proved difficult, because of the different patenting laws of the two countries and the further difficulty of having to carry on negotiations at a distance of 3,000 miles. However, I have every hope that this will ultimately be settled. In fact, I constantly expect it to be settled within a week, but something always crops up to interfere with the arrangements.

Until such an agreement was accepted by the Americans and the British, he ended, 'there can be no question of anyone going to America to give or to seek information'.

Chain had by this time given Mellanby more than one example of how American reluctance to collaborate had hindered British work and he was to give more. 'We consider that we have lost at least two months through not knowing details about this reaction', he wrote on 11 April 1944. There seems no doubt that, aided by the patent laws and commercial circumspection, the Americans were dragging their feet. However, the correspondence leaves little doubt that Chain's persistence – or over-persistence – in speaking up for Britain did as much to hamper his case as to help it. 'Chain is very anxious about the American position,' Robinson told Mellanby in March 1944, 'and I think it would be wise to send him to USA to see Richards, Roger Adams, Merck and

Squibb as soon as convenient after the agreement is concluded.' Mellanby had reservations, replying to Robinson on the 30th:

I think you ought to put a curb on Chain's desire to go off at an early date to America. It seems to me that with the chemical work going so well and vigorously, his job is to help to complete it. Our prestige in this synthesis is greatly at stake. Although I am as anxious as anybody to co-operate with the Americans, you must remember that they stopped the flow of information and took up the strong legal attitude with which we have been trying to deal during the last few months.

Robinson now took the same line, saying: 'We don't want to lose [Chain] just now. When the agreement is concluded somebody should visit America but Chain is too useful here to be spared willingly. I transmitted his own request but my own reaction was the same as yours.' Yet when Robinson himself visited the Americans early in 1945 he found the situation much as Chain had suspected. 'Having seen the ARP precautions in New York and Washington,' he told Mellanby, 'a lack of a sense of proportion in the other side does not surprise me at all. But the essence of the matter is that they are not thinking of the Germans and Japanese but of their "contractors" and USA non-contractors.'

The situation failed to improve, and Chain more than once complained to Mellanby about the inconsistencies of what could, or could not, be published as a result of Anglo–US agreements. His complaints followed a cable from Washington to the US Embassy in London claiming that publication of certain material produced by Robinson 'would in effect be giving aid to the enemy and would be incompatible with the commitments of OSRD to its contractors'.

That the protest sprang not only from security but also from American business policies about which Chain was to object for years was revealed in a letter to Mellanby from A. N. Richards, chairman of the OSRD's Committee on Medical Research, which read:

Prior to the establishment of a system of co-operative effort under Government auspices, time and money were expended by private companies, and their rights to discoveries and patents were carefully protected both by law and by private agreements. Even after they made the results of their research available to the OSRD, these companies have continued to give generously of their own time and money. When they made information as to their work available to the OSRD, however, they did so on the assurance that it would be given to others only to the extent required by the needs of the war effort, and that in every case the patent rights acquired in this field by any person receiving this information would be distributed among them in accordance with the equities of their several contributions. We promised to hold their information secret and in trust and we are not authorized to make any disclosures save under the terms of our agreements. We cannot, therefore, make public disclosures which may lead others to discoveries subject to patent in derogation of the equities of our research group.

The American attitude only exacerbated Chain's belief, which he was to hold all his life, that Britain had been badly treated. It was further inflamed in May 1945 when three Americans filed patents in Britain for various methods of producing penicillin by deep fermentation. One of them was a man who had worked in collaboration with Heatley in Peoria but who now filed the patents in London in his own name alone. This group of patents filed in 1945 did much to support the belief that Florey's mission to the United States ended with Britain eventually having to pay large sums to American companies before penicillin could be produced efficiently in the United Kingdom. This was largely irrelevant since deep fermentation on which efficient production depended had initially come from the United States.

In addition to the discussion of the rights and wrongs of the patent situation, a discussion which continued for a decade, there had already been raised the question of who, if anyone, was personally to benefit from discovering the drug and then developing it. The situation had been unique but it had, almost inevitably, been dealt with by methods which had served well in the past, and when Mr Attlee, Lord President of the Council, was asked whether he knew that Alexander Fleming had made nothing whatsoever from penicillin, he replied:

The question of financial rewards for medical discoveries has been carefully examined on earlier occasions with the conclusion that any such system, even if desirable, could not be administered equitably in practice. The policy of the Government is to support medical research work in progress and not to offer payments on the basis of results.

What was in practice a gulf between the scientific or medical world and the industrial world was still as deep as it had been when the war broke out, and it was uppermost in the minds of many members of Parliament who were later to debate the awards to inventors and the large sums awarded for the development of such techniques as radar. However, in the world of science money is not all, and during the closing years of the war there was much speculation on whether penicillin would feature in any of the Nobel Prizes. Financial reward those certainly brought, but this was barely comparable to the prestige which accompanied them.

By 1944 rumours on the scientific grapevine suggested that penicillin would be included in the presentations for the following year, but in view of the drug's complex history there were numerous theories on how the award might be made. Chain, with his customary belief that he would not get his due, felt that he might be left out. He went, in fact, as far as to ask his colleague, Edward Abraham, whether he should not make his contribution more widely known. Abraham advised him

to do nothing, but doubted whether he was convinced that this course was best. In October of that year (1944) it appeared that his apprehension had some substance. Radio announcements, apparently originating in London but repeated by stations in Switzerland and America, led to press reports that Fleming would be (or in at least one case, had been) awarded the Prize for Physiology and Medicine. In some reports it was suggested that Florey might also be rewarded financially but Chain was not mentioned.

There had been a good deal of discussion - as was inevitably the case with many of the awards - and it is now known that the Nobel Committee had initially recommended that Fleming should be awarded one half of the prize 'for his discovery of penicillin', and that the other half should be awarded to Florey and Chain together 'for its curative value in a number of infectious diseases'.

Discussion as to how the award should finally be made went on throughout the summer of 1945. Meanwhile, Chain was preparing for his long-awaited visit to the United States. He wrote to Mellanby on 8 March 1945:

The main object of my proposed journey is to become acquainted with the latest developments in the deep fermentation technique, particularly as applied to the growth of actinomycetes. . . . Finally, it is my aim to get in personal contact with some of the American chemists working on the structure of penicillin in order to discuss with them a number of important questions relating to this problem. Among the numerous points I would like to discuss in detail are nomenclature of penicillin, production of Penicillin III and the biological properties, interpretations of infra-red data and of the experiments with heavy hydrogen of the Cornell group, reactions and properties of the 5-membered Cornell lactam breakdown product of Merck.

Robinson, chairman of the Synthesis Committee, thought that Chain should make the journey but Charles Harington of the National Institute of Medical Research - possibly remembering his contacts with Chain slightly less than a decade ago – had his reservations and wrote to Mellanby:

On the other hand I think it would be unfortunate if Chain were to go to America to talk about the chemistry of penicillin with any sort of official backing from the Council. Some joint Anglo-American discussion of the chemistry of penicillin might be useful, but Chain is not the right person to conduct it.

The suggestion that Chain might not be going to America became an open secret and it was left to Florey to put in the necessary, and probably decisive, word for Chain. 'As [Chain] was largely instrumental in first extracting penicillin and has played an important part in the subsequent chemical work, I trust that there is no foundation for this suggestion', he wrote to Dr A. Landsborough Thomson of the MRC on 5 June. A problem arose from the fact that the Americans were to produce two official figures and it was considered essential that Sir Robert Robinson and Harold King, the Secretary of the Synthesis Committee, should represent the British. Eventually a solution was found by adding Chain to the 'official' two-man party in a status that never appears to have been perfectly clear. No one seems to have been aware of any difference until, in Washington, Chain discovered that while he and his colleagues were staying and eating in the same hotel, his official allowance was $9 a day, compared with his colleagues' $11.

The three men flew from Poole, Dorset, on 21 July and arrived in Baltimore the following day. From there they travelled on to Washington for a series of discussions with government officials and scientists in the firms which were by this time making penicillin in quantity.

In the United States Chain became worried by two things, judging from his letters to Florey. One was the triumphal lecture tour of the country being made by Fleming, who earlier in the year had been asked by the Columbia Broadcasting Corporation to make a broadcast on penicillin and had asked Churchill whether he should do so. The Prime Minister was at first against acceptance but finally took the contrary advice of his Minister of Information, Brendan Bracken, and the broadcast was duly made.

Fleming, Chain reported to Florey, was being accompanied on his tour by a Ministry of Supply 'chaperon'.

The Oxford work is of course never mentioned by him. It will take a great deal of very considerable efforts to get things into their proper perspectives, and I will do what I can though I am under no illusions about the difficulties and delicacy inherent in the present situation. I came here fully prepared to find the usual distortions of the history of the penicillin discovery, but I must confess that I was staggered to see how far these distortions have gone through the systematic and carefully planned efforts of Fleming.

Although impressed by the American success in producing penicillin in bulk, and by individual Americans, Chain had his qualifications on wider issues. In the same letter to Florey he wrote:

I hope I have not given you the impression that I think that everything is rosy in this country. Far from it. The fight is very hard, harder than in England and more ruthless. You have to succeed here or go under completely. I think that I should hate to live in New York, but nevertheless one cannot but admire the enterprising spirit and the achievements of the American scientists.

Shortly afterwards he was mollified by the announcement from Stockholm that the Nobel Prize for Physiology and Medicine would be split equally and awarded to Fleming, Florey and himself 'for their discovery of penicillin and its curative value in a number of infectious diseases'. This, according to Robert Robinson, who could write as one above the *mêlée*, 'was a joint appreciation of the merits of three of the chief actors in the penicillin drama. Franklin said that "Luck is the bonus that accrues to industry". Fleming was certainly industrious, and how very lucky he was has been accurately described in detail by Chain [in his *Thirty Years of Penicillin Therapy*].'

The award was announced while Chain was still in the United States. Among the congratulatory messages was one from Anne Beloff, whom Chain had first met after being 'rescued' from the mental home at the time of his appendicitis. In 1942 she had taken a degree in chemistry in London. Uncertain what to do next she had conferred with her sister Nora, who knew Chain and suggested asking his advice. Chain had advised that biochemistry was one of the specialities of the future, and had told her that Rudolph Peters, Whitley Professor of Biochemistry in the university, was seeking an assistant for research into the biochemical effects of burns. Anne Beloff took her D.Phil. while working on the research in Oxford, became a frequent visitor to Chain in the nearby William Dunn School and when the work with Peters was completed took a post in Harvard, whence she sent her congratulations to Chain. 'Dear Ernst,' they ran. 'I have become sufficiently Americanized to consider the use of the surname an unnecessary formality. I hope you don't object.'

# —7—

# POST-WAR OPTIONS

The end of the war marked the start of a new stage in the demand for penicillin as well as an ending of the restrictions imposed on information about its manufacture. At the same time it opened up new and far more ambitious prospects for Ernst Chain, a great part of whose working life had been concentrated on this one particular aspect of biochemistry. He had limited experience outside it; but in the science of making and using to best advantage penicillin, and later its successors, his experience was unique.

On 1 January 1946 the scores of reports on penicillin which had been written with the blessing of the British and US authorities from 1942 onwards were declassified. They were not published, but copies were filed at scientific libraries in Britain and the United States, and penicillin production became limited only by the comparatively small number of patents which had been filed to cover various aspects of manufacture by deep fermentation.

Although the fighting had ended there was only a small drop in the overall demand for penicillin. The slack was quickly taken up by the needs of European civilians, undernourished by years of enemy occupation and racked by disease. During the war there had been considerable argument about to whom the penicillin, short in supply at the best of times, should be made available, and it was even proposed at one point that its use to combat venereal disease should be restricted to key troops such as fighter pilots, tank crews and commandos. Now, in the territories that Allied troops took over from the enemy, the priority problems were of a different kind: should penicillin, still not sufficient for everyone, have priority in the treatment of venereal disease in troops or be used to help seriously ill children. A doctor wrote in the *British Medical Journal*:

I confirm from personal experience that penicillin was used to treat gonorrhoea in Germany in 1946–8 while German children died with pneumonia, meningitis, etc. The special centre in which I worked frequently had to turn away distraught parents begging for this drug, often bringing their dying child as proof of their desperate need. Their only hope of obtaining this drug was via the Swedish and Danish Red Cross and the delay invariably meant death to the child. Sex in this context did have priority over the sick child, but of course the child was unfortunately on the wrong side of the war.

UNRRA – the United Nations Relief and Rehabilitation Agency – bought and made available to Europe a number of penicillin production plants, but it was soon evident that a huge and growing market existed for the drug that would only be satisfied by private pharmaceutical companies or by national government agencies. In the post-war world the Americans were quick to consolidate the advantages that the wartime situation had given them.

The Americans are profiting by this situation not only to enhance their prestige vis-à-vis the Russians who have no penicillin at all [went one cable about penicillin from the British authorities in Sofia to the Foreign Office in London] but to consolidate their own situation as a humanitarian and altruistic people by distributing this drug in large quantities to camps, medical officers and others who have need of it. Unsuccessful applicants to us have often been able to satisfy their requirements by addressing themselves to the Americans. And now we learn that the Americans are expecting 100,000,000 units by air this week. Nor is this inconsistent with American policy of kicking with one hand and patting with the other.

To be fair, it must be admitted that economics and ethics were equally entwined in British reactions. Britain, the Ministry of Supply was told by the Foreign Office in January 1946, should release supplies of penicillin to Bulgaria 'both in order not to lose a future market and to give a tangible form to British humanitarianism to offset American gestures in this field'.

Even when total supplies were sufficient to meet demand, problems arose, both from the earlier Anglo–US agreements and from the different production costs in different countries. While distribution of penicillin through British hospitals had hitherto been free, it was clear that charges would now have to be made. But what charges? The Ministry of Supply suggested a minimum figure of £5 per mega-unit and a top figure of £10. The Americans, however, appeared able to export to Britain at £2 10s per mega-unit, while Canadian supplies were costing only £2 5s per mega-unit to produce. These figures, and the varying positions taken up by private firms and by governments, made their frequently competing aims even more tangled than they had been during the final months of the war.

This situation faced Chain with a personal problem which he never entirely solved. His experience with the Medical Research Council had embittered his attitude to official agencies and for the rest of his life he would inveigh, at the slightest excuse, against the ineptitude of civil servants and the 'faceless men' to whom he attributed a high percentage of the world's shortcomings. On the other hand he had not been over-impressed with the activities of the pharmaceutical industry in general. There were exceptions, and his overall view tended to change as he appreciated better the wartime problems with which they had had to cope. In the post-war world Chain was therefore torn between advocating a national antibiotics centre for Britain, which he saw as possible with the advent of a Labour Government and the National Health Service, and support for the country's most adventurous pharmaceutical firms. He also had divided feelings about the exact tasks that should be attempted. 'I lost interest in the field [of new antibiotics],' he was later to say, 'feeling that it was not only too late, but also inappropriate, for us to try to compete with giant pharmaceutical companies, infinitely better equipped than ourselves for searching for new antibiotics – which had become mainly an organizational task.' He thought that it would, instead, be a good idea to try to modify the penicillin molecule to get penicillins which were active against an increasing number of resistant staphylococci. There was little chance of Oxford providing the equipment and this compounded Chain's belief that it might be better to move elsewhere.

If the situation presented one problem, there was also another. With all the loyalty of a refugee for his host country, Chain was anxious that the financial benefits from penicillin should accrue to Britain – an anxiety which was constantly arousing his anger at what he believed was official laxity in letting the United States benefit from the early work. Yet in contrast there was his deep and almost religious belief that penicillin offered a God-given relief from human suffering and that it should be developed and used without regard to country, finance, or national or personal prestige. Chain's activities during the immediate post-war years therefore present a confused picture in which he is trying to expand the uses of penicillin – and later its successors – in a variety of diverse and sometimes overlapping ways.

His psychological ability to consider moving out of the purely academic field was partly due to a growing disillusion with prospects at

Oxford. 'I can see no prospect for an adequate development of my work within the framework or the organization of this university,' he wrote in a draft letter to an unknown correspondent late in 1945, 'and I feel that the years in which I am able to make contributions in science are running short'; was there any chance, he added, of his building up a biochemical department in the London School of Hygiene and Tropical Medicine? The suggestion of a major development originated at least partly in Chain's realization that chemical engineering expertise would be required for the deep fermentation techniques which he correctly believed lay at the heart of future penicillin production, from his own mastery of this particular subject, and from his knowledge that the very considerable funds involved were unlikely to be coaxed from the University of Oxford. It also seems likely, although no proof exists, that a break with Florey would in any case have been agreeable. On Florey's part, little of the wartime disagreement appeared to have lingered. For Chain a sense of subdued grievance remained.

Partly for this reason the immediate post-war years saw Chain involved in a succession of projects. Some were aimed at setting up a flourishing government-supported antibiotics industry in Britain. Others were planned to support such an industry in various parts of Europe, or even in Russia, and it required a man of enormous energy to deal with so many, often overlapping, projects. Chain the juggler, keeping half a dozen scientific balls in the air at the same time, became a familiar figure in the later 1940s.

His task was sometimes made more difficult by the contradictions in his make-up. Asked how Chain might fit into one new position, Florey answered:

He has great charm of manner, is a first-class musician, and can be socially very successful. As he speaks a number of languages well he is at his best at international gatherings. He is, however, somewhat egotistical and for that reason he might not be to everybody's liking, though he has friends in Oxford and elsewhere.

In spite of his continuing disillusion with the Medical Research Council, it was to the Council that Chain turned in November 1946 in the hope that the benefits of penicillin might at last be successfully pursued. Sir Edward Mellanby agreed that he should submit ideas for an MRC Committee on Antibiotics and Chain did so late in November 1946. The needs for such a committee, with which he began his proposals, provide a striking proof of the extent to which the subject had grown since he and others had almost tentatively discussed the potentialities of penicillin in *The Lancet* some six years previously:

It seems certain to me that progress in the field of chemotherapy will be bound up to a large extent with a progress in the field of antibiotics and a growing number of research workers will be drawn into this field. Apart from finding new antibiotics of practical use (a line of work which I personally do not consider very promising) there are numerous problems deserving immediate attention which are connected with the study of antibiotics already known, in particular, streptomycin and penicillin.

At the top of the list Chain put investigation into the methods of increasing the yields of such substances. Secondly, it was important to discover how the fermentation process could be so organized and controlled that when it produced two kinds of penicillin, one more effective than the other, production of the more effective was kept to a maximum and production of the other to a minimum. Thirdly, it was necessary to find ways of increasing production of yet a third kind of penicillin which, it had been found, could be modified into semi-artificial varieties with specialized uses. Finally, there were awaiting solution various problems of a technical nature on which production on an industrial scale still depended.

An MRC committee was necessary, Chain continued, in order to co-ordinate work in Britain, keep contact with developments abroad, promote grants and give advice. And, he added, 'to foster the erection of a pilot plant for the production of antibiotics, which is essential for many of the problems indicated above and without which we shall not be able to compete successfully with the Americans'.

Although nothing came of these proposals, Chain had by no means abandoned the hope that Britain would put herself on the antibiotics map. So deeply did he hope for this that in the autumn of 1949 he prepared memoranda outlining a state-owned organization for making penicillin and sent them in succession to Mellanby, his successor Sir Charles Himsworth, and finally to Aneurin Bevan, the Minister of Health.

His case, including the proposal which appeared to fly in the face of his distrust of the Civil Service and almost everything in which it had a hand, was first made in a ten-page memorandum which outlined the history of penicillin since Fleming's work in 1928 and strongly attacked the pharmaceutical industry for its failure to produce penicillin in the early 1940s.

Chain was equally critical of the department in the Ministry of Supply which had been set up to control penicillin, and of the government contracts set up towards the end of 1945. His main ground for criticism was that in Britain work was concentrated on 'the old surface method and quite a lot of money and time was spent on this type of production which already had been shown conclusively in America to be totally inefficient and long since superseded by the deep culture fermentation method'.

There was, in Chain's view, only one real way of altering the situation:

The author suggests that a state-owned penicillin factory would be a great asset to the nation for several reasons. 1) The state would become independent of private enterprise for the supply of one of the most important and most frequently-used drugs in medicine. 2) It should produce this drug at a lower cost than it is achieved [*sic*] by private enterprise in this country. 3) A penicillin factory in order to be able to run efficiently and to keep up with developments must be provided with a well-equipped research laboratory. This laboratory could serve as a model laboratory for pharmaceutical research in this country and could become the nucleus of a state-sponsored larger research unit for other branches of pharmaceutical research which in the opinion of the author is equal in importance to other government-supported research institutions such as the Experimental Station at Porton, the Centre for Atomic Research at Harwell and the National Physical Laboratory at Teddington.

The author considers that without such a research unit this country is not in a position to compete in quality and quantity of any new inventions with other countries, in particular the USA and Switzerland.

Nothing came of the proposal. But here, as in other fields, once Chain got his teeth into an idea he hung on with a bulldog tenacity more to be expected of the prototype Englishman than of the self-styled 'temperamental Continental'. He now wrote to Aneurin Bevan, enclosing a four-page outline for a national biochemical and pharmaceutical research centre, saying:

I know that there will be a lot of opposition from vested interests in academic, administrative and industrial quarters, and this opposition could not be stronger than that which came from vested interests in the medical profession against the Health Act which was broken so successfully through your unrelenting energy and determination.

Chain's project was ambitious, although no more so than was required. The research centre, he said, should contain, among other things, a large laboratory for structural and synthetic organic work and a first-class library service. The personnel should consist of chemical engineers, organic chemists, biochemists, bacteriologists, analytical chemists and pharmacologists. The research centre should have a strict and rigidly controlled organization and should be welded into a research unit in the biochemical and pharmaceutical field as powerful as any single unit in the US, e.g. the laboratories of Merck and Co. or the Cyanamide Company.

The cost of the project is estimated to be about £500,000. There can be no doubt that if the centre is efficiently run it will produce within a few years discoveries which, even from a purely economic point of view, will amply justify the investment. The American pharmaceutical firms have not built up large research organizations for the sake of philanthropic purposes.

As already suggested on a previous occasion, the research centre could be financed by a large penicillin factory. A well-run penicillin factory is very profitable and could easily finance not only one, but several research centres of the type outlined above. It is certain that a penicillin factory with better methods than those used at present by British penicillin manufacturers could be built which would produce a cheaper product.

This state penicillin factory could then gradually become the nucleus of a state pharmaceutical industry. The number of really important drugs is very limited, and it seems a natural consequence of the Health Act that the state which gives drugs to the public free of charge should have facilities for producing them at a low price, without having to pay for the large profits of the pharmaceutical manufacturers.

The development of a state pharmaceutical industry would be impossible without ample facilities for research.

Nothing came of this proposal, but Chain responded with an enlarged scheme, although he had little hope of its being implemented.

I have been told [he wrote] that Imperial College and the University of Manchester are now toying with the idea to get a pilot plant for chemical microbiology organized, but this talk has already been going on for several years and nothing has happened so far. I am sure that this sort of project which may cost up to half a million pounds needs the encouragement and the stimulus of the government, and I doubt very much whether the present one will look favourably on such a development.

Chain's unsuccessful attempts to gain government support for production of penicillin tended to reinforce his suspicions of official thinking on scientific matters. So, no doubt, although in a perverse way, did the government attitude to patenting which changed after the setting up of the National Research Development Corporation and brought under patent protection the new antibiotic cephalosporin.

The whole patent situation had in fact been made more complex after the secret wartime reports had been made available at the beginning of 1946. Now it became of importance to patent lawyers to establish when specific reports had been consulted by pharmaceutical firms. The increasing complexity is typified by Chain's comment in 1954:

I must say that the idea never entered my head that anyone would think it profitable to make a patent claim for a process such as the butanol crystallization of penicillin salts which involves not a single new step, and it seems to me extraordinary that in Sweden a patent claim is being made by a firm which has not even invented the process, if the process can be called an invention.

Chain's importance in the post-war antibiotics industry which speedily developed did not rest only on the part which he had played in discovering penicillin's possibilities, and on his fame as a Nobel Laureate. There were two other characteristics which separated him from Fleming and Florey. He had a genius for solving the problems of chemical engineering which were to be inseparable from the expansion of the antibiotics industry. In addition he had a businessman's instinct for intuitively sensing what would be economically viable and what would not. These capabilities, added to his quality as a biochemist, made him of unique use to the world's pharmaceutical industry once it appreciated the potentialities of antibiotics. Little wonder, then, that in the next three decades he was to become industrial consultant or adviser on collaborative research to a large number of companies.

Soon after the war he was conferring with Astra, the large Swedish pharmaceutical company with whom contact had earlier been made while he was in Stockholm for the Nobel Prize celebrations. The following year he was advising the firm on the erection of their own penicillin plant and in 1948 he formally accepted a consultancy with the company involving not more than two meetings a month for a fee of not less than 1,000 guineas a year. This was to be the start of a collaboration which lasted until the end of his life more than thirty years later and, through Astra's links with Iran, led him to advise on the supply of penicillin to the Iranian Army.

While the early negotiations with Astra were continuing, Chain also opened negotiations with Russia and Czechoslovakia, the latter having unexpected repercussions a few years later. The initial advance from Russia was made by Dr N. Borodin, a Soviet biologist attached to the Russian Trade Delegation in London who had worked for a while at the William Dunn School in Oxford. Borodin had officially told the

British authorities that he was anxious to obtain details of penicillin production but had run into difficulties due to the patent situation and to the agreements which the British had made with the Americans. He had little more luck when he visited the United States and found essential information kept from him. Alfred N. Richards wrote as follows to Shapley in a letter which spells out the problems which Britain was also to have:

The explanation of this decision was such as to convince me of its soundness in the light of the fundamental fact that our economic system is built on competition. The processes which are kept secret constitute not only a highly valuable asset to the possessor but is [sic] a stimulus to competitors to the strenuous exercise of inventive ingenuity. Such a request as that which concerns us if made by an American who was connected with industry or by an American [sic] would certainly not be granted unless contracts were in effect which required it.

Undeterred, Borodin returned to England and attempted to circumvent the difficulties by hiring the services of Ernst Chain.

The greater part of his adviser's work would be carried out in London and Oxford, Chain later wrote, but he would be prepared to visit the Soviet Union from time to time.

I am certain that on the basis of my advice a modern workable penicillin plant, similar to those in existence in England and the USA, of the desired capacity of 500 to 600 billion units per month could be constructed in collaboration with the Soviet engineering and biochemical staff in charge of the project [he wrote to Dr Borodin on 27 January]. The average yield of penicillin activity in the tanks can be expected to be 400 to 500 units/ml in 3-4 days and the average overall yield of dry alkali salt of benzylpenicillin about 40-50 per cent. This corresponds to the average yield obtained in modern English penicillin plants.

The payment proposed was a substantial premium plus £3,000 a year and the refunding of all travel and clerical expenses. One stipulation was that no use should be made of Chain's name without his special consent.

Agreement was finally reached and on 8 July 1948 Chain wrote to the Trade Delegation of the USSR saying:

This is to certify that I shall deliver the memorandum concerning the production of penicillin, mentioned in clause 1 of the agreement between TECHNOPROMEMPORT and myself, on a date not later than four months after the signing of the agreement, and the memorandum on streptomycin, mentioned in clause 2 of the said agreement, on a date not later than six months after the signing of the agreement. . . .

But Borodin fell from favour, and the project was still-born.

Chain's willingness to enter the commercial field produced a reaction in the scientific fraternity which has not entirely disappeared a third of a century later. It was typified by a letter to Dr F. G. Morgan of the Commonwealth Serum Laboratories, Victoria, by Florey who while admittedly allergic to Chain at this period seems to have reflected an opinion held by more than one of his colleagues. 'I have reason to doubt that Dr Chain has anything really useful to offer to those who are manufacturing penicillin,' he said, 'and if he had he would be wanting to charge you a stiff fee.'

While negotiations were continuing with the Russians, Chain was asked by the Czechoslovak Minister of Health in President Beneš's Government, Dr Schober, to visit Prague and advise on production of penicillin. 'Before my visit was due to take place', he later wrote, 'the Beneš Government had fallen and the Communist Government had taken over. As the purpose of my visit was not of a political nature, but was concerned with health matters, i.e. the production of a medical drug, I saw no reason to cancel my proposed visit.'

The visit lasted three or four days, during which Chain inspected the equipment for producing penicillin which had been given to Czechoslovakia recently by UNRRA. Similar equipment had been sent at the same time by the same organization to Poland, Yugoslavia, Italy and China. He later wrote that

it was obvious that much of it was obsolete, in particular the extraction part. This did not include counter-current extractors which at that time – being much more economical – had already replaced in many penicillin factories the Sharples centrifuge separators which I myself had originally introduced in Oxford for the extraction of penicillin from the culture field and which in the beginning were used by all firms for the commercial production of penicillin.

Chain naturally advised that modern counter-current extractors should be bought. However, they were at that time made only in the United States, which would not grant export licences, a fact which came to light only at the end of the year. It should, however, have been possible to use a different process and on 26 April 1948 Chain wrote to Dr Schober with details.

The process is patented but we shall be willing to issue a licence to the Czechoslovak Government. The details of the conditions will have to be negotiated with my lawyers.... I have instructed them to get in contact with you. Roughly speaking, the terms will be a sum of £5,000 and royalties of total sales amounting to 5% up to £50,000 and 3% above £50,000.

The visit to Czechoslovakia enabled him to deal with his variable health at the country's spas – 'after very strong treatment I have lost some kilos and am satisfied with the success', he wrote to his wife – and it helped satisfy his latent desire for fine scenery.

The more I see of the surroundings of Marienbad the more am I impressed by the beauty of the landscape. The forests are enormous, almost impenetrable, and have something mysterious about them, something which appeals to me very much. There are unlimited possibilities for walks and I am regretting every day that you are not here with me; you would have enjoyed this scenery as you did in the winter.

However, the most important by-product of this foray to give the Czechs the benefits of penicillin was Chain's conversion to the game of golf. He had never ceased to believe that his lack of interest in sport had been a black mark against him in England and he was now excited that he had discovered an acceptable pastime he could enjoy.

Practically every afternoon we drive to the golf course and you could see me swinging the golf club in a most professional manner. I find the whole business very difficult indeed, but quite amusing. The trainer who teaches me (or tries to teach me) the game has an angel's patience – and he needs it, too. The golf course is beautifully situated, with wonderful lawns in the middle of forests, and the mere pleasure of walking through this landscape is worth the effort. I am determined to continue the game in Rome.

A few weeks later he had become even more enthusiastic, writing: 'I hit almost all balls, and get them a fair distance away. I begin to get very interested in the game and think you would like it too. It looks gracious and elegant and one feels that all the muscles in the body get trained.' But his enthusiasm quickly waned and he never again played golf.

By the time of this visit to Czechoslovakia Chain had finally turned down the last of a succession of pleas to emigrate to Israel and set up there his own biochemical establishment in the Weizmann Institute of Science which in 1948 was replacing the Daniel Sieff Research Institute, set up in the 1930s at Rehovoth (now Rehovot), south of Tel Aviv, with the help of the Sieff, Marks and Sacher families in Britain. In the early days the Institute concentrated on technical bacteriology and pharmaceutical and agricultural chemistry, with emphasis on the use of agricultural products. However, Chaim Weizmann, soon to become the first President of Israel, had a more ambitious concept of what the Institute might do. This was based, Israel Sieff was to write in his *Memoirs*, on

his conviction that the problem of the monopolistic position of oil, such a crucial issue in the future history of the Middle East, could be obviated by the discovery of a method of producing oil synthetically. He believed that if abundant supplies of root starches like manioc, tapioca, and cane sugar could be grown in, say, West Africa, and if a fermentation could be introduced, there would be a large yield of ordinary alcohol for power and the production of butyl alcohol and acetone. These three materials, in large quantities and at a low price, could form the basis of two or three great industries, among them high-octane fuel, and would make the British Commonwealth independent of oil wells. . . .

The new Institute that Weizmann was planning in the 1940s was an ambitious idea, his own brain-child, and had Chain joined it the course which the development and exploitation of synthetic penicillins were to take would almost certainly have been very different.

The man given the task of attracting Chain to what was to become the future State of Israel was Dr Ernst David Bergmann, an organic chemist who had been a Privatdozent at the University of Berlin from 1928 until 1933, and who left Germany on Hitler's coming to power. The following year he had become scientific director of the Daniel Sieff Research Institute, and one of Weizmann's right-hand men on questions of scientific recruitment and, to some extent, of scientific policy. After the end of the Second World War he had on Weizmann's behalf begun to recruit to Palestine as many leading scientists as possible. Chain had been one of his targets even before the award of the Nobel Prize, and Chain's own ambition to make penicillin as widely available as possible supplemented Bergmann's belief that it could be made in Palestine to the benefit of the world in general and of Jewry in particular. He met Chain a number of times in the autumn of 1945 and on 26 October added to a request for a further meeting the comment: 'Going to Palestine seems to offer in the situation recently created an act of faith which one cannot wish to escape.' On 12 December he made a tentative offer whose details had already been approved by Weizmann. 'We are offering you a department in the frame of the new Weizmann Research Center in Rehovoth,' he said. 'The physical size of this department, as well as the equipment, will be left to your discretion.' A new building devoted to biochemistry and biology was to be built. As to salary, Chain could 'write [his] own ticket – of course within the limit of our possibilities'. He was to be given much the same freedom in most other ways. 'There is no objection to your taking some very good young scientists with you, in whom you have confidence,' it was added. 'I need not tell you that we will endeavour, in the future, perhaps more than in the past, to employ graduates of the Hebrew University whenever their standard of learning and intelligence is satisfactory.' Chain had already raised the prospect of making penicillin in Palestine and this was one of the matters which could be discussed.

There is no record of Chain's reply but in April of the following year, 1946, he made his first visit to Palestine, lectured to the Convention of Palestinian Chemists on 'The Chemical Constitution of the Penicillins', and later spoke on the same subject in both Tel Aviv and the Hebrew University in Jerusalem. By this time he was seriously considering uprooting himself from Oxford.

While he was still in Rehovoth he received a revealing letter from Weizmann:

I do not know how much weight my words may have with you when you will be considering your future connection with the new centre at Rehovoth, but I feel I must tell you that it would be a great benefit for Palestine as a whole and for science in our country in particular, if you could make your residence here. Difficult as it may be for you to give up your present position and to take up work in a new country and surroundings as yet unfamiliar, I do not doubt that you would soon feel at home in Palestine. Apart from the material possibilities of work – I am sure that adequate facilities will be put at your disposal at Rehovoth – you will no doubt find stimulus and satisfaction in the contact with new men, all of them eager to draw from you fresh impetus and new inspiration. You may become the founder of a new school of science for our young generation, and your presence here will certainly draw other great scientists to our part of the world. With the help of your authority we might be able to build up in Palestine a local tradition of science of which there is to date only a modest beginning and which had no chance of developing during the last few years owing to our isolated position during the war.

I am sure that all this is not your ambition. But your great discovery had made of you a man chosen to do a great service to Palestine. So much depends on your presence here – in fact everything; if you settle here, then Rittenberg may come as well and others may follow.

This personal appeal was followed by another discussion between Chain and Ernst Bergmann and on 13 August by a semi-formal letter from Bergmann to Chain which offered a salary of £125 a month and gave details of the laboratory space and equipment which would be available. Chain's reply does not appear to have survived but its tone can be gathered from a long letter from Weizmann to Bergmann in October in which he reported that Rittenberg had decided not to join the Institute and that this 'may endanger Chain's coming'. From indeterminate letters and telegrams Chain appears to have had difficulty in balancing the needs of Israel against the future of antibiotics. Weizmann was obviously reluctant to consider 'no' as a final answer and on 24 January 1947 told James de Rothschild that Chain would 'join our staff when the new Institute is built'.

This appears to have remained Chain's intention throughout 1947, even though he had various other irons in the fire. On 15 January 1948, after a long talk with Chain the previous day, Weizmann wrote to Weisgal of Chain and Berenblum: 'Both are first-class men and I was delighted to find them so keen to get out to Rehovoth and start work with us', and as late as February 1948 Bergmann was writing in the confident assumption that Chain would be settling in Rehovoth in the not too distant future.

He appears to have felt for a while that the new Weizmann Institute might offer an unfortunate counter-attraction to the Hebrew University which had been founded on Mount Scopus in Jerusalem in 1921. Such fears were damped down by Weizmann who in December 1947 wrote to his supporter, Israel M. Sieff:

It seems to me that the best both Dr Chain and Dr Berenblum can do to help the University (and I have spoken to Dr Rittenberg in the same sense) is that they come to Palestine and help us to make the Institute in Rehovot an institution of such standing that its spirit will automatically influence the life of the University.

Whatever Chain was planning, his decision was finally settled by the Arab invasion in May 1948 of the State of Israel, set up following the end of the Mandate, and by an even more attractive prospect in Europe. While Chain was even at this date an ardent supporter of an independent State of Israel, he was an equally firm believer in the development of antibiotics in general and penicillin in particular as a factor in alleviating the ills which beset the human race. Whether that development could take place in a state disrupted by war was in 1948 highly questionable, and he now turned to other things.

However, the first Arab–Israeli war was not of itself decisive in dissuading Chain from coming to Israel and in January, when the Arab invasion had been repulsed and the situation in Israel had begun to stabilize, Ernst Bergmann was writing to him saying: 'the point in your letter which Dr Weizmann (and myself) liked best was the expression of your reiterated desire to come and work in Rehovot'. Although Chain's letter to Weizmann does not appear to have been kept, his thoughts of coming to Israel were not merely passing ones as is made clear from Bergmann's which said that the government and army were anxious to establish an institute devoted to Immunology and Epidemiology in the widest sense of the terms, including Bacteriology and Virus Research, as a part of the Weizmann Institute of Science. Chain, he added, would 'feel completely and absolutely happy [there] and that is more than can be said about most places in this world'.

In 1948 Chain, still negotiating with Czechs and Russians, still anxious to set up an indigenous British antibiotics industry, finally decided not to join Weizmann in Israel. Instead, he took up what he rightly saw as the best existing opportunity of investigating the potential of antibiotics despite the massive outlay of men, money and materials which he knew this would demand.

Before leaving Oxford in 1948 for the new post which would enable him to utilize his abilities to the full, and in which he was to consolidate his reputation, Chain completed his contribution to a major two-volume history of the penicillin enterprise which was published in 1949. It was an account to which he was later to refer enquirers, but it was one with which he was by no means satisfied as he later revealed:

In order to get the historical account in the form in which it has appeared in print, and is approximately, but only approximately correct, I had to fight a real bitter struggle for practically every phrase and, in some cases, every word. You simply cannot imagine what travesty of the true facts was the historical account they had prepared and wished me to sign. The story which was finally published was a compromise, not entirely satisfactory, but at least acceptable to me, and for those who are interested, it is possible to understand, more or less, what really happened.

With this letter, which Chain wrote to a colleague in 1960, there went a nineteen-page catalogue of amendments, many of them expanding on his criticisms of Florey. Whether the account had added up to a 'travesty of the true facts' depends on the viewpoint of the reader and is perhaps a striking illustration of the fact that a handful of observers, each asked to describe the same incident, will give different versions of it.

Certainly Florey had an entirely different version of events. As early as the summer of 1946 he had told Chain: 'It is quite clear that I cannot carry on any further acrimonious conversations with you [about the book] as they lead to no progress and waste time and energy which I cannot afford.' Two years later he wrote a 2,000-word letter to Chain complaining about delays in writing or revising the text of the book. He objected that Chain's claim that he had fulfilled his obligations was 'absurd' before adding,

and the suggestion that you would have written the chapters that Abraham did if you had known they were to be signed does not bear examination on either ethical or practical grounds. In fact, but for the arrangement with Abraham, you would have received an ultimatum from the publishers about the non-production of your chapters, which was holding up the book.

Even were the various drafts available, even were the subject not one on which genuine differences of opinion were held, it would be difficult to balance the rights and wrongs of either side in an argument of this sort. Any writer who has collaborated with another knows how intractable the problems can be, and dealing satisfactorily with a number could well look impossible. In this particular case it seems likely that Chain's propensity for taking on as much as, or more than, he could cope with, clashed with Florey's wish to see delivered on time the version of events as he had seen them. Even had the two men not developed a mutual allergy to each other much of the trouble might well have arisen naturally.

Despite the bitterness in the summer of 1948 there was on both sides some feeling that emotions had been getting out of hand and on leaving Oxford Chain wrote to Florey a letter which gives perspective to their past disagreements.

My dear professor,

To my regret I could not say goodbye to you personally as you were in London on the day of my departure. So I have to do it by letter.

I am very sorry that our personal relationship has deteriorated so much during the last years; I think the reason for it is mainly the general imperfection of human nature. I have always deeply regretted this development and I hope that as time goes on the unpleasant episodes - which, after all, were not frightfully important when looked at from a broad viewpoint - may gradually sink into oblivion and we shall remember only the exciting and unique events of the time of our collaboration which a curious fate has destined us to experience together.

With best wishes for your personal success in the future and the development of your Department,

I remain,

Yours very sincerely,

E. Chain

Chain's feelings were more than an emotional spasm as he showed in a letter to Florey a year later when he finally resigned from his Oxford post.

Thus an episode in my life has come to an end which has been rich in elating emotions such as very few people are privileged to experience.

I shall remember with great pleasure, and always with gratitude, the first years of our association in which the foundation for the subsequent work was laid, and shall try to forget the bitter experiences of the later years which I am sure will shrink into insignificance as time goes on.

In return, Florey wished him success and added: 'I only trust that the difficulties of running laboratories will not disillusion you too soon, but I am sure it is best that you should run your own show.'

# —8—

# AN INSTITUTE
# IN ROME

The burying of the hatchet by Florey and Chain in the autumn of 1948 came as Chain left Oxford for what was to be a prestigious and newly created appointment in Rome. In 1947 he had accepted an invitation from the British Council to lecture in Italy on the discovery of penicillin and in particular on the work which had led to the elucidation of its chemical structure. In Rome he spoke at the Istituto Superiore di Sanità at the invitation of its director, Professor Domenico Marotta.

'I now saw this Institute for the first time,' he later wrote, 'and gained the impression of a large building containing many beautiful but rather empty-looking laboratories; though lavishly equipped they showed little sign of original scientific activity.'

Professor Marotta was something more than a brilliant chemist. He was also an astute administrator-politician, a 'Garibaldi of Italian chemistry' as he was called, who had succeeded in welding Italy's chemical societies into a national unit in the face of great opposition. As head of the Institute he had built it up from being largely an analytical and control unit into what was virtually the nerve centre of Italy's Ministry of Health. Its main building had been completed in 1935, aided by a grant from the Rockefeller Foundation, and its eight floors now housed eight departments working on biology, biochemistry, therapeutical chemistry, chemistry, microbiology, parasitology, public health engineering and physics. To this centre Marotta had attracted a staff that included Giuseppe Penso, virologist and discoverer of phage viruses, which require bacteria in which to replicate; and Alberto Missiroli, the malariologist and chief architect of Italy's anti-malaria campaign.

Marotta explained to Chain how well aware he was that Italy had drifted far behind in the development of modern biochemistry, due largely to her lack of contact with Anglo-Saxon countries before the war as well as during it. Chain has written that

A further argument in favour of the organization of a biochemistry department at the Istituto Superiore di Sanità was, he pointed out, that he had just succeeded in securing the services of the pharmacologist Daniel Bovet, formerly of the Pasteur Institute in Paris, for the establishment of a new department of therapeutic chemistry, and that all concerned felt that the close neighbourhood of an active biochemistry research group would be of great benefit to the development of this new venture.

On being taken round the Institute, Chain was shown the components of a penicillin production plant built by UNRRA and presented to the Italian Government after the war, together with $300,000 for its erection and initial running. The Government had actually signed an agreement with UNRRA for the plant to be built and put to work in the Institute; however, most of its components were still unpacked, Marotta clearly had little idea of what was involved, and Chain was soon being questioned. He already had experience of other UNRRA penicillin plant: he had not been impressed, and he warned Marotta that if work was started with the plant available the only certain result would be a serious financial loss for the Government.

I suggested, however, [he went on] that Professor Marotta would make a real contribution to European science if he would use his influence to get permission to use the UNRRA funds and some of the equipment they had supplied for building, instead of an inefficient penicillin production plant, a fermentation pilot plant for research in the field of chemical microbiology for the study of substances of biochemical or biological interest and of microbial origin. I added that such fermentation pilot plant would considerably strengthen the biochemistry department which he told me he had the intention of organizing.

There seems little doubt that Marotta was even at this early date hoping he would be able to tempt Chain to Rome. It is difficult to imagine that Chain himself was not well aware of this although he later wrote that it was to his 'great surprise' that some six months later he received an invitation from Marotta. The Italian had discussed Chain's comments with the authorities and now asked whether Chain would consider a formal offer to come to Rome, set up the penicillin plant and organize and direct the proposed department of biochemistry.

Chain responded cautiously, but was prepared to discuss the proposal in detail. Marotta responded with a London to Rome air ticket and a few weeks later Chain was discussing the move that was to govern the next fifteen years of his life.

The Italian offer appeared to have some obvious disadvantages. But

Ernst Chain as a young boy in Berlin.

Chain (seated, second from right) with staff of the State Gymnasium, Berlin, 1924.

Chain with other members of the William Dunn staff, Oxford, c. 1940. Front row, left to right: Isaac Berenblum, Edward Duthie, Howard Florey, Duncan Gardner, Lieut. Col. R. Bridges; second row: Regine Schoental, Miss E. Stubington, John G. Stephens, Miss Jean Orr-Ewing, Ernst Chain; third row: Edward Abraham, Joseph Trueta, John Barnes; at the back, Norman Heatley.

Chain with other Oxford workers, c. 1942. Left to right: Edward Abraham, Wilson Baker, Ernst Chain and Sir Robert Robinson.

Mrs Sacharina, Chain's cousin who helped him in his university years in Berlin and looked after him in Oxford.

Professor Domenico Marotta with Chain (far left) and Sir Alexander and Lady Fleming (far right).

Presentation of the Nobel Prize by the King of Sweden to Ernst Chain, Stockholm, 1945.

Ernst Chain with Donald Callow.

Ernst Chain with Professors Marotta, Berenblum and A. Katzir at the Weizmann Institute.

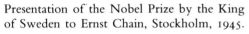

Anne and Ernst Chain with Professor Marotta (front row) and colleagues at the Istituto Superiore di Sanità in Rome.

Ernst Chain and Dr S. Waksman, discoverer of Streptomycin.

Queen Elizabeth the Queen Mother with Ernst and Anne Chain and their twins Judith and Daniel at the opening of the new Biochemistry Department at Imperial College in 1965.

Ernst Chain at the piano in his Oxford home.

Ernst and Anne Chain with their three children, Benjamin, Judith and Daniel, and David Ben-Gurion, first Prime Minister of Israel, at Kibbutz Sde Boker in 1968.

Ernst Chain (second from left, front row) and colleagues in the fermentation pilot plant at the Istituto Superiore di Sanità in Rome.

Ernst Chain with his wife and children on holiday in the west of Ireland at Mulrany, Co. Mayo, in 1967.

Ernst Chain.

it was a fundamental of Chain's character that he could be outspokenly blunt. As he has written,

My reply was that I was not sufficiently well acquainted with conditions in Italy to commit myself at this stage for a long-term period, particularly in view of . . . all the comments I had heard about the country – which I told him frankly were highly unfavourable; in fact, all my colleagues in England without exception, had strongly advised me against taking a job in Italy and to distrust all promises made in that country, as in general people were thoroughly unreliable and had the habit of breaking contracts when it suited them, without hesitation or any qualms of conscience. Furthermore, many people believed that Italy was at that time on the verge of an economic collapse.

Chain therefore needed much persuading. He pointed out that the creation of a major research centre such as Marotta envisaged would be extremely expensive and that no one could guarantee spectacular results such as those which had come from the William Dunn School during the war.

There was, moreover, a further point which might have weighed heavily with anyone of less independent mind than Ernst Chain. Rome had little background of biochemical research and many colleagues in Oxford pointed out that anyone starting a centre such as Marotta had in mind would from the first be labouring under great disadvantages. Chain disagreed, and later explained:

I have always held the view that in order to do creative work, it is not essential to live in a place where an atmosphere of creativity has been a tradition for centuries. On the contrary, it is possible in such places to be overwhelmed by too much tradition, as one can be overwhelmed by too much reading; and one finds oneself, under these conditions, rapidly thinking along the lines of others and losing one's own originality. It has always seemed to me that it is possible to implant creativity anywhere where there is the will by the collaborators to accept it, provided one provides the necessary leadership by bringing to the place new and fruitful ideas, and one has the financial backing to transform them into reality.

This is what Chain now set about doing, buttressed by the financial backing which Marotta was so adept at conjuring from the Italian Government. To start with, he obtained leave of absence from Oxford for a year. That would be long enough for him to build up the new department and the fermentation pilot plant. If things went wrong he could return to Oxford with only a year lost – 'unfortunate, but not a catastrophe', as he put it. If all went well, the period could be extended.

Next he asked his assistant, Donald Callow, whether he would accompany him to Rome and help design and build the plant for the major centre that was planned. 'He said I could have time to think it over,' Callow remembers. 'But I said I needed no time for that. I'd be glad to go with him.'

The reaction says a good deal for the confidence which Chain had built up during the preceding decade, but it also reflects the size of the opportunity offered. This was considerable since even at the end of the 1940s biotechnology was a comparatively new subject and experience of industrial fermentation, which would have to be simulated with pilot plant in the new centre, was almost entirely limited to the brewing industry and the manufacture of citric acid. The Rome centre, which would be used for a wide variety of experimental work, therefore held out great prospects for a young man who would start by designing it from scratch.

During the spring and summer of 1947 Chain and Callow designed the laboratories to be built in Rome and in September Callow left Oxford for Italy. Chain followed in October – on his honeymoon since he had just married Anne Beloff, the biochemist he had met before the war and with whom he had been intermittently in touch in Oxford.

Some while earlier, on being firmly offered the post in Rome, Chain had asked Anne Beloff whether she would consider joining him there as his professional assistant and helping him to build up the new Institute. She had been as uncertain of the prospects in Rome as many of Chain's friends had been and nothing came of the proposal. Matters might have remained like this had not Anne Beloff been invited to join Chris Anfinsen, of the Harvard Medical School, and his wife on a Swedish holiday and had not Chain been visiting Astra in Sweden at the same time.

Chance now took control. During a voyage round the islands from Stockholm, the boat's engine failed. While most of the party decided to land, Anne Beloff and Ernst Chain preferred to stay on board. And, in the unusual environment of a stranded boat in the Baltic, Chain proposed and was accepted.

The marriage at Hampstead Synagogue on 7 October 1948 was to be as successful as Chain's career in biochemistry had been. The happiness of the marriage produced some surprise among many of his friends, not because of any mistrust in the personal or professional qualities of his wife but because, as she is willing to admit, few friends thought that any woman would put up with his temperament for long. The secret of success lay not only in the strength of their mutual affection but in the complementarity of their professional interests and the thick stratum of tolerance which lay beneath Chain's almost cultivated idiosyncrasies and extravagant expressions of opinion.

Ernst Chain was in his early forties when he married, Anne Beloff some fifteen years younger. A son, then twins – a boy and girl – complemented their household during the 1950s, and Chain's happiness as a family man, reinforced by his children's love of music and their dedication to Jewry which he actively encouraged, was a factor which friends felt he rated even higher than his dedication to biochemistry. Few, recalling his years in Rome and later in London, would fail to describe how virtually all professional activity would stop for a short while when the children were welcomed back home from school in the afternoon. Most felt, also, that his professional career had at last come safe to port after the difficulties and danger that not even a Nobel Prize could entirely disperse.

The problems which faced Chain in Rome in the autumn of 1948 were very different from those with which he had had to cope in Oxford. It was not merely that the scale of the operation in Rome would be larger; it would also be wider-ranging. In the William Dunn laboratory the emphasis had been on production of penicillin; in Rome the problems also included those of devising and perfecting fermentation equipment that could be run, as efficiently and as economically as possible, on a semi-industrial scale. Here, in fact, was the development of biotechnology, a discipline which if it existed at all was largely confined to the brewing industry.

It was mainly with these requirements in mind that Professor Marotta had written to the deans of a number of Italian universities asking for the names of the most promising microbiologists, geneticists, biochemists and chemical engineers who had graduated within the previous few years. From the names he was given a few were selected for interview by Chain before he took up work. Among them was Dr (later Professor) R. Falini, a chemical engineer who was to be largely responsible for designing the equipment with which Chain was to work in Rome. Falini had been mainly concerned with heavy chemicals and was surprised by the questions which Chain asked him during the interview: questions concerned with potential mechanical, hydraulic and electrical matters, all of which were to figure largely in the demands of bio-engineering. Chain was satisfied with the answers and before the end of 1949 Falini joined the group which was to produce and operate the unique equipment in the Institute.

Before work could begin Falini had the task of erecting, and seeing if it was feasible to operate, the UNRRA plant which had been given to the Italians at the end of the war. As preparation for the job he went to Sweden to inspect the Astra plant which had been built there on Chain's directions some two years earlier. Eventually, as Chain had feared would be the case, the UNRRA equipment was found to be so out of date as to be useless for most practicable purposes. The Rome plant had therefore to be built from scratch.

It was decided that the new laboratory-scale pilot plant, on the sub-ground-level floor of the Institute, would at first contain three 150-litre fermenters which would themselves be seeded from cultures grown in flasks in a laboratory to be built as a new floor on top of the existing Institute. These were soon added to, and eight fermenters with their ancillary plant were eventually available. The full-scale research plant, contained in three buildings quite separate from the main Institute, housed two 18,000-litre fermenters, two 5,000-litre fermenters, and a number of seeding tanks linked together to allow the maximum flexibility in their use. There was also, as part of the Institute, a new power station to serve the centre which was able to investigate new substances on a laboratory scale, produce them first in pilot-scale quantities and then on a semi-industrial scale if necessary.

When Chain arrived in Rome the laboratories were still under construction and he began work in the basement while building was continuing overhead. On a wall inside this building there were framed four quotations from Pasteur that Chain told friends expressed 'basic principles of [his] own approach to science' – a framed doctrine that he later brought to London with him.

1 *La science est une et c'est l'homme seulement qui, en raison de la faiblesse de son intelligence, y établit des catégories.*

2 *Dans les champs de l'observation le hasard ne favorise que les esprits préparés.*

3 *Permettez-moi de vous donner un conseil que je me suis toujours efforcé de suivre et qui consiste à rester le plus longtemps possible dans un sujet. En toute chose, je crois, le secret du succès est dans les longs efforts. Par la persévérance dans la recherche, on finit par acquérir ce que l'on appelle volontiers l'instinct de la vérité.*

4 *Il n'y a pas de sciences appliquées. L'union même de ces mots est choquante. Mais il y a des applications de la science, ce qui est bien différent.*

While he was still moving into the new Italian premises in 1949 he was elected a Fellow of the Royal Society. He had been proposed by Florey five years earlier and the only amendment to the recommendation had been one proposed by Fleming who suggested that the original description of Chain as 'jointly responsible for initiating the investigations which disclosed the properties of penicillin' should be changed to investigations 'which made it possible to disclose fully the remarkable chemotherapeutic properties of penicillin'.

If the fifteen years that Chain was to spend in Rome witnessed nothing quite as dramatic as the transition during the Oxford years of penicillin from a biochemical curiosity into a unique life-saver, they did, nevertheless, help both to enlarge the influence of antibiotics and give Chain himself a new status in his profession. At the Institute he created a centre to which biochemists came from all over the world to be trained in the production and use of antibiotics, while under his leadership there were held numerous meetings and seminars at which the techniques of fermentation technology were explored. It was here, too, that Chain himself developed his interests in physiological biochemistry largely in collaboration with Francesco Pocchiani, later to become director of the Institute after the end of Marotta's reign.

The misgivings felt by many of Chain's friends and colleagues when he decided to leave England for Italy were thus shown to be unjustified, and it is of interest to note that while he played a vital part in giving both the Institute and Italian medical science an influence they would not have achieved without him, so did the opportunities provided by the Institute under Marotta's control enable Chain himself to widen his own sphere of influence. He was helped, it should be stressed, not only by the availability, in contrast with conditions at Oxford, of almost unlimited funds but by the presence of such men as Daniel Bovet, chief of the Institute's Laboratory of Therapeutic Chemistry from 1947 to 1964 and winner of the Nobel Prize for Physiology and Medicine in 1957. As in Oxford, the cross-fertilization of ideas was an important factor in encouraging progress.

In Rome Chain found the routine to be very different from what it had been in Oxford. Work began at eight o'clock in the morning and continued, with only a short break for lunch, until the afternoon siesta. During this, Chain sometimes played the piano before returning to the laboratory and working there until the evening. One of the problems, particularly during the early days, was the irregularity of the electricity supply, subjected sometimes to lengthy and unpredictable cuts. This played havoc with some operations which could as a result be carried on only during the night when cuts were less likely.

Workers were expected to be present on Saturdays as well as on weekdays. The job in hand came before everything else, and Falini remembers almost three decades later what happened when he got married. 'I was given ten days' leave of absence for my honeymoon,' he says, 'and expected that the tenth day was included. I arranged to report for duty on the morning of the eleventh day but on the tenth Professor Chain was making excited enquiries as to why I had not yet turned up for work.'

In the deep fermentation pilot plant which was to give the key to practicable penicillin production the basic problem was that of providing, in a condition sterile enough to prevent contamination, sufficient supplies of oxygen to the micro-organisms suspended in the broth. The problem exists in two halves, the less intractable being that of ensuring that the oxygen is mixed with the micro-organisms both quickly and evenly. More difficult was the provision of filters. The Americans had tackled this empirically and Chain was the first to approach the situation scientifically, experimenting with filtration fibres of different materials and of different dimensions. Eventually it was found that the best results were obtained by a certain mixture of glass wool having a fibre diameter of six to seven microns and of asbestos fibre with a diameter of one micron. The material was compressed into discs which together formed the filter through which the oxygen was forced into a stainless steel vessel holding the biomass.

The task-force of from fifteen to twenty young engineers and scientists which Chain assembled eventually enabled him to produce the necessary pilot plant. All its members, including the Englishmen Pirt and Callow, and the Italian Falini, agree that he was a hard taskmaster but one who had the great quality which Falini has summed up as that of a 'mentality-maker'. Chain encouraged everyone to do their jobs in the most efficient way not only because that was necessary for the best result but because the practice instilled the right attitude to scientific work.

Falini remembers one incident after an experimental filter system had been developed and had to be tested for 500 hours, during which readings would be taken every hour. By sleeping in the basement, where the system had been set up, Falini found that this could be done. But one night he missed a reading. 'I was young then,' he says, 'and could not see that one missed reading among the 250 or so that had already been taken could make any difference to the test. But Chain was furious. So much so that he insisted on the experiment being started again from hour one. As I got to know him better I realized that he did it as much to train me as for any other reason.'

Chemical microbiology, to the problems of which Chain's new Institute was to be devoted, was concerned not merely with the investigation and production of antibiotics but with all the processes by which enzymes act as catalysts to change the rate at which chemical reactions take place. Many of the microbial substances involved are produced in only minute quantities and for this work pilot plant facilities are essential. At industrial levels large fermenters are required and since many of the fermentations are aerobic – requiring the presence of free oxygen – extensive knowledge of aeration techniques is also demanded. The efficient running of the Institute was thus an extremely complex operation and the exploitation of its possibilities made it necessary to employ not only microbiologists, geneticists and biochemists but also chemical and electronics engineers.

Chain's own family background of chemical engineering was thus brought into play from the opening of the Institute, and it is significant that many of its staff remained impressed for years by the success with which he welded men from different disciplines into an integrated team. As inaugurated in June 1951, in the presence of the Italian Prime Minister, the Centre of Chemical Microbiology included about twenty chemists and biochemists, three physico-chemists, nine microbiologists, and two chemical and two mechanical engineers, a staff served by mechanics, glass blowers, electronic technicians and some forty general and laboratory technicians.

All were involved in the almost ceaseless invention or development of new equipment and instruments the need for which had hardly existed before the rise of biochemistry. They included heat-sterilizable glass electrodes for continuous measurement and recording of pH during fermentation; and sterilizable electrodes for continuous measurements of dissolved oxygen in fermentation media in the presence of bacteria and filamentous fungi.

The work steadily reinforced Chain's reputation not only as the man who knew more about the chemistry of penicillin than most people, but as a leading expert on the best ways of producing it most economically. His authority had been tacitly admitted even as he was beginning work in Rome, and towards the end of 1948 his help was invoked by the World Health Organization, which had taken over much of UNRRA's work, with results he could never have expected. The WHO was responsible for ensuring that the penicillin production equipment donated earlier to Czechoslovakia, Poland and Yugoslavia was being used as efficiently as possible and at the WHO's request Chain therefore travelled to Geneva where, on 19 February 1949, he met experts from the three countries. All agreed that the lack of Podbelniak counter-current extractors was the main problem. These extractors utilized a tall column in which two immiscible liquids were passed against each other. An elaborate system of baffles enabled the penicillin to be separated from its impurities, and in the then state of the art the use of the Podbelniak extractor could make all the difference between the success or failure of a production unit. The WHO agreed to find ways of providing the currency for purchase in the United States, and in Chain's words 'everyone went home very satisfied from this meeting thinking that the main difficulties were overcome and the way open for economic production of penicillin in the countries concerned, in accordance with the wishes of WHO'.

However, a shadow of coming events could soon be seen. Chain later wrote:

Very soon WHO learned that the United States State Department refused to grant export licences for the counter-current extractors for Poland and Czechoslovakia. It transpired that some people in the State Department thought that these machines could be used for the concentration of bacterial toxins. This, of course, was nonsense, as all bacterial toxins, in the present state of knowledge (1951), are proteins and as such are insoluble in organic solvents. In any case, there is no fundamental difference between a counter-current extractor and a Sharples centrifuge, and all operations for which the counter-current extractors can be used, could equally be carried out with Sharples centrifuges, only less efficiently.

At Geneva, Chain was invited by the Czech delegate to visit their country as he had in 1947. He was to do so three times, the last in 1950, and by then he had become, through these visits and his work in Rome, a specialist in making, with WHO help, whatever use was possible of the outdated UNRRA equipment. It was natural, therefore, that he should be elected chairman of a Committee of Experts on Antibiotics which the WHO set up 'to deal with research in this subject (antibiotics) and in technological problems in general'. Collaboration with American firms producing penicillin or making equipment was obviously essential, and in the spring of 1951 Chain was briefed to join a WHO mission to the United States. His instructions ran:

Your first task will be to interview the directors of the research laboratories listed in the report of the Expert Committee on Antibiotics with the object of creating an international research group collaborating in an intimate manner, sharing problems, sharing technical and scientific knowledge and sharing personnel whenever considered desirable. The aim being to bring about a situation in which the subject of antibiotics will develop in the freest scientific atmosphere to the advantage of this field of science and to render full assistance to such member nations as desire the aid of WHO in the production of antibiotics.

There can have been few missions more in line with Chain's ideals and few which he was better qualified to carry out. Early in 1951 he applied for a visa to the United States consul in Rome. His mission was explained to the consul who was asked by the WHO to issue the visa. Nothing happened. As the weeks passed both Chain and an assistant director-general of the WHO stressed the urgency of the matter. Still nothing happened and it was only months after the deadline for departure that he received the standard official notification from the vice-consul saying that a visa could not be issued, but giving no reason.

The only clues to the situation were provided by a later statement in America that the visa had been refused under the Internal Security Act, and a letter to Chain in June 1951 from Brock Chisholm, then director-general of the World Health Organization:

I am very sorry to have to pass on the information to you that it will not be possible for us to complete arrangements for you to visit the United States of America for the WHO at this time. While I have not been able to get any details, it would appear that the difficulty is that there is a strong movement in the United States towards qualifying biological information, perhaps even all biological information, as security material.

In the McCarthy era, the decision was not a passing one. In March 1952, after Chain had renewed his application, he was told by the WHO: 'I am very sorry to say that I have just been informed that the Department of State's attitude has not changed. It regrets that it is unable to reconsider its decision not to grant a visa.'

Chain himself, by this time strongly anti-communist, was in no doubt that it was his series of visits to communist Czechoslovakia which had caused the trouble. He later wrote:

I have repeatedly searched my own conscience whether I did right to give my help to put the Czechoslovak UNRRA-donated penicillin plant into functioning order, or whether I should have refused to go to Geneva and to Czechoslovakia, and should have declined to have anything to do with this project.

I still think that I did the right thing. Our work on the discovery of the curative power of penicillin was published *during the last war* in a professional medical journal and was thus made freely accessible to all. Is anyone going to deny to me, one of the authors of the penicillin discovery, the right to help a nation with which we are not at war and one which asks for help, to make available this important drug for the treatment of the sick?

Chain wrote a long letter describing the affair but American friends pointed out that moves were already being made to change the current visa position. He was, reluctantly, dissuaded from publishing the letter, but the injustice, as well as the stupidity, rankled for years.

By this time Chain had successfully set the Institute on the path that was to make it the most important research group of its kind in Europe. That continuing task would have been enough for most men. Yet one of his characteristics was an apparently limitless ability to take on additional work in his own particular field and an inability to admit that there was a limit to the problems that one man could solve and to the plans he could hope to carry out. It also tended to blind him to the sometimes counterproductive effects of his own enthusiasm. This was demonstrated when, in the summer of 1951, he renewed his plea for a British antibiotic centre in a lengthy memorandum which he sent to Sir Solly Zuckerman, then making proposals for the reorganization of Britain's post-war scientific research. 'As you know,' Zuckerman commented to Himsworth, by this time head of the Medical Research Council, 'I am fully aware of the shape of the axe which Chain grinds, and I would not have interested myself in the matter at all if it were not for the faint possibility that there is substance to the idea which he wishes to see shaped.' Himsworth also was cautious, writing:

[Chain] is, as you know, an enthusiast on this topic; and none the worse for that. Inevitably, however, he presents a partial picture of the considerations. If there were a possibility of this memorandum being regarded as the last word on this particular subject, it might be dangerous. I would suggest that you did not circulate this officially. It is, however, only right that your Committee should be informed of Chain's point of view. I would be inclined to let them see it informally and inform them that it is a point of view and that other people of equal eminence in this field, would have additional points to make which would certainly alter the total picture.

One thing that could never be doubted was Chain's determination to help found an antibiotic industry in Britain. Yet the plan which he proposed to Zuckerman in 1951 was, like his previous proposals, to make no immediate headway, and before his ideas for a British-based centre for antibiotic research could be implemented almost a decade was to pass. However, during that decade his enthusiasm was to produce results in Rome in two rather more specialist spheres. One was the development of animal biochemistry, the second was research in chemical microbiology associated with the pilot plant. In both he was able to deploy his varied experience in chemical engineering and was able to design, or supervise the design of, machinery which would operate on a semi-industrial scale in the laboratory.

In the field of animal biochemistry it was decided initially to carry out studies on the mechanism of insulin action. Insulin, a peptide hormone (containing fifty-one amino-acid residues), is produced by specific cells in the pancreas and controls the blood glucose levels. Thus in the case of excessive insulin activity, low blood glucose (or hypoglycaemia) occurs, whereas a deficiency of insulin leads to high levels of glucose (hyperglycaemia) as occurs in diabetes.

Chain undertook these investigations in collaboration with his wife, Anne, who had already some background knowledge in the field, having previously spent two years in the Department of Biochemistry at Harvard Medical School, where some of the original studies on insulin action, using isotopically-labelled $^{14}C$ glucose, were carried out. When studies were started in Rome it was already known that insulin stimulated the uptake of glucose and the conversion of glucose into glycogen (a carbohydrate storage material) in isolated rat diaphragm muscle. The aim now was to obtain a quantitative balance-sheet of glucose metabolism in isolated muscle in the absence and in the presence of insulin. For this purpose an automatic scanning device, which scanned bidimensional paper radiochromatograms, was developed in collaboration with the electronics department of the Institute. Thus, all the metabolic intermediates in extracts of muscle or in the incubation medium, formed from $^{14}C$ glucose following incubation with the latter, could be separated by bidimensional paper chromatography and quantitatively measured. By also collecting and counting the $^{14}C$ in the carbon dioxide ($CO_2$) produced during incubation, it was possible to obtain a complete balance-sheet of glucose metabolism. This led to the conclusion that in muscle insulin stimulated specifically the synthesis of glycogen and other oligosaccharides and had no influence on glucose catabolism (breakdown) either to lactic acid or $CO_2$.

The two current theories on insulin action at that time were (1) that the hormone's ability to increase the transport of glucose into muscle cells was solely responsible for the increase in glucose metabolism (the permeability theory), and (2) that insulin acted on the enzyme responsible for the first step in glucose metabolism involving its phosphorylation to glucose-6-phosphate (the hexokinase theory). Using the techniques outlined above, and incubating the muscle with increasing concentrations of glucose, and with $^{14}$C-labelled glucose-6-phosphate and glucose-1-phosphate, gave results which demonstrated that neither of these theories could explain the specific action of insulin on glycogen synthesis. The results also suggested that there was a pathway for glycogen synthesis from glucose-1-phosphate which did not involve a reversal of the phosphorylase action, the enzyme which breaks down glycogen to glucose-1-phosphate. This conclusion was later confirmed by the discovery of Leloir and his colleagues in 1957 that glucose-1-phosphate reacts with uridine triphosphate to give uridine diphosphate glucose (UDPG) which is the precursor of glycogen synthesis.

The specific action of insulin on synthetic reactions was confirmed by similar studies in brown adipose tissue, in which it was shown that insulin stimulated both fat and glycogen synthesis. Other investigators during this period demonstrated that insulin promoted fat synthesis from amino-acids in muscle.

These results led Chain and his colleagues to propose a new theory of insulin action: that the hormone acts by raising the energy level of the cell derived from oxidative processes, thus stimulating energy-requiring synthetic reactions.

In addition to these studies on insulin action, investigations on $^{14}$C glucose metabolism in slices of brain cortex and pituitary gland were carried out, again using the automatic scanning device for bidimensional radiochromatograms. It was found that glucose was converted in brain cortex tissue to a number of amino-acids; glutamic acid, aspartic acid, y-amino-butyric acid and alanine were identified. Although the presence of free amino-acids in brain tissue had been known for some time, this was the first evidence that some of these were derived from glucose.

In the isolated pituitary gland it was shown that glucose was transformed into alanine, glutamic aspartic acid and a small amount of proline, where y-amino-butyric acid was absent. Some of these amino-acids also appeared labelled in a protein fraction of the pituitary gland and, as was not the case in the brain cortex, some labelled glucose was incorporated into glycogen and oligosaccharides.

All the research on animal biochemistry was carried out in collaboration with a group of young Italian biochemists which included Francesco Pocchiari.

Much of this research on animal biochemistry carried out in Rome laid the foundation for later research by several groups at Imperial College in the MRC Metabolic Reactions Unit. This unit was composed of groups working on insulin action in adipose tissue and muscle, on cardiac metabolism using a perfused rat heart preparation (work was also supported by the British Heart Foundation), on fat and carbohydrate metabolism in perfused livers from normal and diabetic animals, on amino-acid metabolism and function in the brain. Another group was meanwhile working on hypothalamic hormones and mechanisms of neuro-endocrine integration.

It was not only in the investigation of metabolism and the basic processes by which life is maintained that Chain's experience as a chemical engineer was utilized in Rome. The same experience was equally of use in developing successful techniques for fermentation, the chemical change on which the production of antibiotics then entirely depended, as it still largely does. An important factor in aeration, the basic process on which successful fermentation depends, is the concentration of dissolved oxygen while the culture media is being mechanically agitated, and only after long study was a novel instrument developed in Rome to measure this satisfactorily. It allowed the collection of important data while the fermentation was continuing, relating oxygen diffusion rates with power consumption under different methods of air dispersion, as well as the effect of oxygen concentration on the production of different substances.

At the same time a new aeration system was developed for use in laboratory and small pilot plant fermenters. In conventional systems air is bubbled through the culture fluid by a sparger. In the 'vortex system', as it was christened, air was sucked into the fluid by a vortex created by a fast-rotating propeller blade, greatly reducing and in some cases completely eliminating the foam formation that could disrupt other systems.

These engineering innovations enabled Chain to carry out with the maximum efficiency in Rome the work which had first seized his imagination in Oxford in the 1940s, the production and understanding of the whole new range of drugs already known as antibiotics. He wrote:

We have studied the relationship between aeration, power consumption and geometrical forms of the fermenters. We have carried out extensive investigations into the nature of the penicillin fermentation, the citric acid and kojic acid fermentation, have isolated a number of new mould metabolites, among them the nitrosophenol, ferroverdin, the wilting toxin fusicoccin. We have discovered a method for producing simple lysergic acid derivations in submerged culture in yields up to several mg per ml, from which lysergic acid can be prepared in high yield.

Chain's investigations in Rome in animal biochemistry and on chemical microbiology provided a main focus for his activities. From the mid 1950s onwards, however, he was to be increasingly involved in events which eventually brought him back to London, the next milestone in his career. They had started in 1954 when he met Sir Charles Dodds at the International Biochemical Congress in Brussels. Sir Charles, director of the Courtauld Institute of Biochemistry at Middlesex Hospital Medical School since 1926 and the holder of numerous other prestigious posts and appointments, was one of those rare men who had gained and retained influence in both medicine and industry. In Chain's words he had 'started to have contacts with industrial organizations at a time when this was not at all fashionable and, in fact, rather frowned upon by academic, and in particular medical, circles'. With his regular new Bentley, his fashionable West End flat and his membership of three London clubs, Dodds was hardly the typical consultant. Yet he was the man who gave advice to a number of important companies. Very much a man after Chain's own heart, Dodds followed up the meeting in Brussels by visiting Chain in Rome, inspected the Institute and wrote to him in April 1955. 'You may remember', he said, 'that when we talked in Rome I mentioned that an organization with which I was associated were anxious to consider the possibility of producing citric and tartaric acid in large quantities by a fermentation process. You said that you would be prepared to consider a meeting for a consultation.'

The firm was the Beecham Group, probably the world's largest user of tartaric acid, the main ingredient of health salts. In the 1950s Beecham were anxious to ensure that there would be no interruption in their supply of this invaluable raw material; they knew that it could be made not only by chemical synthesis but also by the microbiological conversion of glucose, although it was largely obtained from grape residue after wine production, and began to speculate on whether the latter method of manufacture might not be worth investigation. They called for advice on Dodds who pointed out that Chain was running in Rome a department capable of undertaking any investigation involving chemical microbiology.

In Rome Chain agreed to meet in London the Beecham chairman, H. G. Lazell. He was impressed, writing to Dodds shortly afterwards that Lazell 'had that spirit of enterprise and initiative which gave British industry its leading position in the world but which one, unfortunately, encounters rarely here. One wishes there were more people like him around.'

The meeting, held on 18 May, was attended by other members of the Beecham staff, as well as advisers including Sir Ian Heilbron who during the war had taken part in penicillin work while at Imperial College. The firm had previously decided to diversify beyond proprietary medicines – those which could be obtained without prescription – since the public was becoming increasingly sceptical of such products and of the claims made for them. The firm should, it was suggested, branch out into the production of medicines which could only be obtained on doctors' prescriptions. During the war Lazell had been involved in the making of penicillin-impregnated pastilles which had been used by RAF doctors before and after operations on men whose mouths had been injured. Would it not be possible, he asked, to put on the market some form of penicillin pastille? Dodds advised caution, realizing no doubt that information on penicillin was still in its early stages and that, quite apart from anything else, production costs could fall dramatically.

Despite this qualification which appeared to hang over Beecham interest in penicillin, Chain became from this period onwards increasingly involved in two sets of Beecham plans, one concerning tartaric acid and the other dealing with antibiotics in general and penicillin in particular. In the not too distant future it might be possible not only to synthesize at least some of the various penicillins now known to exist but also to produce 'tailormade' varieties for special purposes. Much experimental work would be required but while Beecham were building the equipment for it in Britain investigations could be started with the fermenters already available in Rome.

Both the plan for tartaric acid production and that for penicillin had one factor in common since it was agreed that each would benefit if a small team of Beecham biochemists first spent some months in Rome, working under Chain's supervision. When they returned to Britain they would be able to carry on with the fermentation plant that Beecham would have erected in Britain for whatever production was decided upon.

There were further discussions between Chain and Beecham, and he was visited in Rome by Sir Ian Heilbron, by now Beecham's permanent chemical adviser, who was impressed not only with the fermentation equipment but with Chain's abilities as a guide, 'doing six of the seven hills of Rome in one afternoon', as he described it.

Before the end of the summer it was agreed that Beecham should send one microbiologist and one biochemist for not less than a year to the Institute in Rome where they would work under Chain's instructions. A second microbiologist and a second biochemist were later added, although neither was a Beecham employee at the time he went to Rome.

Lazell's published book, *From Pills to Penicillin*, records:

Our negotiations with Ernst's lawyers over his consultancy agreement were long and tortuous, but these did not hold up our collaboration and we had our first formal meeting attended by some of our consultants, scientists and commercial men in May 1955. There followed a series of meetings for the purpose of determining the direction our work should take.

While Chain was obviously anxious to consolidate his position in the industrial field this was by no means his only motive in taking on additional arduous work. In the academic world he had already interested himself in the expansion plans for the Imperial College of Science and Technology, and the linkage of the industrial and academic worlds which he was constantly advocating is made clear in a letter he wrote to Heilbron while negotiations with Beecham were continuing:

I think we will have no difficulty in coming to terms with the Beecham Group and I hope that with their help it may be possible to build up a modern unit of industrial fermentation which will be able to take up completely any new development in this continuously expanding field and to hold its own with any other single unit in the world; you know this has been my wish for many years, and I am certain that it can be done.

The main difficulty I see for future developments in this field on a broad scope is that of manpower; this difficulty may be eventually, I am afraid, the limiting factor. It seems therefore to me of the utmost importance to create a school in England for the formation of biochemists of a suitable type – i.e. well versed in the techniques of chemical microbiology with a good basis of organic chemistry, biochemistry, and microbiological engineering.

This is the reason I am so interested in the Imperial College expansion scheme; Imperial College seems to me to be the obvious place for the development of a biochemical school of this type. . . . You will, of course, understand – and I hope Linstead [the Imperial College rector] does – that my interest to see a powerful school of chemical microbiology growing up at Imperial College is not a personal one; I am quite all right where I am; but I am convinced that it is a real necessity for the country just as I was convinced fifteen years ago that it was vital for us at that time to create pilot plant facilities for development work in the field of antibiotics and that failure to do so would lead to serious economic losses to the country, as in fact it did.

Once the details of Chain's consultancy had been settled, it became necessary for him to advise on the lines which the Beecham research should take. He believed that in view of the work which had already been done it was too late to start investigating further moulds and similar organisms in the hope of finding new antibiotics; an enormous effort had already been expended in that area, both during and after the war, and the results had been modest. A better plan, he suggested, would be to intensify the work on which he had already started in Rome; an attempt to modify the penicillin molecule, particularly with the aim of obtaining penicillins to counter the action of the enzyme penicillinase which was produced by staphylococcal strains in hospital wards, and which effectively removed the therapeutic effect of the antibiotic. Chain has written:

I took the view that this enzyme was *solely* responsible for the resistance of the staphylococcal strains to benzylpenicillin, and was convinced that it would be possible, by suitably changing the side chain of the penicillin molecule to obtain penicillins with changed affinities to this enzyme so as to make them insensitive to its action. I suggested to the Board at Beecham that they should engage a team of scientists to work on the modification of a penicillin, p-amino benzyl-penicillin, which can be obtained by the usual penicillin fermentation techniques by adding the suitable precursor - p-amino phenylacetic acid. I suggested that the new members of the team assigned for the task should be sent to Rome to join my colleagues and participate in this work, which had already been started in my laboratory, making use of our fermentation pilot plant facilities while a similar plant was built at the Beecham Research Laboratories. This proposal was accepted.

The work of a private British company thus became inextricably entwined with that of the Italian government institute. Both sides were fully informed of the quite legitimate arrangements being made. But even if Italy had not then been a country in which any weapons available were used in the complex political battles continually being waged, the possibilities for future misunderstandings might have been appreciated.

After satisfactory arrangements had been concluded with the Italian authorities it was agreed in November 1955 that the Beecham team should try to make p-amino-benzylpenicillin, a penicillin which would lend itself to chemical manipulation of the amino group, either by direct attack or by conversion to p-hydroxybenzyl penicillin and subsequent chemical action. Meanwhile, it was also agreed, the Chemical Development Department at Brockham Park would prepare the necessary precursors, p-aminophenylacetic acid and p-aminophenylacetamide. A hundred grams of each should be ready as soon as possible and production should then continue up to a kilogram.

The British team consisted of Dr Rolinson, Mr Batchelor, Dr Richards and Mr Tridgell. The secondment to Rome of Beecham staff was of Dr Rolinson and Mr Batchelor. The additional assistance provided by Dr Richards and Mr Tridgell came subsequently and neither of these gentlemen were originally employees of Beecham at the time they went to Italy. To start with they had to make do with shake flasks but before the end of the year they were using a 300-litre fermenter and Chain was able to send 10 gm of p-amino-benzylpenicillin to Brockham Park so that the chemists could start modification experiments. Meanwhile, he had provided Beecham with designs for small-scale fermenters and had even arranged for some of the equipment to be made in Italy. A great deal of progress had thus been made when, early in 1957, the British scientists returned from Rome to Brockham Park.

It was here, in the early summer of 1957, that the crucial steps in enlarging the usefulness of penicillin were taken. There had been two methods of ascertaining the extent to which penicillin was present in the fermentation brew, one biological and one chemical. The biological method was basically similar to that devised by Heatley in which bacterial activity was compared with that of a standard penicillin solution. The other was a chemical method which involved the reaction of the penicillin with hydroxylamine to form the corresponding hydroxamic acid and a colorimetric estimation of the latter after the addition of a ferric salt.

These two methods of assay would normally give similar results. However, it was found in Rome that when both were used on the brews being produced for Beecham, the two yielded different results, the chemical method indicating the apparent presence of more penicillin than was shown by the biological method. 'We believed at the time', Chain wrote, 'that the substance in question was some penicillin with very low activity, such as penicillin with an acetyl side chain and as we were busy with the preparation of amino-benzylpenicillin, the matter was not pursued further at the time.' The original observation of the discrepancy, made by Dr Rolinson and Mr Batchelor whilst in Rome, was not followed up to provide an explanation until they both returned to the UK in 1957 and the material on which they originally worked in order to explain the discrepancy was actually prepared at Brockham Park.

There they were again struck by the fact that the two methods used in assaying the material did not agree and that the discrepancies were the larger when no precursor was added to the medium. A Beecham report on their work says:

It appeared then that in the fermentations there was a substance which had the attributes of a penicillin, reaction with hydroxylamine, destruction by penicillinase, but did not appear to be able to inhibit the growth of the test organism in the biological assays. It was significant, too, that the smaller the amount of precursor the more there appeared to be of this substance. Discussions with the chemists, Mr Doyle and Dr Nayler, led to the supposition that the substance might be a penicillin with little or no antibacterial activity or, on the other hand, it might be the core of the penicillin molecule without a side chain, i.e. the substance 6-aminopenicillanic acid. The existence of such a substance had been postulated as being perhaps one of the stages by which the penicillium mould built up a penicillin. The argument was taken further by the chemists in that, if the substance were indeed 6-APA, then it would be possible by a simple chemical reaction to convert it to Penicillin G or Penicillin v . . . and a solution so treated should give equivalent results by the microbiological and the chemical tests.

The fact that it was indeed 6-APA which had been created was proved convincingly by a comparatively simple experiment using paper chromatography. The culture fluid containing the substance was phenacetylated by treatment with phenylacetylchloride, and benzylpenicillin was shown to appear after the treatment. This could only mean that in penicillin fermentations conducted in the absence of a side-chain precursor acid, the mould formed the free nucleus of the penicillin molecule which was transformed by phenacetylation into benzylpenicillin. The implications were exceedingly great. If supplies of the penicillin nucleus could be provided, virtually unlimited new semi-synthetic penicillins could be produced without the restriction of having to modify chemically p-amino-benzylpenicillin. Instead, it would be possible to use the nucleus as a foundation on which to create a virtually unlimited number of new and previously unknown penicillins with new and novel properties. At a meeting of the Beecham research panel at Brockham Park on 30 July, the existence of these exciting possibilities was formally admitted and it was agreed that investigation of them should take priority over all other work.

The extent of the possibilities was underlined by Chain who wrote:

Any side-chain acid could be introduced into the 6-aminopenicillanic acid molecule, the only limitation being the ingenuity of the organic chemist to invent new suitable side-chain acids. The situation was not unlike that in 1935 when Trefouels, Bovet and Nitti had discovered that the active part of the azo-dye prontosil molecule, shown by Domagk to possess chemotherapeutic properties against bacterial infections, was its sulphanilamide moiety which could be chemically modified in any direction.

Now, in a somewhat comparable way, it did at last look as though it might soon be possible to create tailormade penicillins.

However, problems still remained, notably that of getting the 6-APA from the fermentation broth. For 6-APA was amphoteric; in other words, it acted under certain conditions as an acid and other conditions as a base. In addition, and to make matters even more difficult, it was hydrophilic, readily forming a solution in water, so that it could not be extracted from the fermentation liquor by organic solvents. As if these facts did not present sufficient problems, 6-APA was found to be unstable to heat and in solution, while its yield was only about 20 g from 400 l of fermented medium, and obtaining that amount took from ten to fourteen days.

At Brockham Park Beecham had built one of the most modern and efficient fermenters in the world. But the 90-gallon equipment produced, during one complete run, only seven-tenths of an ounce of the penicillin nucleus, although the industrial experts were thinking and talking in terms of hundredweights. In fact before the end of 1959 this difficulty was very largely removed by the discovery at Brockham Park that the isolation of the penicillin nucleus by splitting off its side chain did not have to be accomplished by the slow and costly fermentation process. It could, instead, be carried out enzymatically by the comparatively simple addition of a particular enzyme to the culture. Such enzymes, Chain was to write, made the nucleus 'as easily accessible as the natural penicillins themselves'. Termed penicillin amidases, they were found in soil streptomycetes and in bacteria, the former acting predominantly on phenoxy-methylpenicillin, the latter predominantly on benzylpenicillin.

The first enzyme capable of removing side chains of penicillins was described by Batchelor, Rolinson and myself [Chain has written]. . . . The enzyme acted preferentially on phenoxymethylpenicillin and was later replaced by an enzyme from E. coli acting specifically on benzylpenicillin, discovered by the Bayer group, but our streptomycete enzyme was of great historical importance, for it made possible the preparation of the first large amounts of 6-APA from which methicillin, the first penicillinase-resistant penicillin, was prepared. The particular side chain of this penicillin, 2,6-dimethoxy benzoic acid, was actually suggested by Heilbron. Ampicillin, with its phenyl-glycyl side chain, was made at my suggestion to obtain a compound most closely related to p-amino-benzylpenicillin which had been shown to display some activity against Gram-negative organisms; it was one of the first semi-synthetic penicillins made, its antibacterial spectrum was described by Rolinson and his colleagues; according to expectation it did exhibit activity against Gram-negatives. Its synthesis at a reasonable price proved to be difficult because of the difficulty of removing the protecting carbobenzoxy group by catalytic hydrogenation – the catalyst being poisoned by the sulphydryl group originating from the dimethyl cysteine moiety of the penicillin molecule, and in this synthesis Doyle and Nayler made their most important contributions.

Most of the new products eventually to become available fell into one of three groups: the acid stable group which could be administered orally; the penicillinase-resistant penicillins; and penicillins exhibiting a broad antibacterial spectrum. Some acted against bacteria which had not been affected by earlier varieties; some could be administered orally under easier conditions. Some were excreted at different rates, while in many other ways the therapeutic use of penicillin was given a new dimension.

The 6-APA discovery from which these benefits were to flow was to have more than scientific repercussions. Chain later wrote:

I had a tremendous amount of unpleasantness in Rome following the announcement of the 6-APA discovery at Brockham Park, and so had Professor Marotta. We even had to face an official government enquiry, and though I managed to fight the issue successfully, there was a lot of ill-feeling among my colleagues who resented the fact that I did not inform them, as indeed I could not – about the progress of the work at Brockham Park, though the original observation of the discrepancy between chemical and biological assay was made by them in collaboration with Rolinson and Batchelor, and was discussed between them extensively and it had been decided by all concerned to follow it up at some later convenient time when the pressure of work was less strong than it was at the time.

The 'unpleasantness' at the end of the 1950s was merely a foretaste of the events which were to follow a few years later. By the early 1960s Chain was deep in negotiations which would bring him from Rome and was busy creating, at Imperial College, London, a centre for bio-chemical research which was to become as internationally famous as the Institute he had created in Rome. Professor Giordano Giacomello had taken over at the Institute from Professor Marotta, who had reached retiring age, but there was every indication that the work which Chain had begun some fifteen years previously would continue to expand and to increase the reputation of Italy throughout the scientific world.

Then, in 1964, Marotta, his successor, and a number of other officials at the Institute were arrested on charges of misappropriating funds. While the charges came without warning they were explained by the convoluted state of Italian politics; furthermore, a hint of what might be expected had been given the previous year by the prosecution of the chief administrator of the Italian atomic agency. The situation was easily exploited by those who had over the years been offended by the manner, decisive or arrogant according to viewpoint, in which Marotta had built up his organization until it had become a power in the land.

Chain was involved in the case since it was maintained that his laboratory had been established by presidential decree alone, not by statute, and only as a consulting group. Thus, it was held, it had been illegal for it to be granted money and for it to employ Institute staff. Just what part, if any, the link with Beecham seriously played in the case is unclear, but as early as 11 August 1963 *L'Espresso* had published an article claiming that 'even the Nobel Prize winner, Ernst Boris Chain, who is in charge of the antibiotic section (of the Institute) has patented and ceded to an English firm a process studied for the account of the Institute and in collaboration with its technicians'.

Chain protested that he had taken out no patent and the paper prepared to issue an apology. Then the charge was repeated in the Italian Parliament by the communist deputy Signor Messinetti, who mentioned the name of Beecham, and the paper's attitude hardened.

Meanwhile, the prosecution against Marotta and Giacomello continued and both were found guilty, although it was admitted that neither man had benefited from any of the payments under scrutiny and that an Italian Government had, in any case, authorized such payments. Both men were given heavy sentences: Marotta's being six years eight months imprisonment (of which he served only a few days) and a fine of 1.5 million lire (about £90,000). Chain had offered to give evidence for Marotta – an offer which was refused – and his attitude is illustrated by a letter which he wrote after the case to Professor Trabucchi:

It should be clearly stated that these grants (from the US Department of Agriculture and the National Institute of Health) were given to me personally and not to Professor Giacomello; his role was limited to signing cheques at my request and in strict agreement with the clauses of the contracts which I made with the American authorities. It seems to me an incredible injustice, of an almost nightmarish nature, that someone should be sent to prison because *I* accepted an American research grant – which, after all, was clearly in the interest of the Italian State, and not damaging, as the prosecution tried to make out.

While Marotta and Giacomello were preparing an appeal against their sentences – eventually made unnecessary by an amnesty of June 1966 commemorating the twentieth anniversary of the Italian Republic –

Chain was waging his own battle with the Italian authorities. During the trials of Marotta and Giacomello the government prosecutor had repeated allegations of Chain's conduct. No ordinary rebuttal being possible, Chain thereupon cabled the minister involved, Signor Ricciardi, protesting against his allegations.

Chain's threat to take the offensive himself had almost farcical results. The public prosecutor's office first made Chain's cable public and then passed on the documents to a lower court at Velletri, to find whether a case could be brought against Chain for insulting the Italian judiciary. However, this was a matter for which the authorities at Velletri appeared to have little heart, since they at once maintained that they were unable to trace Chain's address. Moreover, it was claimed to be no temporary difficulty, and although the scientific world well knew of Chain's new enterprise which had by this time been started in London, Velletri was still maintaining in February 1966 that Chain could not be located for service of the necessary papers.

At that point proceedings disappeared in the legal murk. The charges against Marotta and Giacomello were dropped at the time of the June 1966 amnesty and no more was heard of the dispute between Chain and the Italian State. The whole business had done the Italians no good and considerable harm, and it was largely due to Chain's reputation that the Istituto retained its own reputation in the years that followed. He, meanwhile, was creating a new sphere of influence where he had always hoped to build one – in the Britain to which he had come in 1933.

# —9—

# THE CALL OF JEWRY

After Chain's move in 1964 from Rome to London, where he became head of a new Biochemistry Department at Imperial College, many of his friends noted a dedication to Jewry and an interest in Zionism far more pronounced than it had been when he had left England in 1949. Although this increased interest was to continue until his death a decade and a half later, it is pertinent to describe it here. He had never forgotten the Jewish overtones of his early life in Berlin, the fact that his father had been for fourteen years a member of the B'nai B'rith, and that as a member of the Jewish community he had been set apart from those who were not, even in the days before Hitler came to power. Nevertheless, he had grown up as a traditional rather than a 'strict' Jew. He did not decline to work on Saturdays; although regularly attending Jewish services he did not rigidly conform to Jewish dietary customs and he did not wear the small skull-cap that was one of the visible outward signs of the Jew. And even in the 1960s he was still not a strict orthodox Jew.

Nevertheless, a study of his public speeches and pronouncements reveals a feeling for the Jewish religion and an attachment to Israel that had steadily grown over the years, and which gave the man who came to London in 1964 a *persona* slightly different from that of the Ernst Chain who had left Oxford in 1948. The survival of Israel itself in the face of repeated threats, and its increased influence in the world, were factors in Chain's feelings. But to this, it has been suggested, there was now added a belief which strengthened as his children grew up. This belief, it can be claimed, was one result of the increased thought that in his later years he was able to give to matters outside the boundaries of his own professional everyday life. Contemplation of the Holocaust, whose full enormity only became apparent in the post-war years, also had its effect.

One visible result of these influences was Chain's support for Jewish institutions, described in 141 files among his papers and continuing throughout all the post-war years. Yet this sprang from his unqualified commitment to the Jewish beliefs that increasingly suffused his life. The pervasiveness of these beliefs in his thoughts was brought out in a speech which he made in 1976.

The Jews are fortunate to have inherited a particularly strong 3,000-years-old religious tradition which is their lifeblood. Judaism, as presented by the laws of the Torah [the hand-written scroll of the five books of Moses (the Bible from Genesis to Deuteronomy) which is housed in the Ark of the synagogue], is a gigantic code of behaviour worked out in minute details so that it is relevant to all imaginable situations which can occur in human life. It is also a comprehensive and deep philosophy of life whose essential principles were enounced in the Torah, but which were elaborated in the later biblical writings and the rabbinical commentaries: the midrashim [a collection of rabbinical commentary on the moral teachings of the Bible], the Talmud, the medieval and later rabbinical writings.

Judaism is based on the belief that the laws of the Torah were transmitted to Moses by divine inspiration. We are required to accept two basic transcendental beliefs: 1. the concept of one almighty all-pervading Hashem, the Creator of the Universe, to whom no shape or form can be attributed, and 2. the concept of divine revelation through which his presence, his relationship with the Jewish people and his commandments to them were communicated to a few selected persons, among them Abraham, Moses and the prophets.

These beliefs had their impact, both direct and indirect, on Chain's approach to much scientific work. He once said:

The essence of our belief cannot be scientifically proved, but this does not mean that its truth value is inferior to that of scientific theories which . . . have the habit to be disproved in the course of time. I consider the power to believe to be one of the great divine gifts to man through which he is allowed in some inexplicable manner to come near to the mysteries of the Universe without understanding them. The capability to believe is as characteristic and as essential a property of the human mind as is its power of logical reasoning, and far from being incompatible with the scientific approach, it complements it and helps the human mind to integrate the world into an ethical and meaningful whole. There are many ways in which people are made aware of their power to believe in the supremacy of divine guidance and power: through music or visual art, some event or experience decisively influencing their life, looking through a microscope or telescope, or just by looking at the miraculous manifestations or purposefulness of Nature.

There was one practical way in which Chain's stronger identification with Jewry made itself increasingly felt after his return from Rome to

England. This was the strengthening of his links with the Weizmann Institute whose offers he had turned down during the immediate post-war years. The part that he would have been able to play in Weizmann's grand scheme had then been balanced against the greater use of penicillin which Chain rightly considered his own unique combination of chemical expertise and industrial know-how could better encourage outside the Institute. He continued to feel, scientifically, and in the wider field of human benefits, that this decision enabling him to use his influence on the widest possible field had been manifestly justified. But as his feeling for Jewry increased – for an amalgam of reasons which he himself may never have satisfactorily analysed – it would have been unnatural had he not counterbalanced, as far as was possible, his decision to let the Weizmann Institute fight its initial battles without his help. He did so by becoming in 1954 a member of its Board of Governors, by later joining its executive council, and by sheer force of personality helping to steer it through the dangerous waters of scientific policy which had to be navigated from the early 1950s onwards.

There were three ways in which Chain's presence among the men influencing the policy and activities of the Institute were to be particularly useful. One was that this influence began to be exercised as the barriers separating biology from other disciplines began to be removed by scientific and technological advance. The successful production and use of penicillin in particular and antibiotics in general had rested very largely on the removal of such barriers in the William Dunn laboratory and Chain was admirably equipped to cope with such matters as they spread throughout the post-war scientific world. Secondly, there were the links with industry which he had encouraged, as far as he was able, even while still working at Oxford. These had been close to Weizmann's heart when he founded the Institute and were to become increasingly important in the post-war scientific world despite the suspicions of them which still governed the attitude of many academics.

Thirdly, there was the force of Chain's personality which could sway an argument more decisively than that of most men. 'A useful irritant' is the phrase used of him by more than one member of the Institute's Board, an indication that as a governor he was as outspoken as he was elsewhere. J. B. S. Haldane, who had eased him into his first job in England, was affectionately known as 'the cuddly cactus'. For his part, Chain was frequently described as 'the hedgehog', a reference not only to the multitudinous points of his upstanding hair but to his potential prickliness in argument, but it is notable that personal disagreements with him rarely mutated into personal dislike. Only when his anger was aroused by what he believed to be natural injustice did the reaction break the bonds that usually bound him close even to his professional enemies.

From the end of the 1940s Chain had looked on the Weizmann Institute as an essential factor in building up the State of Israel, and this gave to his enthusiasm for the work there a quality which heightened his normal interest in scientific research. The fact that his association with the Institute involved regular visits to Israel was part of the attraction, despite the fact that these visits ate into an always overcrowded life. He always returned, first to Rome and then to London, as he put it on one occasion, 'inspired and stimulated as we always are after having touched the soil of Israel'.

There were normally six Governors' meetings a year and Chain would usually leave Rome or London for them on a Friday, spend Saturday in Rehovot, followed by Sunday and the first half of Monday in discussions at the Institute and be back in Rome or London by Monday night. Sometimes he was able to combine a visit to the Institute with attendance at a meeting of the Board of Governors of the Hebrew University. The concentrated effort that this required is indicated in a letter from Chain to Margalit Sela, first wife of the Professor Sela who subsequently became head of the Institute:

As I told you in Meyer's house just before I left for London, I should like to spend two or three days after the Jerusalem meeting at the Weizmann Institute and devote this time entirely to scientific discussions with various people in the laboratories. In particular, I should like to spend a few hours with Berenblum and his colleagues; Feldman, and his colleagues (to continue our talks); your husband; Ephraim Katchalski and his colleagues; David Samuel and the people in the organic chemical department. I should also like to have a talk with the Yedda people.

It is clear from Chain's extensive correspondence that he frequently acted as a useful link between the scientists and their ideas at the University of Jerusalem and those at the Institute, an application of the ideas which Weizmann himself had wished to encourage when he set up the Institute after the Second World War. This was a matter which had to be handled with considerable tact, as was another concerning the Institute alone of which Chain was fully aware. 'I do not think that the function of the Board of Governors [of the Institute] is to take responsibility for the conduct of research in its various departments, except in the informal manner in which this is done extensively and successfully as at present', he wrote to Israel Sieff who later, as Lord Sieff, was to become chairman of the Governors. 'No scientist of standing could possibly accept interference in his research programme from outside.' However, he did suggest that the minutes of the meetings of the executive council might be circulated to scientific members of the Board of Governors who wished to receive them. This would, he went on, 'enable those taking an interest to make suggestions of a professional nature throughout the working year instead of limiting this possibility to the annual meeting of the Board of Governors as is done at present'.

In this delicate matter of settling how far scientists at the Institute should be allowed to go their own way, and how far they should be kept within an overall plan of research, Chain successfully encouraged his own ideas, a success which was the result of a tact and diplomacy which elsewhere tended at times to be submerged by his tidal waves of enthusiasm.

There was another matter – the relationship between scientific enquiry and religion – which might have caused him trouble and disappointment as the growth of his Jewish faith coincided with a greater possibility of influencing the course which the broad stream of scientific investigation should take. That there was neither trouble nor disappointment was due to his firm belief in the point of view which he outlined in a speech made when he accepted a Doctorate of Philosophy Honoris Causa from Bar-Ilan University, Israel.

It must be remembered that, quite apart from the ephemeral nature of scientific theories, pure science is ethically neutral. No value of good or bad is attached to any natural constant, or, for that matter, any scientific observation in any field. However, in our relations to our fellow-men – and this includes, in particular, the applications of scientific research – we must be guided by an ethical code of behaviour, and pure science cannot provide it.

In the search for an ethical code of behaviour we have to look for more lasting values than scientific discoveries or theories. We, the Jewish people, have had the extraordinary privilege to have been given a lasting code of ethical values in the divinely inspired laws and traditions of Judaism which have become the basic pillars of the Western world. These laws and traditions have lasted over three millennia and will remain a guiding force for the Jewish people and many other nations as long as one can foresee.

It is difficult not to believe that Chain's devout attitude influenced, at least in part, his assertion that certain specific theories were overturned rather than amended by technological progress. Thus he could talk of Newtonian physics being overturned by Einstein, whereas what Einstein had shown was that Newtonian ideas were valid only in circumstances which were restricted, even though these circumstances did appear to permeate everyday life. So, too, with Darwin's theory that evolution was the result of, among other processes, the survival of the fittest, a belief qualified rather than destroyed by the development of genetics and biochemistry. 'Only one theory has been advanced to make an attempt to understand the development of life, the Darwin–Wallace theory of evolution,' he said as late as 1972, 'and a very feeble attempt it is, based on such flimsy assumptions, mainly of morphological-anatomical nature that it can hardly be called a theory.' And after dealing with certain evolutionary examples he added, with a vigour that would do credit to a modern Creationist rather than an accomplished scientist: 'I would rather believe in fairies than in such wild speculation.'

There were at least three factors in Chain's dismissal of Darwin's theory of evolution. One was his general dislike of theories which could not be experimentally tested.

In general [he wrote to one correspondent] I cannot work up too much enthusiasm for any theory, knowing that theories are ephemeral and, as new facts are discovered, must be dramatically changed or discarded. In my view they have no absolute value, and their usefulness consists essentially in their capacity to stimulate new experiments. This is, at least, the criteria by which I judge them.

To illustrate his point he would quote the case of prontosil, the first antibacterial therapeutic agent. This was the ultimate end-product of attempts to follow up the idea of Paul Ehrlich that it should be possible to find an antibacterial dye which could fix itself specifically to the microbial cell and thus kill it without harming the host. However, after prontosil had been discovered it was found that its antibacterial effect was not related to its colouring properties but to one of its colourless components, sulphonamide. 'The importance of the discovery of prontosil', Chain pointed out, 'was in no way diminished by the recognition that the theory of its action and that of the whole approach leading to its discovery were wrong.'

As far as evolution was concerned, some of his letters can give an impression which his elder son believes could be totally misleading. He has said:

I am quite certain that *at no time* did my father believe in a fundamental creationist theory of evolution. I think it would be seriously misinterpreting his views if you did deduce this from his writing. There is no doubt that he did not like the theory of evolution by natural selection – he disliked theories in general, and more especially when they assumed the form of dogma. He also felt that evolution was not really a part of science, since it was, for the most part, not amenable to experimentation – and he was, and is, by no means alone in this view.

Scepticism was reinforced by his view that a belief in natural selection – like, he felt, too great a reliance on molecular biology – would make men feel that they understood everything. How directly such views were linked to his religious beliefs is open to endless argument, but it is clear that he never resolved the apparent dilemma of religion versus evolution that many had resolved even in Darwin's day.

It was not only Darwin among the natural scientists who failed to pass Chain's religious scrutiny. Another was Konrad Lorenz, of whom he spoke in a speech-day address to Jews' College in London in 1972.

It is easy to draw analogies between the behaviour of apes and man, and draw conclusions from the behaviour of birds and fishes on human ethical behaviour, but all these analogies are superficial and have no general significance. Of course there are similarities between all living matter, but this fact does not allow the development of ethical guidelines for human behaviour. All attempts to do this, such as Lorenz' studies on aggression in animals suffer from the failure to take into account the all-important fact of man's capability to think and to be able to control his passions, and are therefore doomed to failure right from the beginning. It is the differences between animal and man, not the similarities, which concern us . . . the various speculations on cosmogony which are advanced from time to time, are nothing more than an amusing pastime for those proposing them.

When it came to speculation about the origins of life, Chain's religious beliefs and his scientific background tended to reinforce each other, as he made clear in answer to a request to write a foreword to a book on the subject.

I have said for years that speculations about the origin of life lead to no useful purpose as even the simplest living system is far too complex to be understood in terms of the extremely primitive chemistry scientists have used in their attempts to explain the unexplainable that happened billions of years ago. God cannot be explained away by such naïve thoughts.

A few weeks later he replied to a further request by writing:

Though I agree with your views on evolution and the importance of belief in God, I regret that I cannot write a foreword to the book as I am deeply involved in the Judaistic religious tradition and do not believe that Christian beliefs have contributed advances to the essential basis of Jewish ethics.

It was not only in science that Chain's personal advocacy led him to support causes that were not always popular. Self-help had been important to his personal survival and success, and he believed that the same course was necessary for Israel as he made clear on being asked to sign a petition to U Thant protesting about the persecution of the Jews in Arab countries, to which he replied:

I do not feel that a letter to U Thant, however strongly worded, is the answer to this problem. Personally I consider the United Nations to be a completely useless and anachronistic organization, and to be disregarded as much as possible. Mankind would not suffer to the least degree if it disappeared altogether.

Chain's scorn of the United Nations extended to its allied bodies, a fact not concealed when, on being asked to sign a document supporting Unesco, he wrote:

Frankly, I have felt for a number of years that the United Nations and their special agencies, in particular Unesco, have completely lost the purpose and direction for which they were created, and are beyond recovery in this respect.

I therefore feel that it would be better for the world, and in particular for the Western world whose values we cherish, if they were abandoned as quickly as possible. I believe any attempt to reform them to be an utter waste of time. No useful purpose is solved by deluding oneself into believing that peace and international collaboration can be achieved by supporting a Utopian pseudo-organization with no realistic basis as are the United Nations now and have been for many years, where the representative of Guinea-Bissau and similar countries and the United States, Great Britain and France have the same vote. . . .

Chain's strong feelings for Israel also tended to qualify his views about Russia. By now strongly anti-communist in outlook, he had nevertheless been ready after the war to help in bringing penicillin to the Russians. Visits to Russia had tended to qualify his views of the Soviet system but as he wrote to his elder son he felt what he called the strength of the Russian genes in his blood, and to the end of his life hoped that some *rapprochement* between East and West would be possible. He wrote from Rome to a Russian scientist in 1959:

I have for many years now tried to do everything within my power to promote closer scientific relations between the Soviet Union and this country, and still believe that this is the best way towards creating lasting friendships and overcoming prejudices.

Yet the growing persecution of the Jews by the Soviet Government in the 1970s was something which he could not – indeed, did not wish to – ignore. His reaction, however, was rather different from the outright public condemnation of many Jews. In 1976 he accepted without qualm foreign membership of the Academy of Sciences of the USSR, an action which brought a protest from the National Council for Soviet Jewry of the United Kingdom and Ireland. In reply to this protest he wrote:

I personally believe that the step I took will act as a bridge between the West, and, in particular, the Jews, and the Soviet Union, and will do much more good than ill for the Jews in the Soviet Union. I had a special phone call from President Katzir [of Israel] welcoming my election, and the Chief Rabbi expressed to me his satisfaction with this move. I have been in Russia a number of times and am fairly familiar with conditions in this country. On the basis of personal experience I hold the view that people like myself can achieve the best results by quiet personal intervention in specific selected cases, and I have done, and shall continue in future to do, everything possible within my power to help in individual cases.

Chain's belief in cautious diplomacy may have been justified, however much it disturbed some of his colleagues, and it was certainly a policy which he followed consistently as relations between Russia and her Jews continued to deteriorate. This policy was exemplified when he was asked his views on a proposal to make the Russian physicist Andrei Sakharov an Hon. PhD of the Weizmann Institute, and replied:

Personally, I am most definitely opposed to such a move. Saccharov [*sic*] [who is generally credited with having helped produce the Russians' hydrogen bomb] has not been involved in active science for many years and cannot possibly be awarded an honorary degree on his scientific merits. The award would be a political action, and in my view the Weizmann Institute should keep away from this type of politics which can do no possible good to Israel or the Jews outside Israel. Such award will only exacerbate the already noticeable increase in tension between academic circles in the Soviet Union and Israel and it not only will make it much more difficult to get Jewish scientists from the Soviet Union to the Weizmann Institute, but also would create difficulties for the many Jewish members of the Soviet Academy of Sciences. I cannot see that such a step will contribute in any possible way towards the improvement of the cultural relations between the Soviet Union and Israel which we all desire. I am, of course, in full sympathy with the feelings of revulsion of the scientists at the Weizmann Institute against the methods used by the secret police against the dissidents, both Jewish and non-Jewish (Saccharov belongs to the latter), but just to give vent to one's feelings of revulsion is not good politics and does not lead to any changes in Soviet policy we all desire.

The need to keep feelings of revulsion in hand was illustrated by his own reactions to the treatment of the Jews in Europe when Hitler was in control. All his life he blamed himself for his failure to help from Germany his mother and his sister, and his post-war visits to Germany, particularly to Berlin, aroused mixed feelings. But his inclination to give all men the benefit of the doubt was shown when he acknowledged a copy of the autobiographical book by Werner von Heisenberg, the physicist who was in charge of Germany's wartime nuclear effort. Chain wrote:

Certainly Heisenberg was exposed to the most terrible conflict of loyalties imaginable and it is impossible to pass judgement on people in his position. His decision to remain in the inferno of Hitler's Germany, despite the obvious advantages which emigration offered him, seems to me to have been a very courageous one. Whether he could have better attained his aim to reconstruct German science from its ashes after the end of the war by staying inside Germany, following Planck's suggestion, than from the outside, is a question to which it is not easy to give an answer. Personally, I am glad I did not have to face the dilemma.

He maintained a questioning interest in the consequences of history which had led Germany towards 1933 and the events which had swallowed up relatives and friends. 'Did you read the book *Gold and Iron* by Fritz Stern, an American historian?' he asked Leonard Wolfson in September 1977. 'Based on the letters between Bismarck and the banker Bleichröder. The book changes completely our outlook on the Bismarck period and the Jewish problem in Germany and makes it possible to predict everything that happened in Germany under Hitler.'

Chain himself went back to Berlin in 1954 with his wife and Mrs Sacharina. He had mixed feelings about going, and the ambivalence was repeated when he was there. He wrote:

[The city] in its present state is such an apocalyptic sight that no human imagination is strong enough to visualize it, . . . destroyed to the extent of 90 per cent or more. It is a dismal, terrifying sight, yet I could not feel sorry for a moment. I had no feeling of pity or sympathy, but felt only that this terrible physical destruction was just some sort of retribution for the horrible crimes committed, some sort of external symbol of the Nazi period. Strangely enough, the house where I was born, near the Chemical Institute in the Centre, and the two houses where I spent most of my childhood, still stand intact, although there is a lot of destruction around them. I visited the Institute in the Charité where I worked until I left Germany; it was hit by a bomb at the top floor where my laboratories were situated, is rebuilt and made into a very nice commonroom. The Institute is in the East sector, completely cut off from the West; I was one of the rare visitors from 'the other side' and got a very warm welcome. I think Berlin is finished as a town for many years. I doubt whether it can ever be rebuilt. I thought I would feel sentimental about Berlin but I did not; I felt rather a sort of repulsion. I doubt whether I shall visit the place again; I did not like the spirit of the place, nor did I like the people.

His wife and his cousin appear to have felt much the same, certainly about East Berlin, and he wrote to a friend that 'both of them disliked the atmosphere intensely and were glad to get home'.

His post-war views on Nazi Germany were outlined in more detail in a letter to Axel Springer, the German publisher. He had, he wrote, 'very similar views' on many important and cultural subjects.

In spite of the horror of the Hitlerite period which drove me from Berlin at the end of January 1933 and which cost the lives of my aged mother and of my sister, who had to remain in Germany, I have never been able to nourish an unforgiving hatred towards Germany. Instead, I had always regarded the events as a human tragedy in which Germany had fallen unreservedly into the trap provided by the times, one in which the wave of destruction had swept beyond German boundaries. However, such events had already taken place many times to other people in the history of man and will probably happen again in the future, probably with the help of the improved technology being perfected for mass-destruction. It would be much simpler if man could attribute guilt for such a catastrophe as that of the Hitler era to a single nation and by its removal prevent its repetition in the future. Unfortunately, the reality is by no means so simple and such hopes are dangerous illusions. While the crimes of the Hitler regime were taking place in Germany, the outrages of Stalin's tyranny were taking place in other countries, and in comparison with those gigantic mass-persecutions, whose victims numbered millions, the atrocities of the Hitler regime were but amateur undertakings.

I have always been convinced, and still am, that Germany has made an important and unique contribution to the development of European culture, in music, philosophy, literature, science and medicine, and will continue to do so. The assumption is that men are to be found, as indeed they already are, who will be ready fully to involve themselves in establishing and maintaining the freedom of the spirit as well as the formation and support of a spiritual elite, these foundations for the success of every conceivable initiative which will otherwise be condemned to be stifled.

Springer, Chain concluded, was one such man who he hoped would help 'the voice of the true Germany to be heard once again in the forum of European nations'.

Whatever Chain's reflection on the moral problems facing Germans in wartime, whatever the exact mix of reasons behind his increased support for Jewry from the mid 1950s onwards, one outcome was a determination to bring up his children securely within the Jewish faith and as accustomed as possible to Jewish ways. He ensured this not only by choosing good schools for their early education but by arranging for extra-curricular Jewish tuition and following it up as they made their way to, and through, university. Typical was the choice of Rabbi Horowitz, head of the Jerusalem Academy of Jewish Studies, and the decision that Benjamin should spend six months there before becoming a biology student at Cambridge. Chain was outspoken in his praise of Horowitz, and wrote:

I am quite certain of one fact. If we get too far away from the basic ethical laws of Judaism, Israel as a country and the Jews living in the diaspora are doomed, and sooner or later they will disappear. Rabbi Horowitz is one of the rare people who can get the values of Judaism across to young people, and he can get them to accept that they are as valid today as they were when they were formulated 3,000 years ago.

Chain's twins spent some months on *kibbutzim* in Israel before completing their education in Britain, and while Benjamin and Danny both opted for biology it is significant that Judy qualified as a teacher in Jewish history.

Their father constantly stressed the need to strengthen the specifically Jewish education of young Jews in Britain, and wrote to a friend:

I, too, believe that in the absence of positive steps towards [this], the Anglo-Jewish community will disintegrate completely and will eventually just disappear through assimilation. The consequence of this will not only be the irreplaceable loss of priceless cultural-ethical values, but will also lead to a loss of support for Israel from this community.

Teachers were needed as much as money, he went on, and in a revealing sentence wrote: 'We must have appropriately trained teachers who can transmit to the young that the traditions of Judaism are not archaic and dusty, but have great relevance to the problems facing us in the modern world.'

Chain's devotion to Judaism was exemplified not only by his personal attitude to, and relations with, his children but at many points in his professional life. When he visited Argentina, Chile, Uruguay and Brazil in 1963, he made a point of visiting Jewish communities, bolstered up their morale, as he put it, and even went so far as to state that this was one of the purposes of his journey.

The feeling for Jewry certainly suffused the latter half of his life, growing stronger as his years advanced, and epitomized in the following speech, entitled 'Why I am a Jew', which he made at the World Jewish Congress Conference of Intellectuals in 1965.

While we have witnessed astonishing technological progress over the last 4,000 years, human relations have remained essentially unchanged since the time the Torah was written, and have to be regulated by very much the same laws.

For this reason the fundamental teachings of Judaism, as expressed in the Old Testament, and developed by the great sages of the Middle Ages, one unitarian Almighty, benevolent, all-pervading, eternal divine force, of which the spirit of man was created an image, is for me still the most rational way of accepting man's position and fate in this world and the Universe, . . . is entirely reconcilable with modern scientific concepts. It gives us, above all, an absolute measure of good and evil, an absolute scale of values without which no orderly human society can exist, and which no philosophical system, and certainly no scientific method can give us. . . .

The firmly established scientific fact that all life processes, the most primitive as well as the most highly developed, have a number of common basic biochemical features and that there has taken place a long evolutionary development of life of which, in certain aspects, man is the culminating point, is as acceptable to Judaism as are the astronomical findings of the movements of the planets in the Universe or of the electrons round the atomic nucleus. . . .

In the diaspora a large part of the effort must be directed towards keeping the Jewish identity and preventing assimilation. Assimilation is a loss of orderliness, and therefore a step towards an increase of entropy, i.e. chaos. It is most important to realize this and to understand that we benefit *most* the community among which we are living by *preserving* our identity, and not by losing it through an equalizing assimilation process.

Overall, the position which he maintained throughout his life was summed up best if briefly in a letter to his elder son in 1973: 'Though I am not too keen on fanatics, I feel very strongly that Jewish traditions are very important and are a rallying-point in a shifting world.'

# −10−

# IMPERIAL COLLEGE

It was a man already convinced of the salutary intellectual role which Judaism should play in the world and of the equally beneficial role which was Israel's destiny who in 1964 finally left Rome for London.

There were many reasons for a return to Britain which pulled against the attractions of the prestigious institute which he had built up from scratch in Italy. Important among them was his deep feeling that any benefits his work might produce should accrue to Britain, the country which had accepted him in 1933. To this there was added an emotional attraction which had grown stronger with the years. 'Whenever he came back to Britain on visits from Rome,' says the present Lord Sieff, 'it was clear that he missed this country.' Other friends have emphasized that however great the professional advantages of the Rome Institute they were always mentally balanced by isolation from Britain and a lack of the quintessential British atmosphere with which he continued to have a love–hate relationship.

Chain's emigration to Rome in 1948 had followed Britain's failure to provide the funds which he knew were necessary to secure her a place in the international world of antibiotics, but he had never given up hope that the situation would change. By the early 1960s there was also the fact that Professor Marotta, without whose influence the Institute would never have been so well-funded, was approaching the age of retirement. Whether his successor would be able to draw on support, which Chain once described as unlimited, was uncertain, while Chain no doubt had suspicions, if no more, about the political storm which was to break. Thirdly, there was a personal reason for returning to Britain. Both Chain and his wife liked Italy and particularly Rome where living conditions were pleasanter than they had been in the austerities of post-war Britain. But Chain had always admired the British educational system with its comparative freedom from government interference – a point he was often to emphasize in the later years of his life. If his children could be educated in Britain that was a matter which weighed heavily in the scales. It was a matter about which he sought the views of close friends, and from New York in 1958 he told his wife that two such friends were 'strongly in favour of our going to London, mainly because of the children'. One particular aspect of education was that in Italy Chain's children would be brought up in schools where the Catholic influence was strong. The predominant religious influence, he was determined, should be Jewish.

It was therefore with interest that as early as the autumn of 1953 he received a letter from P. M. S. Blackett, Professor of Physics at the Imperial College of Science and Technology. Blackett was already a power in the corridors of science policy; Imperial College, Britain's leading institution in technological education, was planning major extensions of the fields in which it operated and Blackett now set in motion the machinery which was eventually to govern what one of those extensions should be. He proposed that Chain should meet the Rector and some of Blackett's colleagues. They could discuss the need for developing the engineering aspects of microbiology in England, possibly at Imperial College. He knew, he added, that there were several people at Imperial College who were keen that something should be done.

Shortly afterwards Chain met the rector, Air Chief Marshal Sir Roderick Hill, and it was arranged that Professor D. M. Hewitt of the College's Department of Chemical Engineering should visit Chain's laboratories in Rome. Hewitt was enthusiastic and on 26 November 1953 wrote to Chain from London: 'I now see clearly the great potentialities of microbiological work and I certainly think it is a development which the Imperial College should take very seriously into consideration in connection with the forthcoming expansion plans.'

This was a beginning, but it was only an early step along a path that had to be followed for a number of years. Patrick Linstead took over the rectorship following the death in 1954 of Air Chief Marshal Hill and throughout 1954 and 1955 Chain sounded out various colleagues as to what the possibilities at Imperial College really might be. Among those obviously anxious that Chain should return to Britain was Sir Charles Dodds, who appears to have raised with Blackett the fact that the College's Chair of Biochemistry had remained vacant since the departure of Professor A. C. Chibnall during the war. Dodds told Chain in November 1955:

I had a long talk to Blackett today about the position at Imperial College. I understand, not only from him but also from other sources, that the question of a Chair is quite open. I think the best thing would be for you to write to him direct and fix an appointment with the rector. I think this will come better from him as a member of the staff than from myself as an outsider. I have told Blackett that I will do anything I can to help.

There was, apart from Chain's personal interest, another and wider reason for keeping alive the prospects for biochemistry at Imperial College, as Chain had emphasized when writing to Dodds about Beecham's plans for setting up a penicillin production plant.

The question of personnel will come up again and again and I feel – as I have felt strongly for some time – that no really satisfactory solution to this problem will be found unless adequate academic training facilities in this complex branch of biochemistry are created in Britain. In this connection I am most interested in the Imperial College expansion scheme and want to ask if you have heard anything further about it. Yesterday I saw Theorell who stayed with us overnight, and he told me that at present *three* pilot plants are going up in academic institutions in Sweden, one in the Karolinska Institute, one at the Technical High School and one at the Microbiological Institute. All of these are more or less modelled on the pilot plant which we erected here in Rome, the one at the Karolinska Institute will have one or two fermenters of 20,000 l capacity. Isn't it a terrible pity that until the present time we have nothing of the kind in England, despite everything that has happened? From where will British industry draw the properly trained biochemists and microbiological engineers which undoubtedly it will require in ever-increasing numbers? . . .

By the first days of 1956 Chain had prepared a memorandum for the new rector outlining the department he envisaged at Imperial College and explaining why Britain had fallen behind in biochemical research. It was, he maintained, largely an attitude of mind, adding:

This attitude of mind shied away from any problems involving complex and costly equipment, believing that the most worthwhile results could be by improvisation and simple methods, and it completely failed to appreciate the importance of engineering methods for biochemical research, believing that problems involving methods of that kind were tainted with industrialism and therefore a job for industry, but not for the academic laboratory.

He pointed out that Imperial College was the biggest training centre in Britain for chemical and mechanical engineers and was therefore an ideal place for the department which was needed.

However, it was only when Chain's plans were studied in detail that the investment involved in setting up such a department, and the building and running of the essential pilot fermentation plant, were properly appreciated. The Imperial College plans for expansion in the 1950s were ambitious, but it was now seen that biochemical research on the lines Chain envisaged would need funds, if not equal to those required for nuclear research, at least of a very sizeable magnitude. 'Taking all the various aspects into consideration,' Chain was told on 30 April 1956, the conclusion had been reached that 'the College should not develop an institute of the scale which you mention, but it will develop a bio-chemical department on a more modest scale which will have a link with engineering.' Blackett agreed, if reluctantly, and to Chain it must have appeared that his experiences with the Medical Research Council were to be repeated.

However, he was, as he bluntly stated to Linstead, 'a tenacious fellow'. He continued to lobby for a major British entry into the biochemical field, an aim which for practicable purposes meant a new department at Imperial College, and in April he was rewarded with the news that Linstead had put forward his name for the Chair of Biochemistry. 'I think, however,' he cautiously warned Charles Dodds, 'that many hurdles will still have to be overcome before acceptable conditions for the organization of a Department of Biochemistry can be found.'

The 'conditions' were centred on the provision of the large sums of money involved, and while Chain was thinking in terms of fermenters costing £200,000–£300,000, an unnamed official at Imperial College was writing that 'an annual expenditure of £10,000, excluding salaries, for a department of this size, is rather out of step with the bulk of the College'. The obvious need to raise money tended to reinforce Chain's position since his connections with industry, stretching back almost to the end of the war, were firmer than those of any other candidate. To this, and to Chain's unequalled scientific expertise, there was added his genuine and deep-seated belief that if Britain were to make her mark in the post-war biochemical field Imperial College was by far the best place to make it. 'At present', he told Linstead, it was 'the only place in the country for developing a modern biochemistry unit for the study of those most important aspects of the reactions of intermediate metabolism which cannot be tackled by the conventional laboratory techniques but require the engineering approach and pilot plant facilities.'

As Linstead himself wrote to Professor Alexander Todd, the new centre at Imperial College 'would in some ways be a counterpart of the Institute which Chain has set up in Rome'. However, he continued, 'if such a project were to be fruitful it could only be undertaken with full consultation on what I might call a national level'. With the 'national' level in mind, approaches were now made to a number of companies involved in the fermentation industry, including both Distillers and Guinness who had already helped to set up a microbiological unit at Oxford.

By the time that approaches to industry had begun to produce results, Chain himself had cleared a different hurdle – the problem of his move from the department which he had built up with the enthusiastic support of Professor Marotta. The professor's reaction was quite as co-operative as Chain can have hoped for, and he wrote to Charles Dodds on 6 November 1958:

I have broken the news of the possible change to Marotta. He was wonderful and as gentlemanly in his understanding of the situation as ever, and promised me his active help. He wishes me to carry on as consultant to the Institute for a prolonged period of years and to continue in this capacity to direct the research of the departments I built up. This means in actual practice the establishment of real inter-European scientific collaboration in a novel sense in which it has not been done so far, inter-European collaboration which goes far beyond the usual, rather empty and meaningless talk; and the arrangement may set a model for the future for other organizations, in the way the bilateral Anglo-Italian Congress in Turin, in the realization of which you have had such a prominent part, has set a model. I think the possibilities which are inherent in such a scheme are quite thrilling.

There remained the differences between Chain and the College as to the scale of the new department, and some months were spent in efforts to reconcile them. Chain wanted 38,000 square feet of space, but the College could apparently plan for not more than 20,000-25,000. Chain wanted 27 fully qualified scientific staff and 46 technicians while the College proposals were for 7 and 6, although the numbers might be increased to 10 and 10-15. The Department of Scientific and Industrial Research might provide an additional £10,000 a year for ten years.

But the real sticking-point came when the large fermenter units were discussed. Their cost went well into six figures. The College was unable to provide that amount of money for them and the rector was not optimistic about the prospects of obtaining outside finance. This hurdle was finally cleared by the efforts of Chain himself who conjured the Wolfson Foundation into providing £200,000. Once it was certain that the new plant could be built Chain asked Falini whether he was willing to design a fermentation plant for use in England. Falini agreed to do so and long remembered how Chain had hardly found it necessary to check the plans. By that time he was confident that any member of the task-force he had trained in Rome could do virtually anything that was asked of him.

The Wolfson money was later increased to £300,000, a sum including a further £25,000 for suitable accommodation which would be available to Chain when he took up the appointment to the Chair. 'The house', recorded a note made in June 1959, 'would be made over to Imperial College, but with the reservation that it would be available for Professor Chain as long as he held the appointment.' The difficulty of finding a suitable house at a suitable price on a site conveniently close to the College was eventually overcome by building a penthouse suite on top of the new biochemistry building. Chain and his wife were able to have the new home tailormade to their own plans and eventually moved into quarters that were the envy of the scientific community. The house provided for the director of the Royal Institution in Albemarle Street was the only residence with which it could be compared, and that had not been built to the occupier's requirements.

The chairman of the Wolfson Foundation Trustees was the 1st Baron Nathan whom Chain had known for many years, both as a personal friend concerned with Jewish affairs and as a partner in Chain's firm of lawyers. In November 1958 Chain had made a case to Nathan for the Foundation's support for biochemical research. Many of the developments he had forecast earlier had already taken place, he said.

For instance, the complete structure of insulin has now been established . . . and not only has the complete structure of the enzyme ribonuclease been established (it is composed of about 120 amino-acids) but it is now possible to establish the chemical differences between ribonucleases of different animal species which lie in the type and the arrangements of the 120 amino-acids. This is a fantastic achievement, made possible only by the application of automatic analytical devices, and represents another example for my thesis that if we want to be in the forefront of events in biochemistry in Britain, and not to remain always at the periphery, we must never shy away from the problems because they require more complex equipment than the 'string and sealing wax' technique admits, and for this reason it is so vitally important to set an example by building a biochemistry department at Imperial College which is not afraid of tackling biochemical problems because they cannot be solved by test tubes alone, but require chemical engineering and electronics methods. I am sure that once the first institute of this kind is built, other universities will follow suit. . . .

Chain was pleased for more than one reason that it was the Wolfson

Foundation which had finally come to the rescue, as he made clear in a letter to Isaac Wolfson on 30 January 1960:

I am very glad that your name should be associated with it so prominently. This cannot but have favourable repercussions on the Jewish community as a whole and especially in Britain. I also see, as I wrote to you before, many possible benefits for Israel which could arise from the close connection, through my person, with the biggest and most powerful technological and training research unit in Europe. I know that Jewish affairs are as close to your heart as they are to mine, and we have therefore many common interests.

However, the Wolfson grant which paid for the fermentation pilot plant by no means solved the financial problems of the new Imperial College department. On 26 January 1960, it is true, Chain received from the Senate of London University an invitation to take up the Chair of Biochemistry which he accepted by return, and the appointment dated from October 1961. But before he took up residence in October 1964 a number of other bodies had become involved in setting the new department on its feet. By the summer of 1962 the University Grants Committee had approved a plan to build an entirely new biochemistry department which would be linked to the Wolfson laboratories containing the pilot fermentation plant, and voted £250,000 for capital equipment.

In the same year Charles Dodds proposed that Chain should apply for support from the Fleming Memorial Fund which had been set up after Fleming's death in 1955, to which Chain replied:

My basic feeling about making an application . . . is that in view of the entirely negative and hostile attitude which I have taken – I believe, of course, rightly – to this whole enterprise, it would not be proper for me to ask the Fleming Fund for financial support for my work. But I may be wrong in this, and would like to discuss the matter with you when we meet before long.

Dodds eventually persuaded him that his personal feelings were less important than the needs of research and in 1962 the Fund gave £50,000 for '(a) the study of regulatory mechanisms with special reference to the mode of action of insulin and thyroxin; and (b) the study of metabolic reactions in nervous tissue, central and peripheral, with special reference to amino-acid-carbohydrate interrelations'.

The following year the Department of Scientific and Industrial Research approved a grant of £100,000, payable over four years, to cover the upkeep of the pilot plant. At the same time the Medical Research Council approved an initial grant of £40,000 for the setting up in the department of a metabolic reactions research unit aimed at studying metabolic reactions in animal tissues and micro-organisms. Further payments of £50,000 were made by the MRC for the work during the next eight years, while between 1966 and 1973 the Council also provided £143,000 to Chain's department for studies on non-specific immunity.

When he had returned to London in 1964 Chain had hoped that he would at last be able to bury his differences and disappointments with the Medical Research Council, and wrote to Sir Harold Himsworth, the secretary:

I am returning to England with the sincere desire to establish the most cordial relations with the Council and to play to the fullest extent, in every way I can, and in close collaboration with this organization, my part to promote biochemical research in Britain. In this task I hope to have the full support and encouragement of those responsible for the organization of medical research in Britain; otherwise – and I am fully aware of this – the whole enterprise is doomed to failure.

Not all his hopes were to be fulfilled, and although many of his enterprises at Imperial College were supported by the Council, and Himsworth became a good friend, his experience tended to confirm his fears that government aid in science and medicine was too often and too easily ineptly handled.

Thus in 1974 he complained about the way in which he had had research applications rejected by the MRC. He also maintained that one training course had been turned down without reasons being given to him. It is difficult to evaluate what substance there was in these complaints, particularly as it is clear that both the MRC and Chain were acting in good faith and with the best of intentions. One clue to the differences between them may be given by his claim that most members of one committee involved were molecular biologists. This was a branch of research to which he believed too much attention was being given and on which he believed too much money was being spent. Whatever the justification for such ideas, if it existed, it does seem that they tended to affect his opinions on many matters.

Chain's frequent and continuing brushes with the Medical Research Council may have been due, at least in part, to his constitutional dislike of operating the grants machinery along the lines that custom laid down; but they were no doubt also due, through an amalgam of different causes, to the dramatic escalation in the costs of research as he was building up the new department at Imperial College. The result was that he faced, from almost his earliest days in London, an inevitable succession of financial difficulties. In 1966 he asked for a further £511,342 from the University Grants Committee, a figure which was first scaled down to £93,671 before being frozen by the government's decision to suspend all university equipment grants. Chain had already planned the courses whose students were to help build up his new department and was among the Imperial College heads who protested. 'We are now left with two alternatives', he said in a letter to the press. 'One is to cancel our courses completely, the other is to give them but omit a large part of the practical training which forms the most essential part of both courses.' He would never have accepted the Imperial College appointment if he had known that such cuts would take place, he said. 'Many of my colleagues in other universities are in the same position,' he told one College official, 'and there may be wholesale resignations and a brain drain to the USA on a hitherto unheard of scale – and I know what I am talking about. I can only hope that the authorities will recognize the warning lights before it is too late.'

It was, moreover, not only training courses which were put at risk by the freezing of equipment grants, as Chain pointed out in a letter written in the hope of securing a grant from the Wellcome Trust. His department, he told Dr P. D. Williams, had work in hand on the production, biosynthesis and mode of action of the ergot alkaloids and the related clavins.

We have recently made some observations on a very specific pharmacological effect of one of the clavins, agroclavin, which was hitherto regarded pharmacologically quite inert [he said]. This effect is, I believe, not only important in itself, but may lead us to an entirely new approach to the mode of action of LSD and thus links up with our studies on the metabolism of central nervous tissues. We face in this field, as in most other biochemical fields of topical interest, a fierce American competition, and it would be really disastrous if we lost once again our initiative in an important development to the Americans. As you know, this had happened to me before in a very spectacular way over the penicillin discovery, and I hope that this sad history will not repeat itself in the ergot field.

The Wellcome Trust felt itself unable to help. There was no change of heart on the government's part and Chain turned, with no more luck, to the Ministry of Technology and the Medical Research Council. It was thus against a background which reflected, if on a different scale, Florey's 'don't buy a glass tube' injunction of thirty years earlier, that he continued his work.

Finally, more general support was to come from the Rank Organization, in circumstances that were later to produce much argument and ill will, the threat of legal proceedings and the suggestion that Lord Goodman should be asked to arbitrate in what Chain described as a major university scandal.

Chain's involvement in what was to turn into a long-drawn-out argument had begun in 1963 when Rank Hovis McDougall Ltd discovered a problem in disposing of the effluent created when gluten was separated from flour. Arnold Spicer, the head of Ranks' research department, sought advice from Chain, and from the enquiry there emerged a quickly growing amity between Chain and Lord Rank, the latter being the only man permitted to address his friend as 'Chainey'. Their views on the virtues of private enterprise and the dangers of government interference were very similar and from 1963 onwards they discussed numerous schemes in which Chain's department at Imperial College might help food technology and especially the production of bread.

Rank became increasingly interested in the scientific approach to food technology and offered to provide £50,000 from the Rank Family Trust towards the foundation of a Chair in Food Technology within Chain's department. This proposal was rejected on the grounds that there was no money to supplement such a gift with the further £50,000 that would be necessary and that, in any case, there was no need for such a Chair at Imperial College.

Neither Rank nor Chain were accustomed to having their ideas flatly rejected and shortly afterwards Rank agreed that £50,000, and the income from this sum, should be put at Chain's disposal to finance research fellowships in his department, or any other research support which he required. The money was never transferred to the College, but kept in the Rank Trust. Nevertheless, Lord Penney, the rector of Imperial College, expressed its thanks for Lord Rank's generosity when the gift was announced. Furthermore – a main source of later dispute – it was agreed between Chain and Lord Rank that after Chain's retirement in 1973 any unused part of the £50,000 would be returned to the Rank Trust unless a successor in the field of physiological biochemistry whom Chain considered suitable could be found, in which case the residue of the £50,000 would be transferred for his use.

Despite the difficulties of funding higher education which in the 1960s were endemic, Chain nevertheless embarked in 1963 on an ambitious series of research and teaching programmes which in the following ten years were to give Imperial College a much-envied status in a new and important field.

To all this there was added what might be called his personal work, the constant stream of letters asking for references or for advice about appointments or promotions. It seemed that by this time Chain had either worked with, or at least knew of, almost every biochemist who could be numbered among the up-and-coming or among those who had already arrived. His experience was called upon as freely as if he had nothing else to do but write lengthy letters. These letters, of which there are scores in his papers, reveal a man often torn between kindliness and honesty, anxious to present the best possible picture but quite as determined not to hide failings. 'He is a hard worker and under guidance will produce the goods, but he lacks originality', ran one typical reference to a man who had worked with him.

We think it will be good for him to get out of the routine of this place into some other laboratory to broaden his horizon, and I think the laboratory to which he goes would not lose by giving him hospitality. But, as I say, he definitely needs guidance, and I think in the kind of work you are doing he would render very useful service. He is a nice fellow and gets on very well with his colleagues. He has a strong social conscience and for this reason has been politically quite active in left-wing movements and trade unions, but of course his political activities are confined to Italy and have not interfered in the slightest with his work. I think you will like him.

From a man already as allergic to the Left as Chain had become, the last sentence was a guarantee of impartiality.

There were three sides to the professional work which Chain supervised. First, there was the long succession of researches which he, and his wife, personally directed and which were not limited to the production and use of antibiotics in all the variety that continued to grow from the 1960s onwards. In addition to this, he became increasingly concerned with the specialist biochemical aspects of food production and storage, including the nation's dietary problems and the country's agricultural planning and future. Secondly, there was the influence which he exercised internationally on the more general progress of biochemistry – largely through the seminars and symposia which he organized at Imperial College and the lectures and addresses which he gave to audiences in the United States and China, in South America and Russia, in fact wherever the prospects for biochemistry were discussed. Thirdly, there was his more general influence on the role of science in education, on the encouragement of collaboration between industry and the universities, and on the role which government could and should play in guiding the activities of science and scientists.

The spread of these activities was in itself enough to complicate life; but complications were compounded when, as sometimes happened, the College, a private company and a government organization were all involved. Then the financial complications could be considerable, even given the goodwill of all concerned. This is illustrated by the agreement signed after Chain had finally arranged for Beecham and the MRC to contribute to his department's work on production of interferon, the protein produced by viruses in many animal cells which itself acts as a protection against such viruses. The document reads:

For their part the Council agree to pay Imperial College one-half of any royalties and payments received by them from Beecham Group Ltd under the terms of the agreement referred to above; from this one-half share Imperial College has stated that it will pay to members of their staff engaged on this collaborative work on interferon inducers the portion of the one-half share of the said royalties and payments for which they are eligible under the rules of Imperial College.

Other complexities of co-operation were sometimes considerable.

Some of the pharmaceutical companies and bigger industrial organizations appreciated the facilities which were now available at Imperial College for the first time, but this was not always so with government bodies. Chain felt strongly that the Science Research Council was dragging its feet and early in 1968 prepared a lengthy paper 'Arguments for increased support of basic biochemical research by the SRC'. The paper outlined the great importance that the subject had acquired during the previous three decades, and the even greater benefits that it was now holding out for industry, and proposed the formation of a Biochemistry Committee at the SRC.

The paper was the precursor of a long correspondence with Brian Flowers, then the secretary of the SRC. There were already in existence 175 research grants in biochemistry totalling £1.25 m in value, as well as 122 research studentships. Flowers felt it was by no means clear that 'even the interests of biochemistry would be better served by giving it a separate Committee', and pointed out that there was, in fact, an Enzyme Panel already in existence.

The reply did not satisfy Chain, who felt there was a certain lack of enthusiasm for the subject in the official attitude but, as usual in such circumstances, hammered away. He was rewarded in January 1969 by an invitation to discuss how the Council could support industrial biology, and a Biological Science Committee was eventually formed.

The aim of the new group was to give specific aid to industry but Chain never believed that industry was given the support it deserved. His feelings were spelt out after a course at Imperial College on Microbial Biochemistry and Fermentation Technology, set up with the Council's help, was first stopped and then resumed only after protests and acrimonious argument. The contretemps, Chain wrote to Dr J. A. Fenley of the SRC,

has strengthened my view which I know is being held by many chemical industrialists and also by some Council members of the SRC, namely that the SRC pays lip service to industry, mainly because the members of the relevant committees are too far removed from industry to understand its needs. It is dangerous for the Research Council to allow such an atmosphere to develop and to give support to their critics by actions which could be interpreted as ignoring the needs of industry.

Certainly the links between industry and the government research councils had become increasingly important during the post-war years and the process was continuing vigorously in the pharmaceutical, agricultural and food industries. By the 1960s biochemical expertise did not lie only at the heart of the production of antibiotics and of vitamin B1 and related compounds. It was concerned with the production of valuable steroid hormones, the oxidation of sugars to citric acid, the production of lysergic acid and other lysergic acid-containing ergot alkaloids, the production of yeast for the brewing and baking industries and of animal feed supplements. It was central to the manufacture of various enzymes, such as amylases, proteinases, peptidases and collagenases and even played its part in mining processes. Biochemistry, with its utilization of radioactive carbon tracers, was being used to study how drugs did their work; it was being used to design new drugs and was each year witnessing fresh uses in food technology and food preservation.

In overseeing, or taking part in, the varied activities that Imperial College work involved, Chain showed a mixture of dislike and enthusiasm for innovation. Thus he never used pocket calculators but stuck to the slide-rule; but was enthusiastic about radioactive isotopes whenever they could be adapted for new tasks. In most things he was extremely practical, claiming that the most important thing for a biochemist to know was how to grease the tap of a burette so that it turned easily. And, he would maintain, there was invariably something to be learned from an experiment that did *not* work as expected.

With his practical turn of mind, and his regular morning enquiry in the laboratory of 'What's new, what's new?', it was inevitable that while building up the biochemical department he should be drawn into the work of many industrial enterprises. Among the more important was Marks & Spencer whose chairman, Lord Sieff, had become one of Chain's friends through their mutual interests in Jewry and the fate and future of Israel. In the middle 1930s the company had formed a technological department which carried out research on the raw materials which it used. In the post-war world, as its activities in food increased, so did the need for first-class biochemical advice. Chain became a consultant in 1961 and for the next fourteen years helped the company in many ways, giving its directors valuable contacts in the field of food bacteriology just as they began to develop the sale of provisions. The use of nitrites in cured meats, the problems of bacteria in chickens and the safety standards to be implemented for cakes containing fresh cream fillings were only some of the matters investigated. With Sir Charles Dodds and Sir Robert Robinson, also consultants to Marks & Spencer, Chain regularly attended meetings of the company's Scientific Committee and advised when a new line of 'perishable' products was being considered. Quite apart from this regular, if not routine, work, Chain was frequently consulted on a wide variety of *ad hoc* problems as they occurred.

During his time at Imperial College he therefore came to typify the new triangular relationship which in the post-war years developed, if only slowly, between the academic world, government departments and some of Britain's major industries. Much depended on efficient tripartite co-operation between major industrial corporations, government organizations such as the Ministry of Technology and the Medical Research Council, and the academic world represented by Chain. But much of the success of this development was due to Professor Blackett, who from the 1950s onwards had successfully occupied both government and academic posts. Few men had more experience to qualify them as 'one of us' by both businessmen and scientists.

The work carried out with the aid of the Imperial College fermentation pilot plant between 1966 and 1972 provides an impressive illustration of what was achieved as a direct result of Chain's development of the Rome Centre. High among it was the production of new antibiotics such as pseudonomic acid and antibiotic 2725. In both cases the structures of the substances were finally worked out and methods discovered for increasing the initial yields.

Chain also developed the possibilities opened up by his discovery in Rome in 1962 that strains of *Claviceps* were capable of producing in stirred fermenters the ethoxyamide of lysergic acid which is readily converted to lysergic amide. Before this, production of lysergic acid – from which it is easy to derive LSD, increasingly important as a psycho-pharmacological agent – was based on its isolation from natural ergot collected in the field from rye which had been artificially infected to produce the ergot. The method was cumbersome and largely uncontrollable and production by controllable fermentation offered obvious advantages. At Imperial College Chain and his team discovered methods of refining the process and increasing the yields.

However, one group of the pharmacologically important ergot alkaloids, including ergotamine, and the ergotoxins, a mixture of ergocormine, ergocristine and ergocryptin, continued to be produced only by existing methods, and efforts were made at Imperial College to find strains and conditions which would produce the same substances by fermentation. Some were successful and a great deal of fresh information was gathered.

More immediately important was the work on fungal viruses, substances which were found to help protect a wide range of living organisms against viral infections. Among the first of these was statalon. This metabolite of the mould *Penicillium stoloniferum* found in the host organism stimulated the production of interferon, a naturally occurring protein which itself inhibited the production of certain viruses. It soon became clear that statalon had considerable potentialities. Methods were developed at Imperial College for its production in fermenters in amounts sufficient for purification and the study of its chemical and biological properties. Purification showed that the ability to stimulate production of interferon was lost as the polysaccharide part of the material became purer, and it was then shown that the ability was due to very small amounts of double-stranded ribonucleic acid (dsRNA) derived from a virus infection of the mould *Penicillium stoloniferum*.

The virus was isolated and characterized by its morphological appearance, its chemical composition and its power to infect virus-free strains of the mould. Similar viruses were found in a number of penicillia and aspergilli. The richest source proved to be the penicillin-producing mould *Penicillium chrysogenum*, and methods were worked out for obtaining it in gram amounts.

Once this technological undergrowth had been cleared away, work continued at the Beecham Research Laboratories and at Imperial College, the former being funded by Beecham and that at Imperial College by the Medical Research Council and by Beecham. The whole investigation into fungal viruses thus provided a good example of co-operative research under different auspices. The Beecham achievement was to produce many hundred grams of fungal viruses – sufficient, that is, for detailed studies of their pharmacological and biological properties. A number of interesting and in some cases totally unexpected phenomena were produced. Thus it was shown that small amounts protected against various viral infections not only tissue cultures but also a series of laboratory animals. In the mouse, one microgram afforded complete protection against the encephalomyocarditis virus and the Newcastle disease virus, and gave a high degree of protection against the influenza virus. In pigs it was found possible to provide a high degree of protection against foot and mouth disease. Furthermore, it was found possible to produce a dramatic anti-tumour effect in experimental leukaemia, lymphomas and some sarcomas.

Chain believed that dsRNA had insufficient specificity and could therefore produce unacceptable toxicity while having beneficial properties. He had a theory that toxicity effects could be antagonized by the use of pharmacological agents. If this were so and the toxic effects could be understood and antagonized, he later wrote,

a significant progress in one of the most important fields of clinical medicine would be achieved. In any case, the double-stranded viral ribonucleic acids evidently stimulate a hitherto unknown immunity mechanism, the study of which should be of great importance. The discovery of fungal viruses and the biological activity of their double-stranded nucleic acid moieties has opened up several entirely new fields of study, with wide perspectives in microbiology, virology, pharmacology, immunology and clinical medicine. It will keep many scientists busy for many years, and is bound to lead to fundamentally important new knowledge in all these areas.

Work of a totally different character, and of a kind which illustrated the need for an instrumentation division in the department, which Chain had always stressed, was that involving the search for lower fungi which could be used as edible protein. After the end of the Second World War the global shortage of cheap edible protein with a high nutritional value became increasingly obvious. Attempts were made by a number of industrial organizations to grow such micro-organisms as yeasts and bacteria, both having a high protein content, on a cheap source as a substitute for vegetables or animal proteins used for human nutrition. These attempts were unsuccessful because of nutritional deficiencies in the case of yeast and high production costs in the case of bacteria.

However, the lower fungi are very similar in their chemical com-position to the higher fungi which have been used as food by man since the earliest times; these micro-organisms can, moreover, be grown in stirred fermenters and Chain, in collaboration with Rank Hovis McDougall, therefore embarked on a screening programme of such micro-organisms in a search for edible proteins. To be of use in the diet they would have to contain not only a high protein content but also a high sulphur amino-acid content. The work demanded the development of new rapid analytical methods for the determination of the complete amino-acid composition of a large number of samples. Responsibility at this stage was handed over to the instrumentation division of Chain's department, the outcome being an instrument which could provide a complete amino-acid analysis of a protein in forty minutes and could thus handle about seventy samples a week.

With the help of the analyser, later made on a commercial basis by the Instrument Division of the Rank Organization, several suitable micro-organisms were found, one of them being a *Fusarium* containing 40 per cent of a protein, some 5 per cent of which was sulphur amino-acid. The *Fusarium* was grown in the Imperial College fermenters in kilogram quantities for extensive feeding trials on animals and poultry and was found to have a nutritional value approaching that of casein. Production of the *Fusarium* was later carried on at the Lord Rank Centre at High Wycombe and work was continued at Imperial College in the search for fungi with even better nutritional properties. A somewhat similar project was later begun on an *Aspergillus* species in collaboration with Tate & Lyle.

Another investigation carried on at Imperial College following its start in Italy was that into the fusicoccins, a group of very powerful toxins produced by the mould *Fusicoccin amygdali* and responsible for the wilting disease of the almond tree. Very little was known about the toxins when they were discovered in Rome, but it seemed likely that they might be of agricultural importance and while work on them was continued in Rome after Chain's departure the investigation also went on at Imperial College. Here, in co-operation with Professor Barton of the Chemistry Department, the toxin was made in Chain's 500-litre fermenters and extracted in the chemical section of the department's pilot plant. The yield was only a few grams in each fermenter but the toxin was active in considerable dilutions.

There were many other activities with potential agricultural or industrial importance which Chain initiated or supported, among them a Shell-sponsored programme of research into the submerged production on a large scale of a powerful insecticidal protein of bacterial origin. Such activities assumed greater importance as he progressively made Imperial College a European centre for biochemical research. They were given greater importance by the *persona* of the man himself. Flying from one scientific meeting to the next with barely time for a meal in between, Chain became a familiar figure who was both respected and enjoyed. His ability to provide an informed survey of a highly technical field was much admired, and the fact that he could provide it in any of five impeccably spoken languages was an additional attraction. Above all, he won influence by his obvious sincerity, by his undisguised conviction not only that his work was intellectually satisfying but that it was helping to make men's lives more bearable.

Admiration and respect came in full measure during the years at Imperial College. But he, as well as some of his colleagues, felt that official recognition tended to come tardily: the result, as his obituarist in *Nature* was to say, of 'his deliberate policy of rocking Establishment boats [which] had made a deep impression in what are termed "influential quarters" '.

There were other indications that in some circles Chain was still regarded as being out of step. He well knew this, as he revealed in a letter to his friend (Sir) Bernard Katz, which said:

It has always seemed to me absurd and incongruous that I am the recipient of high decorations by foreign governments (see *Who's Who*) which I have to display at official national and international functions, whereas the government of my own country has not taken the slightest notice of my existence. If I were to pass on tomorrow my obituary would make curious reading and my biographer would have a hard task to explain these facts away. . . .

Taking all these facts into consideration, I have absolutely no doubt that if my case, with all the considerations outlined in this letter, is ... represented to the Prime Minister by the president of the Royal Society, possibly with the support, which I am sure would be fully forthcoming, of the present secretary of the MRC (a large unit of which – the Metabolic Reactions Research Unit –

is housed in my Department under my direction) and the president of the Royal College of Physicians (of which I am an Honorary Fellow) the whole matter which forms the subject of this letter can be settled in minutes. The outcome of such a step can only be positive and, I know, will be welcomed by many people in this country, and abroad. . . .

Even for a man who felt that he had been officially overlooked during his first quarter-century in Britain, Chain reveals in his letter an unawareness of British ways, since lobbying on one's own behalf can be, if it comes to light, a royal route to failure. However, there is a rational explanation. The early Rothschilds, it has been pointed out, enjoyed their decorations as they rose to fame as well as fortune, not only for the decorations themselves but because they counteracted the vestigial memories of the ghetto which remained in the family. Chain had known no ghetto, but it is clear from his correspondence that more than one incident during his first years in Britain had continued to rankle and he was anxious that they should be counterbalanced as publicly as possible.

His Nobel Prize had come at what was then the early age of thirty-nine. In the following year, 1946, he received the Berzelius Medal and, a year afterwards, two Pasteur medals. He became a Commandeur of the Légion d'Honneur in 1947 and in 1954 was awarded the Paul Ehrlich Centenary Prize. Three years later he received the Gold Medal in Therapeutics of the Worshipful Society of Apothecaries of London and in 1965 was made an Honorary Fellow of the Royal College of Physicians.

These awards, as well as the plenitude of honorary degrees that he collected during his travels, could suggest that official Britain had been tardy in appreciating his work. Official recognition was in fact to come without warning and on 12 May 1969, four days after writing to Katz, he received a letter asking whether he was willing to accept a knighthood in the Queen's Birthday Honours.

Any suspicion that strong left-wing views might have hampered his advancement is totally removed when Chain's public statements are studied.

Even before he began to transfer the centre of his interests from Rome to London in the early 1960s, his influence was becoming increasingly conservative if not formally Conservative. This trend was reflected not only in his political views but also in the way in which he regarded the problems of science, industry and education in the post-war world. Of one well-known journalist of by no means revolutionary sympathies, Chain wrote that the man was too left wing for his taste; and questioned about the Pugwash conferences in 1975, a date by which the organization had worked its passage into respectability, he commented, 'I only attended two [Pugwash conferences] and found them useless and irritating, being completely dominated by ultra-left-wing representatives. I do not believe that the Pugwash conferences have achieved any useful purpose in any of the aims listed in paragraph 4 of the questionnaire.'

In much the same way, his views on such controversial topics as apartheid began to appear singularly different from those to be expected from the young liberal of the Berlin days. A visit to South Africa, he wrote in September 1966, 'amply confirmed the views which I have held for many years that an immense constructive effort has been on balance, most positive and beneficial for the African population'. And to another South African who had been his host he could write: 'If I were a young man again, I would certain consider [South Africa] as a country to settle down in; I think it offers greater opportunities and greater challenges for the pioneering spirit than the United States do at present.' If such views were based on his hosts' cosmetic presentation of the South African situation, they typified the political stance he took up in later life. He was apt to overstate this, often misleadingly, as when he once said that Spain under Franco was the best European country in which to live since it was the one where discipline was best maintained. Those who heard him long remembered the remark, although those who knew him well are confident that he did not intend it to be taken seriously or literally.

His views, surprising in a man who had been quick to see the dangers of Hitler, were to some extent counterbalanced by his attitude to Russia, about which he at times appeared to be ambivalent. However, it was on some of the larger and more controversial scientific matters that Chain was during his later years to adopt attitudes both unfashionable and conservative. The fact that they tended to line him up with an unpopular opposition was possibly an attraction, but the attitudes were based on sincere belief. On evolution, he continued to remain as sceptical as those who had ridiculed Darwin more than a century earlier. It seems likely that his Judaism played its part in this, although he frequently used scientifically grounded reasoning to support his attitude. This came through clearly when, in 1977, he was questioned on evolution by a member of the Life Conservation Museum in the United States, and replied:

I do not believe that evolution is a well-established fact, but on the contrary, in my view its concepts are largely speculative. It seems to me that it is useless to draw conclusions on the mechanism of events which took place many millions of years ago. Modern biology has brought no new fact to light supporting the evolution theory nor has molecular biology. It is irrational and dangerous to believe that problems of the origin of life and its development are to be investigated in a 'rational' manner. The deductions made are very superficial and not worthy of serious consideration.

On being asked to expand, he replied with a sound enough argument that was weakened when he maintained that Newtonian physics had been overthrown, rather than amended, by the 'new physics' of the twentieth century:

It is a big mistake to rely on scientific theories as immovable pillars of truth, particularly in the field of biology, and to base one's ethical attitudes towards the regulation of human behaviour on them. A single new fact which has escaped attention or was newly discovered can upset the seemingly soundest theory. Think what is left of Newtonian physics which seemed to have explained for eternity the basic physical laws of the Universe. One is on particularly treacherous grounds when one tries to translate observations on animal behaviour to the behaviour of men, except on the crudest level.

No valid conclusion regarding scientific theories can ever be drawn by a majority rule. Who tells you that the majority decision is the right one and the minority decision the wrong one? Usually the opposite is the case. Newtonian physics were overthrown by a very small number of modern physicists including Max Planck and Albert Einstein. Biology is so complex and diverse a subject that we have as yet nothing like an all-embracing theory explaining life in its infinitely large manifestations.

The Nobel Prize is no guarantee for wisdom in all spheres of knowledge, but is given as a recognition of a particular achievement in a particular field of science. I would value a majority opinion of Nobel laureates on evolution, which is outside the experimental approach, not higher than that of any other group of intelligent educated persons.

His emphasis on the gaps in human knowledge, particularly concerning the fundamental basis of life, was reiterated when he wrote to Sir Cyril Hinshelwood in October 1966 after reading Hinshelwood's latest book *Growth, Function and Regulation in Bacterial Cells.*

I am always fascinated by attempts to formulate in quantitative physico-chemical terms the complex problem of life processes, though I am aware, as no doubt we all are, of the immense difficulties inherent in this task due to the fact that as the consequence of intracellular compartmentalization and spatial factors in multi-enzyme systems, we have as yet no means to determine the effective concentration of *any* reactant in the cell, whether it be enzymes, coenzymes or substrates. However, such attempts are thought-provoking and lead to the planning of new experiments to test the hypotheses, and this, in turn, may lead to the discovery of new facts and phenomena which is, essentially, our main interest and all we can really hope for. I feel that your own work provides a multitude of such ideas and I admire the power of its intellectual force.

Holding such opinions, Chain naturally had little sympathy with philosophical-scientific speculation on how life began. His attitude was exemplified in his reply after being asked in 1976 to give an opinion on a paper 'How life arose on earth'.

I have read Dr Stanley Miller's paper, but should not like to comment on it in public as I am entirely negative in my attitude to the attempts to speculate on the origin of life on earth on the basis of experiments on substances formed under the influence of irradiation of ammonia and carbon dioxide. In my view these attempts are naïve and primitive, to say the least.

Scepticism ran through many of Chain's reactions to the new methods, new ideas and new techniques which began to infiltrate the scientific world during his years at Imperial College. Thus he could write to Dr Mathilde Krim:

My views on the possibilities of genetical engineering differ from yours, being much less optimistic. It is impossible to explain this in writing, as it would take too long a letter to do this intelligently, but I would very much like to talk to you about this. The main reason for my caution is that for transcription of a piece of DNA to take place it is not sufficient to have this piece inserted in the DNA genome; about 200 proteins are, in addition, concerned with protein synthesis in bacteria, and no one knows which factors are responsible for their synthesis without which transcription cannot occur.

Frequently ready to consider innovations, he nevertheless had a constant fear that too much could easily be made of them and that it was invariably a mistake to stake out too early claims that could later be supported only with difficulty, a lesson no doubt learned from the near-euphoria which had for a while followed in the wake of penicillin. This was Chain's reaction to the growth and popularity of molecular biology, the study of the structure of molecules of importance to biology, which followed the understanding of the double helix in the 1950s and of the genetic code in the following decade. He was willing to agree, as he did in a letter to Dr T. Vickers of the MRC, that molecular biology had 'made some important contributions towards the under-standing of some genetical and immunological disorders, as well as the mechanism of virus infection and replication'. But in prophylaxis and therapy, he maintained, its impact had been minimal.

The aim of both molecular biology and classical biochemistry, as advocated by Chain, was to arrive at an understanding of biological phenomena in chemical terms. Nevertheless, the antagonisms that developed reflected real differences in approach. Molecular biologists concentrated on understanding the basic material (deoxyribonucleic acid – DNA) which carries the genetic blueprint for all organisms, and on describing how this 'genetic code' is translated within each organisms's cells into the biochemical machinery it requires. Chain's thesis was that biochemistry, and especially medical biochemistry, while striving for chemical explanations, should concentrate on higher levels of biochem-ical organization. Biochemistry should be more concerned, he felt, with understanding interactions *between* cells, *between* organs of the body and ultimately between different organisms. The discovery of penicillin, in Chain's view, which involved understanding the antagonistic interaction between a mould and a bacterium, was a classic example of this type of biochemistry.

He was not alone in his views. Biochemists, E. A. Morton had written in *The Biochemical Society: Its History and Activities, 1911–1969,*

have never taken kindly to the expression 'molecular biology'. In this they have resembled Ruskin in his opposition to the Pre-Raphaelite Brotherhood, for although he repeatedly described the name as unfortunate, unwise and even ludicrous, he gave to the word greater understanding and more praise than any other instructed critic of his day. Biochemists have enormously admired – and imitated – the work which they regarded as a splendid blend of biophysics and biochemistry and perhaps fearing a beam in their own eye, have decided after all, 'What's in a name? that which we call a rose By any other name would smell as sweet'.

Chain's opinions were spelt out in greater detail in a paper he read in 1974 to a meeting on physiological chemistry arranged by the MRC, in which he said:

I do not wish to create for one moment the impression that molecular biology has no place in medical research and, therefore, should cease to be supported by the MRC. All I wish to convey is that a proper balance must be struck between the various branches of medical research, and much more emphasis should be put on physiological biochemical research, by the clinical and physiological biochemist, with a view to make advances in *therapy*. There is a tendency to consider this kind of biochemist as a second-grade scientist, and one hears frequently the view expressed that clinical and physiological research is old-fashioned and has just lost its value. This, in my opinion, is a very arrogant point of view; exactly the contrary is true.

At present, research in molecular biology is overemphasized, and this has led to general scepticism towards medical research, as none of the promises made by some of the molecular biologists – that their approach would lead to the cure of cancer, the ideal contraceptive, tailormade drugs – have come true.

However, his feelings on the subject went far beyond what he believed were its distorting effects on medical research. He expressed this forcefully after he had read a paper on 'Social and philosophical implications of molecular biology' written by Dr R. E. Monro. It was, Chain wrote,

a valuable and timely essay on an important issue, namely, whether or not the findings in the field commonly termed molecular biology strengthen the mechanistic concepts of life, so popular during the last half of the past century, particularly after Darwin's ideas of evolution through natural selection. Jacques Monod has recently written a semi-philosophical book on the subject which has been much quoted; he and Crick are the main exponents of the positivist-materialistic philosophy according to which all aspects of life are explainable in relatively simple physico-chemical forms. This approach has always seemed to me to demonstrate a great lack of knowledge of biology on the part of those proposing such primitive ideas.

Here, as at other places in the argument, it is difficult not to believe that Chain's religious views were influencing his attitude to a scientific debate.

As a direct result of his strong feelings, he fought a campaign throughout much of the 1970s for a reduction of the effort, financial and organizational, which was being devoted to molecular biology. In particular he was anxious about what was to happen at Imperial College after he retired. By the summer of 1973 he believed that he had made his point and wrote to Dr J. A. B. Gray of the MRC. 'Our rector has now fully accepted my arguments *in favour* of the continuation of functional biochemistry in this department after my retirement, both in the fields of physiological biochemistry and chemical microbiology and *against* the introduction of any kind of molecular biology, and has stated this in writing.'

However, circumstances changed, and a sub-committee of the Medical Research Council was set up to survey the national position of molecular biology. Chain, who claimed that 'all bar one of the committee are molecular biologists', protested that it was 'farcical that a committee of molecular biologists should decide how much financial support their own subject should get', and continued his own private lobbying to change the situation. Edward Heath, Mrs Thatcher, Keith Joseph and David Owen were among the ministers whose help he sought. And, as usual with Chain, the enthusiasm for his case sometimes drove him to not always helpful overstatement. Thus David Owen was told that the matter was that 'of breaking the power of a self-perpetuating clique of physicists and protein chemists'. And Sir Douglas Black at the Ministry of Health was told, after a long plea from Chain about his successor at Imperial College: 'I have just heard that yet another Chair of Biochemistry has fallen victim to the molecular biology clique, at Leicester.'

Chain's proposition, which he presented to the MRC sub-committee, was that a new body should be set up to assess the support that molecular biology should receive when compared with that for other spheres of medical research, that structural work on the subject be transferred from the MRC to the Science Research Council, and that Britain should withdraw its support from the European Molecular Biology Laboratory at Heidelberg. These proposals, which were not accepted by the sub-committee, were in line with the attitude to science policy in general that Chain pursued and propagated during his later years.

Another subject in which Chain became involved at Imperial College was cancer research. This began in 1967 when he was awarded a grant of £49,200 from the British Empire Cancer Campaign for research into the production of asparaginase. Some dramatic results had been obtained by treating murine leukaemias with it, and there were cases of large tumours disappearing within two or three days. The unique property of asparaginase as a chemo-therapeutic agent was that its effect depended upon the specific metabolic degree of malignant cells, and for some years hopes, later found to be over optimistic, were held out for its use as an anti-carcinogenic agent.

Chain's grant was the first of a series, and throughout the early 1970s his links with the Cancer Research Campaign were close. However, he was the prototype of the man who never failed to ask questions when he felt they needed asking, and as the Campaign's chairman was subsequently to write to him, he had 'not always seen eye to eye with some of [his] colleagues on various issues'. One of the first crises arose when Chain sought to prevent a career staff member of the Medical Research

Council from joining the Cancer Research Executive Committee. His grounds were simple enough. As a member of a body which Chain felt was coming increasingly and unnecessarily under government influence, such a man might be inhibited from giving totally objective advice to the Cancer Committee. He sought the advice of his brother-in-law, Max Beloff, Gladstone Professor of Government and Public Administration in the University of Oxford, and pushed his protests strongly enough to force a review of relationships between the CRC and MRC by an *ad hoc* committee. He wrote to the 2nd Baron Nathan:

Your report is in conformity with the general trend of the ever-increasing government infiltration into all activities in this country, including industrial, educational and all aspects of research. I believe that this trend is a disastrous one, particularly in the research field, where it will inevitably lead to ever-increasing mediocrity.

Chain's strength of feeling on the subject was shown in a memorandum which he drew up, which read:

It seems to me of the greatest importance to protect and preserve, to the best of our ability, the independence of the last research foundations of which the CRC is one of the most important in this country. Believe me, this is not mere rhetoric. The State has the habit to penetrate private organizations insidiously, with imperceptible, but nevertheless very effective and often irreversible steps, and before you realize what has happened your freedom is irretrievably gone. . . . If we do not recognize the threat to the freedom of science arising from the ever-increasing State penetration into its organization, and if we do not take energetic steps to combat it now while this is still within our power, we shall have only ourselves to blame for the consequences of our acquiescence.

The threat of government influence was not the only subject on which Chain found himself at odds with the Campaign. On one occasion he asked for the following comment to be inserted in the minutes of the Scientific Committee: 'Sir Ernst Chain, in relation to the grant made to [a scientist], said he was opposed to the Cancer Research Campaign supporting research in the so-called genetical engineering, because there was not enough substance to it. Many high sounding and sensational promises, resembling more science fiction than science, were made by workers in the field, which had not the slightest chance of success.' And when the chairman of the Scientific Committee proposed that the nomination of his successor should be made by an *ad hoc* committee under his chairmanship Chain described the procedure as 'most improper'.

By this time Chain's relations with the Campaign can be gauged by a letter he had earlier sent to Lord Nathan, which went:

It seems to me quite extraordinary that the secretary-general of the Campaign should ask me on behalf of unspecified 'members of the campaign' to resign from the executive committee. If the executive committee wish me to resign, a proposal to this extent must be made to its members, a good and valid reason for this proposal must be given and the decision carried by a majority vote. Do you agree? I look at [the] letter as an attempt by some people to get rid of an awkward critic.

The epithet typified much of Chain's attitude during the last decade and more of his life. Between his arrival in England in 1933 and the 1970s when he reached the summit of his influence as the internationally known director of the Imperial College biochemistry department, Chain's work had given him wider experience of the context within which science could be pursued in mid-twentieth-century Britain than most scientists had enjoyed. He had acquired strong opinions, which he habitually expressed bluntly, on the place of science and scientists in society, and on the attitudes to them which should be taken by industry, by education in general, and by university education in particular.

The foundation for his policy was what he regarded as the limitations of science which he outlined at the end of his Waley-Cohen lecture, 'Social responsibility and the scientist in modern Western society'. The scientist looking for ultimate guidance in questions of moral responsibility, he said,

would do well to recognize the limitations and fallacies in this respect of the scientific approach, to abandon the status of intellectual superiority with which he has been vested, often against his wish, by wide circles of the lay public, largely as a result of the concepts of nineteenth-century scientific philosophy, and to turn, or return, to the fundamental and lasting values of the code of ethical behaviour forming part of the divine message which man was uniquely privileged to receive through the intermediation of a few chosen individuals.

Reliance on a divine inspiration, part of Chain's Jewish faith, qualified his assessment of what science alone could accomplish, but it was not the only factor, as he pointed out in this lecture:

There is no evidence that scientists *per se* have any greater claim to wisdom than other members of society; there is, in fact, a good deal of evidence to the contrary. The view that scientists are objective, dispassionate, impartial and tolerant, is a myth. They are just as prejudiced and emotional as any other group of people, certainly in relation to matters outside their professional competence, but even in their own fields of scientific research, in relation to the views of colleagues with whom they disagree. Their power of logical thinking is also not above that of other professions. The views of the scientist, therefore, carry no greater authority in major political issues than those of non-scientists.

That the world could and should benefit from a scientific approach to experience he regarded as axiomatic, although he was cautious about recommending how this experience could best be interpreted: He once wrote to the science writer Lord Ritchie-Calder:

The fact that science can do some good when applied in the proper way appears to me to be so well recognized by everyone that to stress it further would simply mean running into open doors. It appears to me that the real issue is how far scientists can and should control the application of their discoveries. As society is run at present they have no influence at all in this matter. Whether this is good or bad is an extremely complicated and controversial matter, particularly as far as medical discoveries are concerned and I am sure you will agree it cannot be adequately dealt with in a short letter to a newspaper.

On the division of science into pure and applied, Chain believed that the distinction was largely artificial. The impulse which led Pasteur to the line of research from which a whole new science was destined to emerge, and which had vast theoretical and practical repercussions, came, he pointed out in his inaugural address at Imperial College, 'from an industrial consultancy job which he was asked to undertake while he was professor of chemistry in Lille, for an industry with as hedonistic an aim as that of wine production . . .'.

In Britain the division, mirrored by the different valuations of education, was particularly strong in the medical and pharmaceutical fields. Chain was particularly aware of this, but also of the fact that by the 1960s the differences were at last beginning to disappear. He made his feelings clear when he wrote to Dr M. R. Pollock of the National Institute for Medical Research on the fact that Sir Charles Dodds had been elected President of the Royal College of Physicians. It was, he said,

an event which, in view of his commercial connections - quite apart from the fact that he is not a practising physician - would have been unthinkable a few years ago.

If industrial connections are now considered reconcilable with the ethics of the medical profession, even for medical people, by one of the most representative medical organizations in Britain, the Royal College of Physicians, then perhaps the MRC could feel justified to take a more broadminded view towards collaboration on their committees of people like myself, who are chemists and not bound by the conventions of the medical profession. Altogether, I am convinced that the movement towards breaking down unnecessary and anti-quated barriers and prejudices will do only good, for both science and industry; we do need the closest collaboration between the two. . . .

His efforts to break down also the distinction between 'pure' and 'applied' science were frequent, and he seized every opportunity to do so. One came at a two-day symposium on 'Food Technology in the 1980s' held at the Royal Society in May 1974. Chain, who had chaired the organizing committee, said:

Food science is a marvellous example of how closely and indissolubly the so-called pure and applied sciences are tied together, how one cannot exist without the other, and how nonsensical attempts are to separate them into 'higher' and 'lower' categories. Look at the impact of the results of, or shall we say, the spin-off for the food industry from low temperature research. Would Professor Kurti, who made so many pertinent and interesting contributions to the dis-cussions, have anticipated when he first entered the field of low temperature research, that he would have found himself one day among the food scientists? . . . The electron spin resonance, developed by physicists for a very different purpose, has become an indispensable instrument for the food scientist for the study of free radicals on exposure of lyophilized food to oxygen. These examples could be multiplied many times in all the sciences listed above and should give food for thought later for the ivory tower scientists - they do exist - who believe that applied science is not worthy of their great minds, and also for the industrialists who think that basic research in any field is a waste of money and time.

Equal in strength to Chain's feelings about the division of science into 'pure' and 'applied' were his views on government intervention in education, a fact which made him an enthusiastic supporter of the Independent University, today the University of Buckingham. His atti-tude to this aspect of the educational problems of the 1960s was revealed in a letter written to Professor Canonica after the Paris riots of 1969.

I am sorry about your student troubles. It is essentially a consequence of the Napoleonic system of State monopoly of education, both higher and lower. Once the educational system gets under political control, one is in serious trouble. Thank God, we have so far managed to keep free from this in this country - though for how long we do not know. I see no solution to the student troubles on the Continent, except gradual denationalization of at least higher education - a very long-term project I am afraid. A reassessment of the false scale of values of our society according to which you are not considered a good citizen unless you have a university degree before or after your name is also essential.

He further expanded his views in an address sponsored by the CIBA Foundation, saying on this occasion:

In the last thirty years I have witnessed a continuing erosion of academic freedom and standards, and an ever-increasing amount of bureaucratic controls imposed on the activities of the universities in this country. The University Grants Committee was conceived as, and indeed represented until about thirty years ago, an independent body designed to be a bulwark between the Government and the universities, but it has become, since the Second World War, almost entirely a tool of the Treasury, as far as finance is concerned. Now, much worse, it has become an instrument of the Ministry of Education, for the UGC now comes under the aegis of the Ministry of Education, as administratively – in my view, and in the view of many of my colleagues a grave error – the universities are now lumped together with the primary and secondary schools though, of course, their problems are completely different, and the purpose of the UGC is now to implement, or try to implement, the general educational policies of the Government. This is certainly a long step towards the continental system.

In Germany, he maintained to a friend three years later,

the universities as Centres of Excellence have already been practically totally destroyed, and German industry would be in poor shape without its own research sources and those of the Max Planck Gesellschaft [the organization reconstituted by the Allies after the Second World War from the Kaiser Wilhelm Institute] which has still managed to preserve a high degree of independence, despite large government subsidies.

Chain was alert in picking out examples of what he saw as an insidious wasting disease in the educational body, and protested vigorously when in 1969 he was asked to provide details for an 'Enquiry into the use of time by university academic staff' issued by the Committee of Vice-Chancellors and Principals of the Universities. Those circulated were asked to give details of their occupation for every half-hour between 8 a.m. and 11.30 p.m., for every day, including weekends. To Sir Keith Joseph Chain wrote: 'It is one of the most ludicrous documents I have ever seen, and really would be quite funny if it did not have such serious implications with regard to the liberty of the individual, and the academic in particular.' To Sir Derman Christopherson, chairman of the committee, he protested:

I have seen nothing like it, and if this document is a portent of things to come, I look on the future of British academic life with the gravest misgivings and forebodings. . . . It is not an effective means for assessing either 'productivity' or 'efficiency' of a university, nor for obtaining a realistic cost analysis. There exist far better direct methods for the latter, as every head of a big commercial organization will tell the statistical economist who has been responsible for devising the absurd document.

It was, moreover, not merely the uselessness of the questionnaire that worried him:

Whether anonymous or not, the questionnaire constitutes an intolerable intrusion and prying into the ways in which academics conduct their affairs. It is an unacceptable effrontery to ask them to give an account of how they spend each half-hour of their days from 8.0 a.m. to 11.30 p.m., weekends included. It really cannot be taken seriously, for if it were it would have to be considered as a serious threat to the freedom of the individual, with rather sinister undertones, conceivable only in a dictatorship, but not in a free democratic society.

After suggesting that if the issue of such questionnaires was the best that the committee could do to protect universities from government interference, then it might be better if the committee did not exist. Chain hammered in his argument with the proposal that such a document 'seriously undermines and still further weakens the prestige of the Vice-Chancellors' Committee'.

Chain had decided views not only on government interference in academic affairs but on many aspects of the ways in which research was being conducted in Britain. In November 1970 there came his 'Suggestions for the creation of an autonomous authority for the administration of scientific research in the United Kingdom'. A seven-page plan for a radical restructuring of the machinery by which the country's scientific effort was controlled, the scheme envisaged an autonomous Authority for civil scientific research under either a chairman who would be governed by a Parliamentary Statute or under a Minister without Portfolio. Beneath its wing would operate the Medical, Agricultural, Science and National Environment Research Councils, as well as a new Biological Research Council and a number of other organizations attached to a variety of ministries.

Basically the aim was to reduce the bureaucratic machinery felt to be inhibiting scientific research and to increase collaboration between the various research councils. The paper continued:

A further advantage of an autonomous Authority for scientific research over the present system is that it could provide a mechanism for quick decisions to be taken to deal with unexpected requirements for personnel, materials and equipment arising in the course of scientific research. Greatest success in scientific research, as in business, is often achieved through unexpected and unforeseen observations made in the course of the investigations which may necessitate a complete turn of the course set at the beginning of the work. Fundamental scientific research proceeding according to pre-established plans is usually un-inspiring and lacks originality. Hence it is most important to have a mechanism available for quick decisions to be taken in the allocation of extra-budgetary funds for unexpected contingencies.

If there was any doubt about the main thrust of the paper, it was removed in one of the concluding paragraphs. 'A very real and acute deterioration of standards of scientific research, particularly in the universities, is already noticeable under the impact of some of the directives issued by ministerial departments under the past Labour Government.'

As his experience continued to widen, Chain became increasingly worried about the stultifying effect of government influence on research. Rooted in his early experiences with penicillin, it was certainly re-inforced in his later years. His views on the value of privately-funded industry compared with industry which depended on government aid were emphasized when he compared industrial and government laboratories and their value for future biological research.

For anyone familiar with the subject [he wrote], there can be no question as to the decision between the two; he will undoubtedly vote in favour of privately owned industrial laboratories for a number of reasons: 1. The industrial laboratories can operate in an atmosphere free from bureaucratic impediments and restrictions. 2. Financial decisions can be taken rapidly without those in charge having to fear in case the research project ends in failure that they may be publicly accused of having wasted public money, and 3. They are units of manageable size and there are many of them, working in competition with each other.

His awareness of the dangers of size came out when he warned in November 1970 of the dangers which interdisciplinary collaboration always had to avoid:

*All* progress in science is made on borderline fields, and requires interdisciplinary collaboration. However, such collaboration cannot be forced upon people, it must come naturally by itself, and it does not help to break down established barriers between disciplines by abolishing names of subjects such as biology and zoology, and call them general biology. You may say that all living matter consists of atoms and, therefore, all biology is really physics. This does not help.

It also does not help to create huge international research institutes in the hope that housing various disciplines in one building will ensure collaboration – it just does not.

During his years at Imperial College, Chain's views on the best relationship between government and industry, on the amount of direction that should be given to scientific research, and on the manner in which it should be given, continued to develop, as did the frequency and outspokenness with which he expressed his ideas. These were given added weight by his ability to compare conditions in Britain with those in other countries, an ability continually being reinforced as he lectured to informed audiences throughout the world and discussed with their members how government and research collaborated in countries outside Britain.

He had for long been one of the world's most popular lecturers on antibiotics and the ways in which they had become known and developed in the modern world. He was the recipient of numerous decorations while learned societies loaded him with honorary awards. Most demanded a lecture, particularly as it became well known that Chain spoke well in numerous languages, had a fund of anecdotes to enliven the most serious material, and could display a rare facility for adapting his lecture as required to the level of the audience.

The extent of his travelling hardly decreased as he grew older and is revealed in the letters with which he regularly informed his family of his doings. Thus to his elder son, Benjamin, he commented in June 1973, from London: 'Next Sunday I am going to Switzerland to open a Congress, then on to Italy for a few days and the following Sunday to Washington.' A few years later, and already into his seventies, he told his younger son, Danny: 'Next Wednesday, February 23, I am going to Stockholm for a few days, and from there to Helsinki for a couple of days, all business. I shall be back in London on March 1. On March 13 I have to go to Frankfurt for a meeting of the Paul Ehrlich Foundation on March 14. On the 20th, there is an Executive Council meeting of the Weizmann Institute I have to attend.'

He had many friends in the United States and hardly a year passed without at least one visit across the Atlantic, while in the summer of 1961 he visited China at the invitation of the Chinese Medical Association and the Academia Sinica. As usual when he travelled abroad, he lectured at a number of universities and institutions, the Departments of Chemistry and of Biochemistry of the University of Peking among them. He later wrote in a report to the Foreign Office in London:

I was struck by the contrast between the very high level of intelligence and erudition of the research workers and the very low level of originality of the research work in all the Institutes I visited.

Most of the research workers I met were extremely bright and well read, and of an intellectual standard equal to anything one can find in the West, and some of the scientists I would even call brilliant. But with very few exceptions . . . I saw not a single really novel line of research worth noting.

Despite this he was, he wrote to a friend, 'one of those who thinks very highly of China and who believes that every effort should be made to improve our relations with that country, difficult as the task has become, mainly because of the crazy China policy of the USA in the last twenty years'.

The visit to China came early in a year of much travelling, and after completing a report to the Foreign Office Chain set off for Moscow where he chaired a meeting on the Biochemistry of Antibiotics at the Fifth International Congress of Chemistry. In September he visited Czechoslovakia at the invitation of the Slovak Academy of Science and in mid month chaired a session on the new antibiotics held at the Second International Symposium of Chemotherapy in Naples. In November he visited New York to receive an Honorary Doctorate of Humane Letters awarded by the Albert Einstein College of Medicine, Yeshiva University, New York, and after returning to Europe visited Paris in the last month of the year.

If this appears a crowded itinerary, it was a typical indication of the way in which Chain, throughout his work in Rome and then at Imperial College, dealt with an internationally mixed bag of academic appointments. Another typical year was 1966 during which he celebrated his sixtieth birthday. In April he visited Copenhagen to address the Danish Society of Pathology and Microbiology on the new penicillins. In May he addressed a symposium held in New York by Merck, Sharpe & Dohme on 'The quest for new biodynamic substances', and in June addressed the tercentenary meeting of the Académie des Sciences de l'Institut de France, at which he represented Imperial College. The following month he was guest of honour of the organizing committee for the Ninth International Congress for Microbiology held in Moscow, and in September gave the opening address on 'The semi-synthetic penicillins' at a meeting held in Johannesburg by the Beecham Research Laboratories. During his visit to South Africa he visited medical research centres there, and in Kenya and Uganda, and also spoke on 'Science in Israel' to the Israeli United Appeal Group in Johannesburg.

Chain's visit to Russia was one which aroused ambivalent feelings. In 1963, during his first visit to the country for some thirty years, he had been approached by a niece whose husband, an economist, was anxious to take up a post in the United States. Chain's letter to America, asking what the prospects were, revealed that he was under no illusions about the position of Jews in the Soviet Union. His relative, he said was

in the tragic situation of a Jew who has lost all contact with Judaism, both on a national and religious basis. Many such people existed in the pre-Hitler days in Germany, and exist now in many countries. In the Soviet Union they are predominant as their nationality in their identity cards is marked as Jewish, but they are prevented from carrying out any activity bearing relation to their nationality. They are faced with a crude and vicious anti-Semitism endemic in Russia since centuries, and in no way different from those of the Czarist days.

Nevertheless, when he wrote in 1972 to the son of the eminent Russian scientist, Professor Skryabin, he could say: 'I also have great faith in the Russian genius which will continue to manifest itself in the future, as it did in the past, and I am convinced that this genius will overcome all the difficulties of the day and continue to produce in the future great humanistic personalities in the field of science, like your father was. . . .'

He enjoyed a visit to Moscow in the autumn of 1975 and in May 1978 wrote to Igor Stepanovich:

It is my great wish to come to the USSR at more regular intervals and more frequently, and to be engaged there in some professional activity. As you know, your country is very dear to my heart and, with all its faults, I do not feel at home anywhere the same way as I do in Russia. My Russian genes are very strong and I would like my son to experience this country too and thus see my attitude to Russia continued in the next generation of our family.

Chain's extensive journeys were not made only to cement professional relationships. More than one of them allowed him to ride his own hobbyhorses. Thus after giving a series of lectures in Vienna he told Professor T. Antoine, president of the Gesellschaft der Ärzte: 'The main purpose of my lectures was to show that ultimately progress in therapy will come only from physiological and clinical observations, and not from laboratories removed from the excessively complex biological reality.'

He was a personality in his own right and this enabled him to support Jewish organizations in a way that he thoroughly enjoyed. After he had lectured on penicillin in Argentina, he told his wife, he 'could not walk in the streets [of Buenos Aires] for five minutes or sit in a restaurant quietly for a meal without someone approaching me to shake hands and express his good wishes – a demonstration of friendliness but a little fatiguing'. Outside Buenos Aires, where he collected $30,000 for the Weizmann Institute, his visits to Jewish communities were particularly welcome. 'To summarize,' he wrote, 'the visit has been successful from every point of view, but particularly from that of the Jewish community which has been electrified by my presence and whose spirits have gone up enormously. I do think that I have done an important public relations job, and everyone here says so repeatedly.'

In 1969 the whole family visited Australia where Chain had been invited to give a series of lectures. It was a longish journey on which he wanted to be accompanied by his wife. But Anne was not anxious to leave the children and as a result parents and children made a round-the-world tour that took in Fiji, Honolulu, New Zealand, New Guinea, Hong Kong and Bangkok.

Much of Chain's travelling continued to be carried out as adviser to either companies or governments. Thus in 1972 he visited Chile after the authorities there had asked whether they should replace their existing penicillin plant with a new one. After visiting the plant, and discussing the situation with the health authorities, he advised P. Dorolle, the deputy director-general of the World Health Organization, that in a forty-five-minute interview with President Allende he had persuaded the president that a new penicillin plant would be uneconomic and the necessary money would be better spent on other things.

As usual, Chain used the Chilean visit to investigate the area's peoples and background and in Peru visited Machu Picchu, the Inca city 2,040 m up in the Andes, unvisited for hundreds of years until Hiram Bingham discovered it in 1911.

In Chile, as elsewhere during his travels, Chain kept his politics to himself. At home, on the contrary, he made little effort to hide his feeling that on a scientific, as well as any political, balance the Left was doing more harm than good. The feeling continued to grow during the 1970s as Chain's tenure of office at Imperial College approached its end. It was not a comfortable feeling but he was lucky in that, however doubtful he might feel about the way that public affairs were going – and at times he was as worried about the future of the Weizmann Institute as he was about Britain's – his personal and family life continued on an even keel. His wife progressed in her researches and his three children all began to show that they would probably be successful in whatever career they chose.

Benny spent some months in Jerusalem studying Jewish ethics and philosophy, won a scholarship to Emmanuel College, Cambridge, where he read biology, and subsequently gained a First. Of the twins, Danny was learning fish-farming on a kibbutz in Israel after being educated at Bryanston, while Judy, 'with very independent but, thank God, not left-wing views' as her father described her, was studying at London University's University College and its School of Oriental and African Studies after an education at St Paul's and Westminster. 'Her subject is Jewish history and Hebrew,' her father told a friend 'and the course is internationally very well known and highly esteemed, but is quite difficult, and Judy has to learn Hebrew and Aramaic to follow it.' He was overjoyed to learn, only a few weeks before he died, that she had been awarded a First.

# –11–

# FINAL DAYS

By the end of September 1973, the year when Chain was due to retire from his Chair, he had not only built up the Department of Biochemistry into an institution respected throughout the world. He himself had evolved from a leading figure in the world of antibiotics into a biochemist with unrivalled knowledge of the machinery, academic, industrial and governmental, which powered an important sector of Britain's scientific research. It was therefore natural that he should be approached when, early in 1973, two major Italian companies made plans for setting up a new European Centre for Biochemical Research. But nothing came of these plans which could well have offered a post almost tailormade for Chain's particular qualifications.

He had of course known that when official retirement came he would no longer occupy the quarters at Imperial College which had been his home since 1963. With the future in mind he had therefore bought a pleasant house on the edge of Wimbledon Common, only some six miles from the College and situated in almost rural surroundings that were rare for the London area. Here he was able to make a fresh home when a different link with the College was forged in 1973. The Wimbledon house was therefore a comforting base throughout the traumatic period during which the future of his professional Chair was debated.

He had also, during his years at the College, reinforced his standing as a man ready to fight his corner in any of the battles which inevitably break out in the conduct of human affairs. This reputation as a scientist who would support with effective pugnacity what he believed to be right was to be strengthened by the commotions which now accompanied his retirement and the appointment of his successor, a series of arguments which were ended only after some years of controversy.

At first glance it might have appeared that the finding of a successor to Professor Chain would not be unduly difficult even when the shortage of first-class biochemists was taken into consideration. In fact, a purely fortuitous concatenation of circumstances created an argument that only narrowly escaped from bursting into public view. As it was, two successive rectors of the College, two chairmen of the Board of Governors, and other members, the vice-chancellors of the University of London, and a clutch of distinguished legal advisers and scientists were all embroiled.

Early in 1972 he told the rector, Lord Penney, that he believed that his Chair should on his retirement be divided into two. This would mean that the two lines of research with which his department was concerned, chemical microbiology and animal physiological biochemistry, might be pursued co-operatively but independently. A continuation and expansion of the department's fermentation plant work would then be possible without affecting the other investigations which had grown up over the years. To Penney, and apparently to most of the College governors, it seemed an admirable plan but it did raise a major problem: how was a second Chair to be financed? No College funds were available and it was unlikely that the Department of Scientific and Industrial Research or any other government body would provide them.

To Chain this difficulty was merely an obstacle to be overcome and before the end of 1973 he had solved the problem with the help of the Rank Organization. Considerable argument later developed over the exact details, argument hardly clarified by the fact that much of it appeared to rest on personal recollection and verbal assurances. However, the necessary sum of £100,000 that was needed was eventually found. Half of it came from the untouched capital of £50,000 provided a few years earlier by Lord Rank on terms which were later to be disputed; the other half came from the Rank Charitable Trust.

Funding of the two Chairs whose occupants were to take over from Chain was not the only problem to be solved. Chain had, virtually alone, been responsible for creating the international reputation for microbiology that Imperial College now enjoyed – and for funding the fermentation plant, by this time valued at more than £700,000 – and was determined that this line of research should be given the priority he himself had given it. He was, in particular, anxious to prevent any increased emphasis being given to molecular biology in the department's work, a discipline against which his opposition had continued to increase. For this reason, if for no other, he felt it right to disregard the English convention under which retiring professors played no part in influencing the choice of their successors.

In Chain's case, however, there was another reason. The first £50,000, he maintained, had been given by Lord Rank for such research as Chain felt should be carried out. It was only at Chain's request that it had subsequently been transferred to the College to support the transformation of one Chair into two, and under the unwritten but fully understood terms of the transaction, Chain maintained, any appointment must have his approval.

Chain's description of events was given in a letter to the rector, Lord Penney, on 13 July 1973, in which he described how Lord Rank had virtually given £50,000 towards the establishment of a Chair for Food Technology at Imperial College.

Lord Rank *insisted* that the sum of £50,000 should *not* be transferred to the College, but kept *outside* the College, and in fact this was the case. If Lord Rank had wanted to give a benefaction to the College, he would have transferred the money to the College, and would not have *insisted* that it was kept outside for *my disposal* only. It was most definitely *not* under the jurisdiction of the College, Lord Rank made it as a further definite condition of the grant to me that the money should be returned to him or his designates after my retirement, unless I was allowed to use it after my retirement for my own research, or I agreed that it should be used by my successor.

The benefaction did not come from the present Rank Trust, but was a personal gift from Lord Rank, *administered* by the Rank Trust. Lord Rank did not ask anyone about this donation, he always acted on his own initiative.

Chain went on to point out that his part in obtaining the endowment of £100,000 for the Chair of Physiological Chemistry consisted in two separate moves.

The first was to obtain the permission of the Rank Trust to transfer the £50,000, given to me personally, to the College towards the endowment of this Chair, the second was to ask the Rank Trustees to complement this sum with an equal sum to make the whole endowment possible. The College was not involved in either of these actions, in fact it did not even know that I had approached my friends at Rank Hovis McDougall for their help. The Rank Trustees agreed to both my proposals, hence I am responsible for getting the whole endowment for the Chair of Physiological Biochemistry, after considerable difficulties, and the College has no part in this transaction, except to ask for the additional £50,000.

To this complex situation there was added the fact that the rector was also to retire in the autumn and that his successor was to be Sir Brian (now Lord) Flowers, a distinguished physicist but a scientist to whom Chain was somewhat allergic. Just what part an outgoing rector should play in the choice of Chain's successor and what part the rector's successor should play was obfuscated by the financial importance of the biochemical equipment and the fact that the succession had been under discussion since the start of 1972. An unofficial committee, set up under the chairmanship of Professor Albert Neuberger to advise the rector, recommended that no appointments should be made immediately and it was only in January 1974 that Chain was told by Sir Brian Flowers that Brian Hartley, a biochemist who had spent thirteen years at the MRC's Laboratory of Molecular Biology, had been appointed to the Chair of Biochemistry. Chain wrote to the rector on 4 January 1974.

In this letter he maintained that he was unhappy about Hartley's appointment, an unhappiness that could well have been accounted for by his own attitude to molecular biology. However, he went on to claim that the appointment was contrary to various commitments on whose basis he had carried out negotiations for the Rank Chair and that it was contrary to various recommendations which had been made by those who had become involved in the appointment over the preceding months. The letter was a good example of how Chain would muster all available forces with determination and energy when he was personally convinced of the strength of his own case. It can also be considered an example of his facility for letting his enthusiasm – either for or against a project – lead him into over-stating his case.

The forthright letter was merely an opening move in a campaign which Chain was to wage until the second Chair was filled, equally to his distress. His case was largely based on the claim that the terms of Lord Rank's initial bequest of £50,000 required his personal acquiescence in the appointment, and he sincerely believed that he had legal as well as moral right on his side in what was to develop into a bitter argument. It was not a new situation for him. 'It seems to be my destiny to be involved in fights throughout my career,' he wrote to Sir Robert Robinson. 'I had my full measure of them in Oxford, then in Rome at the end of our stay, with the Marotta scandal (Marotta died last week), and now here at Imperial College.' He just could not accept what he thought were blatant injustices without raising his voice in protest, even if he thought his chances of succeeding were slim.

He appealed to the governors of the College, to the Rank Trustees and to a number of distinguished scientists. Eventually he suggested that Lord Goodman should be asked to arbitrate in what he described as a major university scandal. None of his efforts produced results. One factor was no doubt the vagueness surrounding the bequest of the first

£50,000; others were probably the vehemence with which Chain followed the course he believed to be right and his determination that the priorities established for running the department he had created should remain unchanged.

The result of the turmoil was an extraordinary series of letters, spread over some four years. The Rank Trustees and Lord Sherfield, chairman of the College's governors, both failed to support Chain while his lawyer warned him that the nature of his interest in the gift from the Rank Trustees did not entitle him to object to the appointment made by the University to either Chair, although that was his best argument.

They were weighty judgements, but Chain persisted in seeing the situation in a general as well as a purely personal context, and a letter to Professor R. K. S. Wood, the College dean, does much to explain the stubbornness with which he pursued the argument.

Since my experience in Germany in the late twenties and early thirties I have never had a high opinion of academics when it comes to showing courage and standing in cases when blatant injustice or impropriety is being perpetrated by the Establishment. With very rare exceptions, academics have always preferred, as first priority, to safeguard their own personal position and to avoid confrontation with the Establishment, even in the mildest form, in the fear of their wrath and vindictive action. All I can say is that my experience over the last five years at Imperial College, for which I have done more than the vast majority of the heads of departments, has only strengthened my views. . . .

And he complained of what he conceived to be the weakness of most academics.

The bitter controversy might have continued with unabated vigour had it not been for the conciliatory efforts of Chain's lawyer, Stanley Berwin, who wrote to Chain on 30 June 1977:

When you first discussed the problem with me, I advised that legally you had no case, though morally you were entirely justified in your complaints. The stage has now been reached where common sense must prevail and you must submerge your differences with the College, not only for your peace of mind but also for that of your family. There are far more important things in life than the perpetuation of your belief that the College has wronged you and the College's belief that they have not. They are two utterly irreconcilable points of view and your strength should be towards progressing your important and valuable work and peace of mind, rather than their dissipation.

Chain finally acquiesced. His three-year Senior Research Fellowship, which had been granted on his retirement in 1973, was not renewed in 1976 but he was offered a three-year Honorary Research Fellowship. He followed the advice of his lawyers and did not bring into the open a dispute that he felt reflected little credit on the College.

'Retirement' was a somewhat misleading word, since the period which followed Chain's release from administrative duties - and from the previous constant need to raise funds for his colleagues - was taken up by increased scientific research. Much of it was a continuation of the work he had inaugurated at Imperial College during the previous decade.

One subject concerned problems of non-specific immunity, particularly against virus infections. Here he continued to work with groups from Beecham Research Laboratories and with former colleagues from the College's Department of Biochemistry. Another investigation - also made in collaboration with research workers from Beecham - was into the anti-viral effects of double-stranded RNA from fungal viruses against pathogenic viruses producing infections in animals and man. A third subject of investigation was the mechanism of an effect, discovered by ICI workers at Macclesfield, of double-stranded RNA on neonatal mice which led to the development of tumours strongly resembling *Lupus erythrematosus* which were found to be inheritable over four generations. This work was being carried out by Chain in collaboration with ICI and workers at the Imperial Cancer Research Fund.

Another totally different line of investigation with which Chain continued during his retirement was the production of edible microbial biomass for human consumption which had been started by, and was being continued in collaboration with, research workers at the Lord Rank Research Centre at High Wycombe. In addition there was the work which he had begun before his retirement for the Shah of Iran's Protein Committee. He continued to advise not only on this but also the Iranian Minister of Agriculture and Mines and the Head of the Army Medical Staff on the use of single-cell protein produced by fermentation for animal and human food and on biomedical research in general.

'Retirement' was therefore a comparative term, although the release from many duties at the College did give Chain a greater chance of utilizing the home which he had acquired a few years earlier at Mulrany in Southern Ireland. In the 1970s he had contemplated buying a plot of land in Jerusalem, building a house on it and settling there on what would have been a semi-permanent basis. The Hebrew University in the city and the Weizmann Institute only sixty miles away would have enabled him to maintain professional contacts. But he considered the price of suitable land in Jerusalem to be too high. He had always hated crowds, had tried without success to find a sanctuary on the British mainland, and had been intrigued when George Woodham-Smith, a solicitor he had met while finalizing details of his move to Imperial College, mentioned his wife's association with Mulrany on the Mayo coast. Mrs Woodham-Smith, author of *The Reason Why*, the epic of the Crimean War, had described the delights and the loneliness of the area, and Chain and his wife spent a holiday there. Next year they rented a cottage and following that decided to build their own home in what they considered one of the most attractive parts of Europe.

Here Chain and his family spent whatever time he could spare from London, flying to Dublin, since he tended to be seasick, and completing the journey by car. At Mulrany he could completely relax, spending his time in the lonely surrounding country or playing on the sixty-year-old Steinway grand piano which had been a priority installation in the house.

The virtually uninterrupted series of enterprises on which he continued to work began to exact its toll and his wife and his friends found themselves increasingly occupied in trying to persuade him that he must work less. Their problem is illuminated by a letter which he sent to a Jewish friend early in February 1976. 'I have to go to Tehran on Feb. 20 and following this to Israel and Switzerland from which I expect to return on March 2. In March, April, May and June I have several other journeys and lectures.'

Impressive seventieth birthday celebrations were held that June. They began with two days of meetings held at the Royal Society at which a number of his collaborators spoke on a variety of biochemical subjects, the lectures subsequently being published under the title *Biologically Active Substances – Exploration and Exploitation*. The symposium was followed by a dinner held at the Middle Temple Hall at which Sir Ernst was the guest of honour. The celebrations were marked by two happy events: one was the receipt of the news that his elder son, Benny, had in Cambridge been accorded First-class honours in Zoology; the other was the opening of the entertainment after the Middle Temple dinner with the playing of piano duets by Chain and his elder son.

From this period onwards he suffered increasingly from sciatica which eventually began to affect his piano-playing, and his breathing difficulties became more troublesome. Yet despite his generally deteriorating health he had no intention of rusticating. 'I do not feel at all like retiring from the scene of physiologically orientated research which at present is in a very poor state in this country and has practically disappeared from the biochemistry institutes of British universities', he wrote to Sir Max Rayne in the spring of 1976. 'It has been replaced by molecular biology which to a large extent is irrelevant to medical research. . . .' He proposed that he should start work in the Max Rayne Institute of St Thomas' Hospital. 'I need an office and secretary, and a laboratory,' he added, but he would not require a salary, and could get support for the work from his industrial contacts. As for his title, that could be something like 'visiting professor'.

He continued to work, and to travel, and even after a heart attack in the summer of 1979 was optimistic about continuing work, as he made clear in a letter to a friend in July. 'At the moment I am sitting at home, doing nothing, at the order of my doctors,' he said. 'In a few days I shall go to Ireland to our house for our summer holidays. I hope that after a month of these I shall have sufficiently recovered my strength to continue my professional work, but whether I shall be in a position to undertake long-distance travel in November is impossible to predict at this stage. I am doing my best to recover as soon as possible, but this takes time.'

Shortly afterwards Chain flew with his wife for the usual summer break on the shores of the Atlantic. But the respite which he had at last granted himself had come too late and he died before the end of August.

# BIBLIOGRAPHY

Sir Ernst's extensive papers written during his long career are listed in the catalogue of his archive produced by the Contemporary Scientific Archives Centre at Oxford.

Bickel, Lennard, *Rise up to Life: A Biography of Howard Walter Florey who Gave Penicillin to the World* (Angus and Robertson, Edinburgh, 1972)

Clarke, H. T., Johnson, J. R., and Robinson, R., *The Chemistry of Penicillin* (Princeton University Press, Princeton, NJ, 1949)

Dean, Alastair C. R., and Hinshelwood, Sir Cyril N., *Growth, Function and Regulation in Bacterial Cells* (Clarendon Press, Oxford, 1966)

Florey, H. W., Chain, E., Heatley, N. G., Jennings, M. A., Sanders, A. G., Abraham, E. P., and Florey, M. E., *Antibiotics. A Survey of Penicillin, Streptomycin, and other Antimicrobial Substances from Fungi, Actinomycetes, Bacteria and Plants* (Oxford University Press, Oxford, 1949)

Hare, Ronald, *The Birth of Penicillin and the Disarming of Microbes* (George Allen and Unwin Ltd, London, 1970)

Hems, D. A. (ed.), *Biologically Active Substances – Exploration and Exploitation* (John Wiley & Sons, Chichester, New York, Brisbane, Toronto, 1977)

Hughes, W. Howard, *Alexander Fleming and Penicillin* (Priory Press Ltd, London, 1974)

Lazell, H. G., *From Pills to Penicillin: The Beecham Story* (Heinemann, London, 1975)

MacFarlane, Gwyn, *Howard Florey: The Making of a Great Scientist* (Oxford University Press, Oxford, 1979)

Maurois, André, *The Life of Sir Alexander Fleming, Discoverer of Penicillin* (Jonathan Cape, London, 1959)

Morton, E. A., *The Biochemical Society: Its History and Activities, 1911–1969* (The Biochemical Society, London, 1969)

Parascandola, John (ed.), *The History of Antibiotics: A Symposium Spon-*

sored by the Divisions of History of Chemistry and Medicinal Chemistry. American Chemical Society Meeting, Honolulu, Hawaii, April 5, 1979 (American Institute of the History of Pharmacy, Madison, Wisconsin, 1980)

Ratcliff, J. D., *Yellow Magic: The Story of Penicillin* (Random House, New York, 1945)

Sieff, Israel, *Memoirs* (Weidenfeld & Nicolson, London, 1970)

Stewart, Gordon T., *The Penicillin Group of Drugs* (Elsevier, London and New York, 1965)

Wilson, David, *Penicillin in Perspective* (Faber & Faber, London 1976)

# INDEX

# Index

Callow, Donald: as Chain's 'pair of hands', 61-2; goes to Rome with Chain, 120, 124

Cambridge, England: Chain at University of, 14-17

Campbell-Renton, Miss: and a penicillin mould, 33

Canada: and penicillin production, 74; and post-war cost of penicillin supplies, 101

Cancer research: Chain and, 32, 179-81

Canonica, L.: Chain writes to, on student troubles, 183-4

Cantaloupe, a rotten: important strain of penicillin detected in, 72

Chain, Lady (Anne) (wife of Ernst Chain), *see also under* Beloff, Anne: Chain writes to, on his health, 110; works on insulin with Chain, 129-31; visits post-war Berlin with Chain, 151-2; and return to England from Rome, 155, 156; and new home at Imperial College, 160; and research, 165, 190; Chain writes to, of popularity in Argentina, 189-90; and Mulrany, 198

Chain, Benjamin (Chain's elder son): on Chain and evolutionary theories, 147-8; Chain writes to, 149, 154; education of, 153, 190-1, 198; Chain writes to, of his travels, 187; at Chain's seventieth birthday celebrations, 198

Chain, Daniel (Chain's second son): education of, 153, 190-1; Chain writes to, of his travels, 187

Chain, FRS, Sir Ernst Boris (1906-79)

CHRONOLOGY

birth, 2; early years, 2-7; becomes naturalized German, 4; choice of career, 4, 5, 6, 11, 15; arrives in England, 7, 9; reaction to life in Britain, 10-11; joins University College Hospital Medical School, London, 12, 13-14; his career at Cambridge, 14-17; his career at Oxford, concentration on penicillin, 18-116; relationship with Florey, 18, 19, 45-6, 47-8, 57, 68-9, 103, 114-16; relationship with Heatley, 23, 40; and World War II, 39; takes British nationality, 39, 46; and the question of grants and financial support, 40, 41, 51, 81, 92-3; his genius for biochemistry, 11-12, 17-18, 45, 107, 134, 165-7, 171, 178; and report on penicillin in *The Lancet* (1940), 51-2, 53, 64, 104; writes history of antibiotics, 54; and efforts to interest drug manufacturers in penicillin, 55-6; and patenting of penicillin, 56-8, 94, 96, 107; his stance on Florey/Fleming dispute, 78; excluded from Moscow mission, 82-3; and penicillin synthesis, 55, 85, 90; and Anglo-US collaboration, 75, 90-1; a suggested visit to USA rejected, 92, 94; an

exchange with Mellanby, 94-5; and the question of a Nobel penicillin award, 96-7; visits USA, 97; and Fleming's lecture tour of USA, 98-9; awarded Nobel Prize (1945), 1, 5, 99, 107; friendship with, and marriage to, Anne Beloff, 99, 120-1; prospects and problems after the war, 100, 102-7; and antibiotics, 1, 54, 102, 103-4, 107, 128, 165, 187; accepts consultancy with Astra, 107; and penicillin negotiations with Russia and Czechoslovakia, 107-10, 114; temporary interest in golf, 110; does not emigrate to Israel, 110-14; contributes to History of Penicillin, 114-15; leaves Oxford (1948), 114, 115-16; at the Rome Institute, 7, 117-41; as family man, 120-1, 155-6, 190; elected Fellow of Royal Society, 122-3; visits Geneva, 125-6; visits to Czechoslovakia, 126, 127; elected Chairman of Committee of Experts on Antibiotics, 126-7; baulked on WHO visit to USA, 127-8; work on animal biochemistry and chemical microbiology, 129-32; and Beecham Group, 132-9; involved in Italian legal tangle, 140-1; leaves Rome, 142, 155; and Imperial College, 134, 139, 142, 156-73, 178, 181, 187, 192-7; offered Chair of Biochemistry at Imperial College, 161; interest in Zionism, 142; and Weizmann Institute, 144-6, 150, 187; receives Doctorate of Philosophy from Bar-Ilan University, 146; his scorn for United Nations, 149; his attitude towards Russia, 149-51; and Nazi Germany, 8, 152; and persecution of Jews, 150-1; visits post-war Berlin, 151-2; his return to England, 155; and Medical Research Council, 162, 163; faces financial difficulties in biochemistry department, 163-5; friendship with Lord Rank, 164; his wide influence, 165-6; his personal work, 165; consultant to Marks and Spencer, 168; and co-operation between academics and industrial world, 10; his honours, awards and knighthood, 173, 187, 188; and Pugwash conferences, 174; and a visit to South Africa, 174; and molecular biology, 176-9, 193; and cancer research, 32, 179-81; his Waley-Cohen lecture, 181-2; and Food Technology, 183, 194; and research in Britain, 185-6; his travels, 187-90; takes family to Australia, 190; visits Chile to advise on penicillin plant, 190; buys future home in London, 192; and his retirement from Imperial College and subsequent turmoil over successor and future of department, 178, 192-7; his after-retirement work, 197; builds a home in Southern Ireland, 197, 199; his seventieth birthday celebrations,